Critical Global Perspectives

Rethinking Knowledge about Global Societies

A volume in
Research in Social Education
Merry M. Merryfield, *Series Editor*

Research in Social Education

Merry M. Merryfield, *Series Editor*

Critical Global Perspectives

Rethinking Knowledge about Global Societies

Binaya Subedi
Ohio State University

INFORMATION AGE PUBLISHING, INC.
Charlotte, NC • www.infoagepub.com

Library of Congress Cataloging-in-Publication Data

Critical global perspectives : rethinking knowledge about global societies /
edited by Binaya Subedi.
     p. cm. – (Research in social education)
  Includes bibliographical references.
  ISBN 978-1-60752-386-4 (pbk.) – ISBN 978-1-60752-387-1 (hardcover) –
ISBN 978-1-60752-388-8 (e-book)
1. Education–Social aspects. 2. Education and globalization. 3.
Education–Cross-cultural studies. 4. Multicultural education–Moral and
ethical aspects. I. Subedi, Binaya.
  LC191.C68 2010
  370.116–dc22

                                                                  2009047644

CONTENTS

CHAPTER 1

INTRODUCTION

Reading the World Through Critical Global Perspectives

Binaya Subedi
Ohio State University

The primary purpose of this book is to invite educators to (re)think what it means to critically conceptualize knowledge about the world. In other words, imagining curriculum in a critical way means decolonizing mainstream knowledge about global societies. Such an approach reevaluates how we have come to know the world and asks us to consider the socio-political context in which we have come to understand what constitutes an ethical global imagination. A critical reading of the world calls for the need to examine alternative ways of knowing and teaching about the world: a pedagogy that recognizes how diverse subjects have come to view the world. A critical question this book raises is: What are the radical ways of reconceptualizing curriculum knowledge about global societies so that we can become accountable to the different ways people have come to experience the world? Another question the book raises is: How do we engage with complexities surrounding social differences such as gender,

Critical Global Perspectives, pages 1–18
Copyright © 2010 by Information Age Publishing
All rights of reproduction in any form reserved.

race, ethnicity, religion, and so on, in the global contexts? Analyzing global issues and events through the prism of social difference opens up spaces to advocate a transformative framework for a global education curriculum. Transformative in the sense that such a curriculum asks students to challenge stereotypes and engages students in advocating changes within local/global contexts.

In an attempt to expand what constitutes legitimate knowledge to be learned within the social studies (Ross, 2006), a curriculum based on critical global perspective advocates four interrelated interventions. First, it argues that educators need to look at the historical factors that have influenced how we have come to understand the contemporary unequal global formations. In the context of social studies curriculum, such a perspective demands that we look at the colonial or the imperial discourses that have shaped knowledge about non-Western societies (Merryfield, 2001). By doing so, it highlights how discourses on race, class, gender, religion, and so on, have always been part of the colonial or neo-colonial imagination (Mohanty, 2004; Rhee, 2006). Indeed, the legacy of imperialism continues to shape the nature of knowledge students in U.S. schools learn about the world. This legacy has "left us with liabilities of an educational nature. Imperialism afforded lessons in how to divide the world" (Willinsky, 1998, p. 13). The historical construction of knowledge about the Third World has always been imbricated in power and racial discourses (Alexander & Mohanty, 1997; Spivak, 1988). As Said (1979) described in his work *Orientalism,* in the Western imagination, the Third World has been historically represented "by making statements about it, authorizing views of it, describing it, by teaching it, settling it, ruling over it: in short, Orientalism as a Western style for dominating, restructuring, and having authority over the Orient" (p. 3). Said went on to argue that Eurocentric academic writings had "a certain *will* or *intention* to understand, in some cases to control, manipulate, even to incorporate, what is a manifestly different (or alternate and novel) world" (p. 12).

Second, a critical global perspective advocates the value of going beyond the nation-state-centered approach to teaching about topics such as history, politics, culture, and so on. It calls for the need to develop curriculum that accounts for transnational formations: an intervention that asks us to go beyond issues that are confined within national borders. Such a practice recognizes the complicated ways the local is connected to the global and vice versa and cautions against creating a hierarchy between national and global issues (Coloma, 2008; Daza, 2008). It also suggests the need to critically examine the pitfalls of forming dichotomies between the local (or the national) and the global or the center and the periphery. In schools, students are inundated with center/periphery representations based on dominant ideas that the Western society "eternally advances, progresses, modernizes" and "the rest of the world advances more sluggishly, or stagnates" (Blaut, 1993, p. 1). Binary oppositions create superior/inferior or civilized/uncivilized ways of looking at cultural practices and do not reveal the complexities of experiences that are connected to issues of power and privilege.

Third, a curriculum based on critical global perspectives asks that we be ethically accountable for the ways we have imagined global societies so that our ways of "including" do not end up excluding the global Other. The idea of "inclusion" in a critical sense demands that we become responsible to how we have theorized or conceptualized local–global relationships. Sadly, "even with the best of intentions, as we will see, it is all too easy to slip into colonizing and stereotyped ways of doing education" (Crocco, Chapter 2, this volume). Thus, the inclusion of critical global perspective is about being reflexive on how we have included the Other so that the very act of inclusion does not appropriate global cultures, histories, and experiences to further claim the superiority of specific national/cultural ways of being. It asks that the act of being globally conscious is about unlearning what we have learned before and is about coming to terms with knowledge that is difficult to understand (Kumashiro, 2004; Subreenduth, 2006). It is about recognizing that "our knowledge is imperfect, provisional, subject to revision in the face of new evidence" (Appiah, 2006, p. 144). Thus, educators may greatly benefit by analyzing self–Other relationships that are always embedded within power relationships (Alcoff, 1991; Fine, 1994). Such an orientation invites us to be reflexive about our own subjectivities and how we are implicated (in different ways) in the contemporary unequal global conditions.

Lastly, a curriculum that values a critical global perspective includes knowledge that has been historically marginalized. It places emphasis on articulating worldviews through "subaltern knowledge," the kinds of knowledge that has been viewed as unworthy to be learned in schools. The value of learning marginalized experiences, histories, and cultures is particularly significant, considering schools often place emphasize on the kinds of global knowledge that fits mainstream ideas on what global ought to be. This is particularly important, considering, as Crocco (Chapter 2) notes, "it seems safe to conclude that many future teachers get little systematic grounding in global education as a regular and required aspect of their teacher preparation." In a K–12 context, global curriculum often serves as what Banks (1997) terms "add-on" curriculum. Add-on frameworks do not consistently or ethically integrate marginalized global knowledge into curriculum and the approaches simply serve as superficial attempts to address global issues in classrooms. A critical approach to global curriculum recognizes that knowledge from a particular culture or a nation-state should not be viewed as being monolithic or simplistic but as being heterogeneous and complex. Too often there is a tendency within mainstream settings to represent or to teach cultures (or histories) of non-Western societies as being homogenous, facile, or too "different" to be taken seriously (Mahalingam & McCarthy, 2000). It is worth noting that, although a critical global perspective attempts to decenter Western episteme, it does not claim the superiority of knowledge that has emerged out of Third World traditions. However, it does ask that we engage with the heterogeneous experiences of people and that we fully recognize the humanity of people who have negotiated Third World histories and cultures.

The chapters included in this book invite us to consider the complicated ways global knowledge is present and absent within social studies curriculum and, in general, in schools. In particular, the book raises questions about the politics of representation that have shaped what and how students learn about marginalized communities in social studies classrooms (Rains, 2006; Subedi, 2008; Urietta, 2004). Indeed, representations are connected to power and power is used to dominate through political or economic means. A critical approach to curriculum would "involve, first, submitting these representations of social relations to deconstruction and critique and, second, reassembling new images that reflect our new political understandings of the relationships in which we are embedded" (McCarthy, 1998, p. 46). Through examining issues of representations, we can ask, as Sensoy (Chapter 3, this volume) does: "What stories are told? How are they told? Who tells whose stories? Whose interests are served? And how does group and individual resistance (or reclaiming of identity) affect social representation?" It is through discussions of representation and knowledge that we can reconsider how national or global events impact how and what students learn in schools.

WHY STUDY A CRITICAL GLOBAL CURRICULUM?

In recent years, a number of educators have indicated how teaching about global perspectives can enable students to critique stereotypes and misinformation about global societies (see Merryfield & Wilson, 2005). Unfortunately, critical ways of teaching and learning about global issues remain marginalized in school settings (Gaudelli, 2003; Kirkwood-Tucker, 2004). This is indeed unfortunate, considering the unprecedented global, cultural, and political changes that have taken place in the world. Even as various scholars in the field continue to emphasize how global perspectives can engender radical ways of understanding the interconnections between local-global issues, the area of global education remains marginalized in the field (Crocco, 2005; Hicks, 2003; Merryfield, 2001). Sadly, whether in the historical or in the contemporary contexts, social studies curriculum in the United States has not been effective in teaching students about the complex formations of global history, culture, and identities.

There are multiple factors that can be attributed to why critical teaching and learning about global issues have been absent within U.S. schools. First, schools emphasize narrow notions of citizenship in which selective events or issues within the U.S. nation-state become the sole unit of analysis to conceptualize notions of culture, identity, history, and so on. And, within the nation-state framework, U.S. national and international policies are romanticized and viewed as an exception: as being independent of and as being uninfluenced by global events. Or that histories and events are taught to glorify U.S. national policies and practices, thus avoiding how the nation-state has been complicit in the development of internal and external colonies (Loewen, 2007). Within such a framework, shaped by narrow nationalistic discourses, critical issues and events that have taken place in non-Western societies often become peripheral. Or global events become selectively significant whenever U.S. national interests are at stake. For instance, during times of war (Iraq, Afghanistan, etc.), we often hear about how schools need to make efforts to teach students about world geography/culture, and students are relentlessly bombarded with media representation about societies being "rescued" through U.S. interventions. Sadly, in the post-9/11 context, too often, any sort of critique of U.S. policies in the international context was viewed as being unpatriotic and as a statement of anti-Americanism (Giroux, 2002; Rizvi, 2004). Kaplan (1993) argued for the need to critique the binary of domestic and the foreign and that we recognize how U.S. domestic policies are interconnected with U.S. international policies and that we "not omit discussions of the United States as an imperial power" (p. 17). As we have witnessed in recent years, it is through the policies of giving/spreading freedom and democracy that the U.S. has justified the occupation of many nation-states (Afghanistan, Iraq, etc.). One may ask: What might be the political and economic implications of the occupations? Sadly, the "imputations of 'backwardness' and 'barbarity' to Third-World communities function to justify their economic exploitation and political domination" (Narayan, 1997, p. 126).

Second, critical global perspectives are devalued in schools because U.S. students are often socialized into learning narrow conceptions of citizenship. Historically, schools have served as a site where students are taught to consume uncritical notions of being an "American." Clearly, narrow ways of theorizing concepts such as patriotism or national identity leads students to develop chauvinistic or ethnocentric identities, which constructs the world, particularly Third World societies, as being a "problem." Unfortunately, Third World societies have been historically represented as a deviant space in school curriculum: a geography that is behind modern Western conceptions of time (McCarthy, 1998). The "Third World as a problem" perspective operates within dichotomous frameworks and creates oppositional relationship between the United States and the non-Western world. Problem narratives place emphasize on exotic issues (seemingly strange cultural practices, etc.) or conflicts (wars, stories on violence, etc.) that are often described as having cultural roots or being deeply ingrained within the cultural practices of a community. Essentially, problem narratives perpetuate stereotypes and such narratives neither provide a range of perspectives on a particular topic nor the cultural context of a particular experience or event.

Mainstream conception of citizenship demonizes Third World societies and it is by representing such societies in negative terms that students are asked to consume a narrow orientation of national citizenship. As Said (2001) argued, the U.S. public is often socialized into consuming, for instance, the "clash of civilization" framework that represents global cultures as always being in conflict and posits that societies "cannot communicate except through opposition, sometimes through even exterminatory relationships" (p. 271). It is worth considering, as Gaudelli (Chapter 8, this volume) writes: "perhaps U.S. schools avoid teaching about the world because a critical study of the world can compel serious conversations about significant changes needed in our society." A more open conception of citizenship asks that we consider a more critical aspect of local–global relationship and come to terms with how we have local as well as global responsibilities.

Third, the absence of learning about critical global issues is connected to the broader issues of knowledge and the politics that has shaped what constitutes appropriate curriculum to be learned in school. Too often, curriculum helps "reproduce many aspects of social life, including the divisions that mark off various 'thems' from 'us.'" (Parker, 2004, pp. 433–434). In other words, intellectual "domestication, not emancipation, is the norm in curriculum work" (Parker, 2004, p. 434). For instance, diverse global knowledge is not taken seriously as a legitimate area of academic inquiry because it is not considered as an intellectually valuable field of study (see Dimitriadis, 2006). Moreover, critical global perspectives do not fit the narrow model of diversity in schools since it challenges "national" interpretation of what constitutes community and belonging. As a result, critical learning about global cultures and world history courses are simply placed on the margins. Unfortunately, differences that are seemingly exotic and unconventional are emphasized since such knowledge become safe and nonthreatening to dominant value systems. The emphasis on exotic forms of knowledge within curriculum trivializes diverse global cultural practices and silences people's experiences. Thus, by avoiding controversial issues, the emphasis on exotic reinscribes orientalistic discourse that perpetuates the myth of the Other being "different" and inferior. When global issues are reduced to exotic cultural habits or practices within curriculum, they are not taken seriously as an intellectual or transformative topic of discussion. Such a mainstream approach to curriculum succumbs to a comfortable method of teaching about global issues and reinscribes neo-colonial notions of differences. Mainstream approaches to teaching about global issues do not engage with questions of becoming open-minded, recognizing the value of engaging with complexity and the need to critique stereotypes (Case, 1993).

CRITICAL INTERVENTIONS

Epistemological Considerations

A critical argument that the authors make is on how epistemological standpoints help us recognize the different ways people read or interpret the world. In a broad sense, epistemology refers to the study of knowledge: how we come to understand what counts as legitimate knowledge to be learned (see Collins, 1991). Valuing or devaluing certain types of knowledge is a political act and is mediated by our experiences, prior knowledge, and the ways we have come to terms with new forms of knowledge. Epistemological standpoints help us tease out the heterogeneous ways we have experienced or have come to know the world since our experiences and prior knowledge influences how we (differently) interpret international issues or local–global relationships (Dillard, 2006; Ladson-Billings, 2004). This is not to suggest that there may not be commonalities across various epistemological standpoints shared by individuals or cultural communities.

It is by learning to value epistemological issues that we learn to examine the differences across perspectives and experiences: a reminder that we cannot subsume differences in how we imagine the idea of universal history or culture. When we analyze epistemological issues, we begin to critique viewpoints that claim the universal nature of history, culture, or experience since historically the category of universal history or universal culture has essentially meant maintaining a European or European American orientation to the understanding of human experiences: an orientation that dehumanized the Other. Within Euro-centric conceptions of the universal, marginalized perspectives are deemed to be inferior and are not included within the category of the universal. As Smith (1999) suggests, historically, "the processes of dehumanization were often hidden behind justifications for imperialism and colonialism which were clothed within an ideology of humanism and liberalism and the assertion of moral claims which related to a concept of civilized 'man'" (p. 26). Thus, claims of cultural universals are never innocent and we may benefit by problematizing how and why a particular universal discourse is being proposed. This is not to suggest that certain concepts, ideas, or experiences across cultural communities do not have universal meanings but that we need to imagine an ethical and inclusive version of universal that foregrounds diverse experiences and knowledge frameworks. Too often, the need to value and to work through differences is marginalized within educational research (Lather, 2007).

By highlighting the value of epistemological issues, we ought to not privilege a certain viewpoint as being superior but point out the need to value (and respect) different perspectives that are shared on a particular social issue. For instance, Subreenduth (Chapter 11, this volume) addresses the politics of knowledge in regard to how people in Western societies have come to read events in the continent of Africa, particularly in relation to South Africa. Addressing epistemological issues, Subreenduth complicates the binary of insider and outsider perspective and points out how one can be an insider as well as outsider within a particular community. Locating the significance of race, Subreenduth describes both the difficulties and possibilities of developing cross-cultural connections across cultures and asks that educators go beyond superficial approaches to addressing cultural knowledge in relation to South Africa. Advocating the need to complicate travel narratives, Subreenduth addresses how a critical orientation of travel can open up spaces to examine power relations across societies and that one cannot subsume one's positionalities and subjectivities when one travels across cultural spaces. Addressing broader questions of knowledge, Zong (Chapter 9, this volume) similarly shares traveling experiences to locate the shifting position of a Chinese immigrant negotiating local/global identities in the United States. Similar to Subreenduth, Zong speaks of how traveling subjects negotiate both insider as well as outsider identities in various locales. Noting the significance of recognizing epistemological differences, Zong explores the value of providing multiple readings of events in China that are circulated in various media outlets in the United States and in China. Essentialist viewpoints and stereotypes, according to Zong, have shaped how China has been and continues to be represented in mainstream media. Similarly, to critique dominant epistemological structures and their canonical knowledge base, Sensoy (Chapter 3, this volume) asks that we come to recognize how the exotic "visual vocabulary, and the ideas about the Middle East that it represents, is found in *both* media and school curricula." Addressing broader issues on mainstream visual knowledge, Sensoy shares personal challenges of dialoguing about the Middle East or Islam via "a fog of nervous anticipation, waiting for that moment when questions about the oppression of women, or the impoverished societies of the region, and backwardness of its people inevitably arise, and I have to answer for 'my people.'"

The study of epistemological issues enables us to critique dominant discourses and also creates spaces to recognize the value of learning marginalized perspectives. Verma (Chapter 10, this volume) raises broader questions on how specific local/global knowledge is included and excluded within school curriculum and the selective learning process excludes those (e.g., Sikh students) who are represented as the local/global Other. Verma calls for the need to include the knowledge Sikh students bring into schools and argues for the greater need to decolonize knowledge that "calls for the need to return to traditional values and morality." This is because, as Verma argues, dominant epistemologies continue to reassert "romanticized notions of Eurocentric values, cultural norms, and traditional knowledge." Hamdan (Chapter 5, this volume), for instance, contextualizes the ways in which Western feminist epistemologies have silenced experiences and knowledge that diverse Muslim women have valued and how Muslim women have been represented as "helpless subjects" within various Western mainstream writings. Hamdan argues that global educators reevaluate how non-Western gender issues are taught in classrooms and reconsider how global educators have included or excluded the complex experiences and histories of Muslim women.

A number of chapters in the book also address how various academic disciplines (such as history, geography, etc.) have devalued marginalized epistemologies and address the need to reimagine disciplinary landscapes in light of various epistemological interventions. Kenreich (Chapter 4, this volume) explores the question of epistemology in relation to the shifting nature of the discipline of geography and how questions of knowledge and experience shape how people come to define space. Ways in which subjects come to read and socially construct space, as Kenreich argues, is a political practice and is inherently connected to power. Indeed, different epistemological standpoints offer different readings of space. Dominant groups may see a particular land as a space to colonize and to "develop" yet marginalized people may view the same space as being connected to discourses on genocide, discrimination, agency, and power.

Ukpokodu (Chapter 7, this volume) addresses the politics of knowledge that has shaped the very meaning of what constitutes global perspectives and how the call to go "global" is often influenced by political and ideological discourses. Advocating the practice of global perspective pedagogy, Ukpokodu is interested in troubling the simplistic ways the continent of Africa is represented in the U.S. curricular imagination and asks that teacher educators critically analyze resources that have often represented the continent within monolithic terms or images. For instance, relying on dominant epistemologies, "textbooks in many U.S. schools and media outlets have presented negative images, myths, stereotypes, and distortions about peoples, cultures, and histories of the Third World, and Africa in particular." Ukpokodu and Zong (Chapters 7 and 9, respectively, this volume) are both critical of the absence of global education scholarship within the field of teacher education and indicate how the absence seriously compromises how teachers are being prepared to teach about diversity and equity.

Differences and Global Perspectives

The second intervention addresses the relationship between social differences and ways of theorizing global perspectives. When we examine issues of social differences such as race, class, gender, and so on, we learn not to treat topics such as identity and experience in monolithic ways. Diverse ways of understanding social differences open up spaces to recognize how essentialist viewpoints foster stereotypes and that the very notion of theorizing "common" culture/world can be fraught with biases and generalizations. A more nuanced approach to understanding social differences calls for the need to look at the intricacies involved in interpreting a particular social issue since there are multiple ways of reading a specific event or cultural practice. Such an approach can enable possibilities to move beyond essentialist ways of looking at cultural differences across cultures and can help us be cognizant of the ways we have advocated global perspectives. A critical approach to examining differences, as advocated by Asher and Crocco (2001), creates spaces to critique both the cultural relativistic framework (the belief that one needs to only understand and not critique a cultural topic) and the ethnocentric view that claims the superiority of a particular belief or cultural system. For instance, when theorizing differences, it is useful to consider how identities function within intersections in the sense that identities (gender, race, etc.) are interconnected. Addressing the intersection of race, gender, and religion, Hamdan (Chapter 5) points out how diverse Muslim women's identities are shaped by multiple experiences in various geographical locales. Hamdan also explores questions of race and how the racialization of Islam in North America functions to represent Islam as being the source of Muslim women's marginalization. Too often, according to Hamdan, Muslim women have been represented as being oppressed in the Western imagination and people who hold the belief that "Muslim women need to be rescued (from their religion/culture) impose their own notions of freedom on Muslim women." Through Hamdan's analysis, educators can examine how topics such as *hijab*, marriage, and education are often evoked to reinscribe the "oppressed" status of Muslim women. Along with mobilizing a critique of dominant Western representations of Muslim women, Hamdan also argues for the need to critique the viewpoints of Islamic extremists who claim to speak for all Muslim women.

Sensoy (Chapter 3) similarly asks that we consider broader questions of difference, particularly how questions of race and religion have shaped how women from the Middle East have been represented in the North American mainstream media. For Sensoy, along with school curriculum, popular culture representations has shaped how K–12 students have come to imagine gendered non-Western subjects, particularly in the context of the Middle East. Historically and in the contemporary context, as Sensoy notes, the representations have commodified the cultural Other and have functioned to consolidate dominant power relations. In other words, representations of Third World subjects are often "co-opted by marketplace-multicultural-ism in which diversity (in the form of costumes, food or dance), become currency in an increasingly competitive market." A critical media analysis, according to Sensoy, involves analyzing not only the intent of a given visual knowledge but also how questions of accuracy and context are addressed in a given representation.

Verma (Chapter 10, this volume) helps us recognize how discourses on gender, race, and religion have impacted Sikh boys' experiences in U.S. schools. For Verma, the experiences of Sikh boys in the post-9/11 racial climate convey how race and religion functioned to marginalize the cultural knowledge students negotiated in schools. Verma argues that the lack of positive intervention made by school officials (in the post-9/11 context) is indicative of how the cultural differences negotiated by Sikh students are actively silenced. For Verma, the ways in which "Sikhs are being represented as exotic and dangerous suggests how Orientalist thinking is prevalent in the United States." Verma points out the need to recognize how race has historically functioned to locate Asian subjects, and in particular Sikh communities, as being the local/global Other. For this reason, in the racialized climate of U.S. schools, Sikh students often struggled to find a sense of community and "described schools as being a place of conflict, tension, and silence." Verma's analysis helps us understand how dominant discourse often selectively codes the meaning of citizenship during times of national crisis and how educators need to challenge rigid conceptions of citizenship. Myers (Chapter 6, this volume) also addresses the question of identity and citizenship in relation to globalization, including the ways students are being socialized to embody narrow national citizenship ideals. Myers points out the value of teaching a more critical conception of global citizenship that accounts for the politics on how students come to affiliate as patriotic subjects. Such a move allows students to conceptualize a more fluid and critical interpretation of national identity, thereby helping students to be critical of how they have come to negotiate their national identity (Dolby, 2004; Osler & Vincent, 2002).

Noting the value of infusing a more complicated notion of gender examination, Crocco (Chapter 2) argues that gender is often subsumed as a category of analysis within social studies curriculum. "To the degree that women are viewed as marginal to the world's history, the mandate to include their voices, perspectives, and stories in teaching global and international topics remains minimal." Crocco argues that educators need to decenter mainstream conception of gender discussion that positions European American women at the "center" and that locates Third World women as peripheral subjects who cannot speak for themselves. Crocco also argues for the need to critique the perception that gender-based problems exist only outside of the United States. Exploring the challenges to infusing world global literature in U.S. classrooms, Crocco notes the intricacies of teaching about gender issues concerning women from Third World societies, especially since students in U.S. classrooms often do not have sufficient knowledge to critique mainstream representations of Third World women. For Crocco, Third World women are both absent as well as present within U.S. media representations. If the oppression of women by the Taliban, for instance, is covered in the media, the representations "may contribute to circulating tired images of downtrodden females from developing nations that support an American sense of cultural superiority."

A critical analysis of difference also opens up spaces to recognize how various theoretical or conceptual traditions posit different readings on differences. For instance, Ukpokodu (Chapter 7) addresses the similar yet distinct interventions sought by scholars who affiliate with disciplines such as multicultural education and global education. Although both fields have valued the importance of working toward social change, Ukpokodu suggests that educators not conflate the interventions advocated by various scholars within both disciplines. Ukpokodu argues that educators should critically examine how both disciplines have come to differently theorize questions of knowledge construction and pedagogy.

Rethinking Local/Global Relationships

An important intervention that the scholars make is by helping us reconceptualize local and global relationships, particularly how we have come to understand the concept of border crossing. For instance, Gaudelli (Chapter 8, this volume) asks that educators rethink the meaning of space and how a critical understanding of space allows us to reconsider how local/global communities are represented through the lens of power. By recognizing the relationship between space and power, as Gaudelli maintains, educators can complicate their subjectivities as they cross national borders, particularly when First World subjects travel to Third World geographies (Wilson, 1988). Yet, educators need to consider how "international travel is helpful in creating dissonance about one's assumptions and confronting the alterneity of life, it alone cannot guarantee that one develops a global perspective." For this reason, Gaudelli asks that global educators infuse discussions on intimacy and aesthetics since such an approach invites critical, meaningful engagements with students. Yet, such engagements are not created through simplistic agreements but "only occurs through discord and tension," which enables us to interrupt superficial ways of engaging with complex social topics. Clearly, discourses on power are connected to how local subjects come to see global events. As Sensoy (Chapter 3) demonstrates, the popular culture discourse disseminated by U.S. media sources influence how people in the United States consume what constitutes "real" culture of the Other. Unfortunately, it is via media (mis)representations that students often get exposed to exotic global topics.

By foregrounding issues of power, Kenreich (Chapter 4, this volume) examines the changing nature of the field of geography and how critical geography can reshape how we have come to read local and global relationships. Similar to various other academic disciplines, the teaching and learning of geography has historically focused on dominant conceptions on what constitutes space. Schulten (2001) explained how the discipline of (U.S.) geography implicitly aided U.S. expansionist policies locally and globally and how the discipline of geography was similarly shaped by U.S. policies and interests. As Kenreich notes, the scholarship within critical geography attempts to serve the purpose of social change and provides a rather complex interpretation of space, including the intricate interplay of race, gender, culture, and social class on theorizing space. The nature of local–global relationship that critical geography advocates is about recognizing how marginalized subjects come to understand space. The analysis that Kenreich provides on American Indian land discourses and urban geography are examples of the interrelationships between race and the nation-building process and how space cannot be separated from economic, cultural, and political issues. Indeed, questions of race and geography are interconnected in the global context as well since various indigenous groups have noted land/space as a critical site to seek cultural self-determination from neo-colonial subjugation (Smith, 1999). Kenreich's examination of women's negotiation of corporate/home space in India speaks about the complex relationship between culture and space and how globalization is reshaping how local subjects negotiate global spaces within unequal power relationships.

Indeed, the post-9/11 landscape has also reshaped the meaning of the local and the global. Noting the problematic silences that circulated in the post-9/11 context, Verma (Chapter 10) argues that educators ought to examine how the effects of events such as 9/11 are read differently across cultural communities. By tracing the experiences of Sikh boys, Verma points out how Sikh students were considered national/global problems since the dominant discourse represented Sikh communities as being deviant terrorist subjects who were a threat to the United States. Verma's analysis explores how state practices and mainstream media portrayals influenced how Sikh boys were represented in schools. Verma also addresses questions of identity and how diasporic subjects negotiate local and global subjectivities that transcend narrow national conceptions of citizenship. The chapter also addresses the importance of including histories and experiences of diasporic subjects, particularly of cultural groups that are not viewed as legitimate citizen communities within multiple geographical spaces. Verma's analysis helps us understand how local and global events serve to racialize students of color and how students feel the need to be visible as well as invisible as a way to claim their citizenship.

Structural issues such as globalization and imperialism impact how we interpret local–global relationships. Globalization and imperialism have local as well as global connections since labor, culture, and capital crosses national borders and differently impact people's everyday lives. Myers and Zong (Chapters 6 and 9, respectively) address the lack of discussion about globalization within social studies curriculum and how globalization is redefining the meaning of local/global citizenship/politics. The chapters analyze how globalization has entered mainstream media yet remains absent within school curricula. Zong points out the need to link how globalization is re/shaping local as well as global politics and calls for the need to address globalization within social studies curriculum. Addressing how events in China may be differently read in the United States, Zong calls for the need to incorporate multiple interpretations of a given social issue so that students become open-minded and critical of essentialist perspectives. Myers traces the ways in which the myths and the realities about globalization are discussed in the media and how skills are currently being defined to prepare students for a local/global economy. Myers's intervention also helps us explore the intricate relationship between national sovereignty and the rise of transnational corporations. Myers (Chapter 6) suggests the limits of theorizing a romantic version of local–global relationships since nation-states remain powerful entities that govern global politics despite the increased flow of knowledge and the movement of people across the world. In fact, "the effect of globalization on world cultures is an uneven process. Not all cultural groups are included in the global village." Myers also indicates how we may better formulate local–global relationships via articulating a more open-ended notion of global history. However, "the case for a global frame has been particularly difficult to make for history education in the United States due to the entrenched exceptionalist view that portrays it as having a historical trajectory that is unique and primarily independent from other countries."

CONCLUSION

The curricular and popular culture constructions of the world to which U.S. students are exposed are the foundation for oversimplified, stereotyped understandings of the world in which we all live. Too often, these representations are full of stereotypes, generalizations, and are essentialist since they do not expose students to multiple experiences of people and the complexities around cultural issues. Because of the political nature of global knowledge that is institutionalized in schools and in U.S. society, the knowledge students learn in everyday contexts does not prepare them to critically challenge mainstream conceptions of global knowledge. The constant exposure to exotic as well as deviant representations of the Third World often socializes students into embodying a superior identity (as superpower subjects) since they are rarely exposed to the humanity of the people in the Third World.

Although students learn about various nation-states and cultures in classrooms, and are influenced by media, rarely are they exposed to complex knowledge that challenges their viewpoints. Classrooms have not served as a place where students can critique what they are being exposed to. Critical interventions can enable students to understand alternative perspectives on historical or contemporary issues. As the authors indicate within the various chapters of the book, critical global perspectives are omitted within the learning about citizenship in U.S. schools and are not part of the everyday school culture. The omission, whether intentional or unintentional, serves to reproduce citizens who selectively belong within the "imagined community" (Anderson, 1983) of the U.S. nation-state. Such (mis)education does not foster the kind of thinking that can genuinely create communities that would work toward local and global social justice responsibilities. What is needed is the kind of social studies curriculum that can foster critical dialogue and action on global issues. Such a curriculum would address how marginalized people have come to experience the world and how the infusion of multiple viewpoints unsettles the hegemony of dominant ways of reading the world. What is urgently needed in social studies research is the kind of intervention that constantly asks us "to rethink the ways in which local/global formations are represented and included in curriculum, teaching and research contexts" (Subedi & Daza, 2008, p. 7).

ACKNOWLEDGMENT

I would like to thank the anonymous reviewers for providing feedback on various chapters. I would also like to thank Melinda Wightman and Carolyn Osborne for reading segments of the book.

REFERENCES

Alcoff, L. (1991, Winter). The problem of speaking for others. *Cultural Critique,* 5–32.

Alexander, M. J., & Mohanty, C. T. (1997). Introduction: Genealogies, legacies, movements. In M. J. Alexander & C. T. Mohanty (Eds.), *Feminist genealogies, colonial legacies, and democratic futures* (pp. xiii–xlii). New York: Routledge.

Anderson, B. (1983). *Imagined communities: Reflections on the origin and spread of nationalism.* New York: Verso.

Appiah, A. (2006). *Cosmopolitanism: Ethics in a world of strangers.* New York: W W. Norton.

Asher, N., & Crocco, M. S. (2001). Engendering multicultural identities and representation in education. *Theory and Research in Social Education, 29*(1), 129–151.

Banks, J. A. (1997). *Educating citizens in a multicultural society.* New York: Teachers College Press.

Blaut, J. M. (1993). The *colonizer's model of the world: Geographical diffusionism and Eurocentric history.* New York: Guildford Press.

Case, R. (1993). Key elements of global perspective. *Social Education, 57*(6), 318–325.

Collins, P. H. (1991). *Black feminist thought.* New York: Routledge & Kegan Paul.

Coloma, R. C. (2008). Border crossing subjectivities and research: Through the prism of feminists of color. *Race Ethnicity and Education, 11*(1), 11–27.

Crocco, M. S. (2005). Teaching *Shabanu:* The challenges of using world literature in the US social studies classrooms. *Journal of Curriculum Studies, 37*(5), 561–582.

Daza, S. L. (2008). Decolonizing researcher authenticity. *Race Ethnicity and Education, 11* (1), 71–85.

Dillard, C. B. (2006). *On spiritual strivings: Transforming an African American woman's academic life.* Albany: State University of New York Press.

Dimitriadis, G. (2006). On the production of expert knowledge: Revisiting Edward Said's work on the intellectual. *Discourse: Studies in the Cultural Politics of Education, 27*(3), 369–382.

Dolby, N. (2004). Encountering an American self: Study abroad and national identity. *Comparative Education Review, 48*(2), 150–173.

Fine, M. (1994). Working the hyphens: Reinventing the self and other in qualitative research. In N. K. Denzin & Y.S. Lincoln (Eds.), *Handbook of qualitative research* (pp. 70–82). Thousand Oaks, CA: Sage.

Gaudelli, W. (2003). *World class: Teaching and learning in global times.* Mahwah, NJ: Erlbaum.

Giroux, H. (2002). Democracy, freedom, and justice after September 11th: Rethinking the role of educators and the politics of schooling. *Teachers College Record, 104*(6), 1138–1162.

Hicks, D. (2003). Thirty years of global education: A reminder of key principles and precedents. *Educational Review, 55*(3), 265–275.

Kaplan. A. (1993) "Left alone with America": The absence of empire in the study of American culture. In A. Kaplan & D. E. Pease (Ed.), *Cultures of United States imperialism* (pp. 3–21). Durham, NC: Duke University Press.

Kirkwood-Tucker, T. F. (2004). Empowering teachers to create a more peaceful world through global education: Simulating the United Nations. *Theory and Research in Social Education, 32*(1), 56–74.

Kumashiro, K. K. (2004). *Against common sense: Teaching and learning toward social justice.* New York: Routledge.

Ladson-Billings, G. (2004). Culture versus citizenship: The challenge of racialized citizenship in the United States. In J. A. Banks (Ed.), *Diversity and citizenship education: Global perspectives* (pp. 90–126). San Francisco: Jossey-Bass.

Lather, P. (2007). *Getting lost: Feminist efforts toward a double(d) science.* New York: State University of New York Press.

Loewen, J. W. (2007). *Lies my teacher told me: Everything your American history textbook got wrong.* New York: Simon & Schuster.

Mahalingam, R., & McCarthy, C. (Eds.). (2000). *Multicultural curriculum: New directions for social theory, practice, and policy.* New York: Routledge.

McCarthy, C. (1998). *The uses of culture: Education and the limits of ethnic affiliation.* New York: Routledge.

Merryfield, M. M., & Wilson, A. (2005). *Social studies and the world: Teaching global perspectives.* Silver Spring, MD: National Council for Social Studies.

Merryfield, M. M. (2001). Moving the center of global education: From imperial worldviews that divide the world to double consciousness, contrapuntal pedagogy, hybridity, and cross-cultural competence. In W. B. Stanley (Ed.), *Critical issues in social studies research for the 21st century* (pp. 179–208). Greenwich, CT: Information Age.

Mohanty, C. T. (2004). *Feminism without borders: Decolonizing theory, practicing solidarity.* Durham, NC: Duke University Press.

Narayan, U. (1997). *Dislocating cultures: Identities, traditions, and Third-World feminism.* New York: Routledge.

Osler, A., & Vincent, K. (2002). *Citizenship and the challenge of global education.* London: Trentham.

Parker, W. C. (2004). Diversity, globalization, and democratic education. In J. A. Banks (Ed.), *Diversity and citizenship education: Global perspectives* (pp. 433–458). San Francisco: Jossey-Bass.

Rains, F. V. (2006). The color of social studies: A post-social studies reality check. In. E. Wayne Ross (Ed.), *The social studies curriculum: Purposes, problems and possibilities* (pp. 147–156). Albany: State University of New York Press.

Rhee, J. (2006). Re/membering (to) shifting alignments: Korean women's transnational narratives in US higher education. *International Journal of Qualitative Studies in Education, 19*(5), 595–615.

Rizvi, F. (2004). Debating globalization and education after September 11. *Comparative Education, 40*(2), 157–171.

Ross, E. W. (Ed.). (2006). *The social studies curriculum: Purposes, problems and possibilities* (3rd ed.). Albany: State University of New York Press.

Said, E. (2001). *Power, politics and culture: Interviews with Edward W. Said* (Gauri Viswanathan, Ed.). New York: Pantheon Books.

Said, E. (1979). *Orientalism.* New York: Vintage Books.

Schulten, S. (2001). *The geographical imagination in America.* Chicago: University of Chicago Press.

Smith, L.T. (1999). *Decolonizing methodologies: Research and indigenous people.* London: Zed Books.

Spivak, G. C. (1988). Can the subaltern speak? In C. Nelson & L. Grossberg (Eds.), *Marxism and the interpretation of culture* (pp. 271–313). Urbana: University of Illinois Press.

Subedi, B., & Daza, S. (2008). The possibilities of post-colonial praxis in education. *Race Ethnicity and Education, 11*(1), 1–10.

Subedi, B. (2008). Fostering critical dialogue across cultural differences: A study of immigrant teachers' interventions in diverse classrooms. *Theory and Research in Social Education,* 36(*4*), 413–440.

Subreenduth, S. (2006). "Why, why are we not even allowed...?": A de/colonizing narrative of complicity and resistance in post/apartheid South Africa. *International Journal of Qualitative Studies in Education, 19*(5), 617–638.

Urietta, L. Jr. (2004). Dis-connections in "American" citizenship and the post/neo-colonial: People of Mexican descent and whitestream pedagogy and curriculum. *Theory and Research in Social Education, 32*(4), 433–458.

Willinsky, J. (1998). *Learning to divide the world: Education at empire's end.* Minneapolis: University of Minnesota Press.

Wilson, A. (1998). Oburoni outside the whale: Reflections on an experience in Ghana. *Theory and Research in Social Education, 26*(3), 410–429.

CHAPTER 2

[HOW] DO WE TEACH ABOUT WOMEN OF THE WORLD IN TEACHER EDUCATION?

Margaret Smith Crocco
Teachers College, Columbia University

In a report published by the American Association of Colleges of Teacher Education (AACTE) in 1994, the organization estimated that "only about 4 percent of the nation's K–12 teachers have had any academic preparation in global or international studies" (Merryfield, 1994, p. 4). Although teacher educators would like to think that the situation has improved since then, many might question whether this is, in fact, the case. Over the last 10 years teacher education has been focused on the "back-to-basics" approach demanded by the standards and accountability movement. Likewise, in response to the tragedy of 9/11, Lynne Cheney and others called *not* for more global education but for increased attention to U.S. history. They argued that studying the world amounted to "blaming the victim" because it implied that U.S. ignorance about Islam was responsible for the attack (Wiener, 2005).

At the same time, the last decade has also seen new calls for global education, to some degree due to alarm about rising threats to America's future

Critical Global Perspectives, pages 19–38
Copyright © 2010 by Information Age Publishing
All rights of reproduction in any form reserved.

from globalization. Whether such rhetoric has actually raised the bar for teacher preparation requirements related to international content knowledge remains unclear. A recent survey on this subject concluded that "Current teachers found the certification and re-certification processes to be lacking in elements related to knowledge about other countries, their interrelationships, and globalization" (Schneider, 2003a, p. 2). Ann Schneider (2003b) also found that "Education faculty may have experience with foreign travel but there has been little encouragement to them to incorporate their international experience and understanding in their teaching" (p. 1). It seems safe to conclude that many future teachers get little systematic grounding in global education as a regular and required aspect of their teacher preparation.

Treatment of women's lives—in either U.S. or global contexts—in teacher preparation programs reflects a similar lack of attention. A recent survey by Jennings (2007) of elementary and secondary teacher candidates in 142 public universities within the United States (representing approximately 23,000–30,000 teachers annually) asked which diversity topics were discussed most frequently in their teacher preparation courses. The results indicate that race/ethnicity is covered most consistently, with special needs and language diversity next. Social class, gender, and sexual orientation are discussed less often (Jennings, 2007). The author cites several earlier studies (Mader, 1994; Campbell & Sanders, 1997; Pryor & Mader, 1998) that confirm lack of attention to gender and gender bias in teacher education programs. Jennings asks whether attention to race and ethnicity tends to "obscure other forms of diversity" (p. 1265). He also notes that the silence about gender exists today despite the large number of female faculty members working in teacher education (p. 1266).

Jennings's results echo those of an earlier study by the American Association of Colleges for Teacher Education, which concluded that there has been a "missing discourse" about gender in teacher education (Blackwell, Applegate, Early, & Tarule, 2000). A contributing factor may be the fact that many teacher education textbooks provide little coverage of this topic (Zittleman & Sadker, 2002). Likewise, another recent study indicates how little coverage of women appears in world history textbooks (Clark, Ayton, Frechette, & Keller, 2005) or is included in state curriculum standards related to human rights (Crocco, 2007).

This is unfortunate since a large body of educational research indicates how important gender is to education (Klein, 2007). In contemporary American classrooms, teachers find growing numbers of female immigrants from around the world who have come to the United States with their families (Merryfield, 2000). Part of their process of socialization to American schooling involves learning about the gendered norms of schools—for better or worse, as the case may be (Olsen, 1998). Bringing attention to gender as part of a world history, global studies, or civics class may provide a safe space for new immigrant students, male and female, to talk about the cultural differences around gender that they confront in the United States.

In this chapter, I attempt to establish a case for the importance of bringing content about the lives of women of the world into teacher education programs. Recognizing the challenges of doing so in an age of accountability, I offer a set of examples linked to commonly taught social studies content drawn from a course I have taught for ten years at Teachers College, Columbia University, in New York City called "Women of the World: Issues in Teaching."

When it comes to gender equity, social studies teacher educators may simply be "uninformed but interested," just like the math, science, and technology professors surveyed in one study on gender in those fields (Campbell & Sanders, 1997, p. 74). Given the long tradition of interest in global education within social studies (Anderson, Nicklas, & Crawford, 1994; Gaudelli, 2003; Kirkwood, 2002; Merryfield, 2002; Subedi, 2007; Tye & Tye, 1992; Wilson, 1993; among others), stimulating interest in gender may simply need a spark. Not only is including women of the world in teacher preparation a matter of social justice, it is also a matter of providing a solid foundation for teaching social studies. To overlook gender in teaching about the world is to offer a partial, stunted, and incomplete view of the world, more misrepresentation than representation. Our teachers—and their students, female and male—deserve better.

The chapter begins by laying out a set of feminist, postcolonial considerations about social studies teaching and learning articulated by Asher and Crocco (2001) and a conceptual framework for teaching about women in global education by Merryfield and Subedi (2003). Both articles provide guidance for avoiding problems often associated with teaching cross-culturally, especially within American educational contexts. Even with the best of intentions, as we will see, it is all too easy to slip into colonizing and stereotyped ways of doing global education. Building upon the principles advanced in these two articles, I then provide a set of examples of bringing women of the world into social studies teacher education. Offering examples drawn from my course allows me the opportunity to engage in a self-reflective as well as sharing exercise. I use the framework provided by the two articles above to see whether the choices I have made in the course embody the principles associated with a postcolonial feminist framework.

A GLOBAL EDUCATION FRAMEWORK
FOR TEACHING ABOUT WOMEN

Asher and Crocco (2001) focus on the tensions teachers face in dealing with issues of gender cross-culturally, especially as they try to redress the invisibility of women in social studies curricula. They advocate for the "middle ground" between ethnocentrism and cultural relativism in addressing women's issues. In other words, they do not advocate abandoning the human rights discourses of the West in favor of extreme forms of cultural relativism, especially an "anything goes" approach that privileges cultural mores above all else. At the same time, they wish to avoid extreme forms of ethnocentrism that use Western social practices as the yardstick by which all other societies are judged. Universalizing all Western values can lead some proponents of women's rights to interpret customs different from those found in Western nations as candidates for automatic rejection. Judging the cultural claims of non-Western societies about an issue such as veiling, for example, can be a complex and tricky business, fraught with problems of insider/outsider status, ethnocentrism, and colonial attitudes about modernization (for more on this subject, see Bulbeck, 1998). In short, a postcolonial feminist framework emphasizes the need to get outside the "cultural paradigms" in which many Western feminists work (Asher & Crocco, 2001, p. 132).

In the same vein, Merryfield and Subedi (2003) emphasize respecting alternative traditions and "moving the center" from American and European worldviews to achieve more equitable representation of the world's peoples (p. 10). Merryfield and Subedi highlight the stereotypes that circulate widely in American schools, which project a one-dimensional portrayal of these women as oppressed. They advocate beginning the process of inclusion by dislodging preconceptions and misconceptions or what they call the "legacy of imperial worldviews" (p. 13).

Presenting a complex, multifaceted, and balanced portrayal of women of the world can be difficult, especially when student teachers enter classrooms believing that all women in developing nations are ignorant, subjugated, poor, heterosexual, and religiously and nationalistically self-defined, especially in highly fluid global contexts. Asher and Crocco (2001) note the confounding impact of media representations that tend to skew depictions of women toward the exotic and sensationalist, creating attitudes about women's lives worldwide that reinforce notions of American cultural superiority. Interrogating the expectations largely white, middle-class student bodies bring into social studies classrooms is critical if teachers are to get beyond reinscribing colonial attitudes about the world's women and exporting cultural assumptions rooted in Western history (for more on these matters and related issues, see, Kailin, 1999; Luibhéid, 2004; Narayan, 1997; Najmabadi, 2006; Paley, 2000).

Asher and Crocco (2001) note four major challenges in getting past the invisibility of women in the social studies curriculum:

1. the tendency to essentialize (i.e., to reduce to inherently female status) certain aspects of women's identities that vary by culture
2. the failure to recognize the important intersections of race, class, sexual orientation, geography, colonial tradition, and culture in defining gender roles
3. the uncritical belief that all individuals share the same needs and desires as Western women, especially regarding relationships between women and men, individuals and the community
4. the assumption that a discourse of human rights can be applied uncritically by Western women to non-Western women without interrogating the Western values that are behind these values. (p. 133)

Such mindsets underscore the need to critique the "framework of opposition" (the hidden curriculum of many social studies classrooms) that positions the West as culturally superior to other parts of the world (Merryfield & Subedi, 2003, p. 13). The "imperial assumptions" resulting from such a stance undercut the need for Westerners to study other societies and cultures (Merryfield & Subedi, 2003, p. 13). To the degree that women are viewed as marginal to the world's history, the mandate to include their voices, perspectives, and stories in teaching global and international topics remains minimal. Moreover, moving beyond the imperial legacies and framework of opposition that shape American classrooms requires rethinking issues of power, dominance, and hegemony and shaking up educators' thinking about what counts in curriculum. This is a tall order.

Merryfield and Subedi (2003) offer a detailed examination of the issues confronting educators, including lack of good information, insider understanding, awareness of the politics of knowledge, of others' experiences with oppression, and experience with radically differentiated power relationships. They warn against teaching practices that are counterproductive, including a general lack of concern for women or girls of other cultures, simplistic generalizations about their lives, reliance on a single perspective (typically one constructed by white middle-class scholars) in portraying women from diverse cultures, assumptions that views expressed by non-Western women are suspect or pose a threat to American life, unwillingness to examine the assumptions of mainstream academic knowledge, and ignoring or glossing over oppression, especially when it places the United States in a bad light (p. 12).

Merryfield and Subedi (2003) then suggest five principles for teaching about women. They conclude their article with examples from second grade, seventh grade, and high school courses. Their principles provide an important set of benchmarks that I will employ here to critique the various approaches I have used in teaching "Women of the World: Issues in Teaching." The course is loosely based on an elective I taught for several years at a high school in New Jersey. Over the years, the readings and strategies selected have changed regularly. Thus, I have a rich database upon which to draw, including one year's experience with teaching the course online. The course typically enrolls between 15 and 20 students; most are pre-service social studies students who are enrolled in a program leading to a master's degree and New York State secondary school teacher certification.

Utilizing the Merryfield and Subedi (2003) criteria allows me to critique the course through a reflective if self-serving examination of my efforts to get women into social studies teacher education. It is my hope that this exercise will be useful for others interested in moving beyond the invisibility of the world's women so prevalent in our field.

In making the invisible visible, Merryfield and Subedi recommend the following practices:

1. Confronting exotica, stereotypes, and misinformation directly
2. Teaching multiple perspectives through primary sources and contrapuntal literature
3. Developing student skills in analyzing how people's norms, beliefs, and values shape their worldviews and the knowledge they accept as truth
4. Teaching about interactions of power, prejudice, injustice, and worldview
5. Providing students with cross-cultural experiential learning (2003, p. 14).

CRITIQUING THE COURSE

"Women of the World" meets once a week for 15 weeks for 100 minutes per session. The reading load is heavy, as befits graduate school, with emphasis placed on discussion, group work, independent projects, and experiential learning. Time spent reading, writing, and discussing with other students outside the classroom compensates for the comparatively small amount of time spent in face-to-face contact. Typically, most students are women, but each year about 10% are men. Although Teachers College attracts a large number of students from outside the United States, they enroll in other programs across Teachers College. Occasionally, however, a few have enrolled in this class, which has contributed greatly to improving conversations in the course, as we shall see. Many social studies students have little background in U.S. women's history. So in teaching about women of the world, I include U.S. women in the syllabus but put this topic toward the end of the semester so that American women are not seen as "setting a standard" for other groups.

Confronting Exotica, Stereotypes, and Misinformation

Teaching global material always means confronting some measure of student ethnocentrism—the view that one's own ways of doing things are "natural" whereas others' practices are "strange." Ethnocentrism derives energy from the stereotypes and misconceptions commonly circulated within the media about women in developing cultures. Over the last 10 years, in particular, dealing with issues concerning Muslim women has been a particular challenge, given the monolithic way in which they have been portrayed in mainstream media.

In terms of such portrayals, we have a "good news/bad news" conundrum. On the one hand, increased reporting about the Taliban's oppression of women in Afghanistan, for example, means that global women's lives are being covered. On the other hand, such stories may contribute to circulating tired images of downtrodden females from developing nations that support an American sense of cultural superiority. Likewise, students may decide that Islam is inherently oppressive to women, a judgment that is neither accurate historically nor valid today across all nations.

Selecting good materials for teaching about women of the world is a challenge that I have written about previously (Asher & Crocco, 2001; Crocco, 2006). Suffice it to say that in selecting readings for "Women of the World," I made several mistakes according to Merryfield and Subedi's guidelines before settling on something better. My first mistake was in assigning the book *May You be the Mother of One Hundred Sons: A Journey among the Women of India* (Bumiller, 1991), and my second mistake was the book, *Shabanu: Daughter of the Wind* (Staples, 1989), which was chosen to replace Bumiller.

First, let me explain the attraction of these books. They each offered engaging, readable depictions of two cultures, India and Pakistan; they were written in English and widely available in affordable paperback versions. Only later, through enlightening and somewhat awkward conversations with women from India and Pakistan, did I discover that they—and other "insiders"—took these books to be prime exemplars of "colonialist literature." Among other complaints, my students felt that the "outsider" status of both authors, American journalists who had spent a few years in the cultures about which they wrote, resulted in superficial, exoticized, and reductive portrayals. In the end, they counseled against using these books again, pointing to the damage done by writing that reinforces stereotypical, especially exoticized ways of thinking about Indian and Pakistani women.

Belatedly, I came to recognize that these books represent examples of the long-standing genre of Western travel narratives about Third World countries, documented in works such as those by Edward Said (1979) and John Willinsky (1999). The two books differed in certain ways but in the end they were seen as similarly colonial accounts of women. Bumiller's book is non-fiction, a journalistic portrait based on her travels around India; Staples's book is a coming-of-age story of two sisters in the "tribal areas" of eastern Pakistan. In both novels, women get beaten by their husbands, yearn for "true love" relationships (and sons), and live lives almost wholly dictated by patriarchy. My students felt both books exaggerated marginal cultural practices and underestimated the authority, agency, and resiliency of women in these societies. In the end, these students felt the books would have profound, negative effects on young American readers, whose prejudicial attitudes would be reinforced rather than altered by these books. They also felt that young Pakistani-American and Indian-American students would be embarrassed by the depictions of their families' countries of origin. In short, despite the good intentions of teachers, cross-cultural enlightenment would be subverted rather than enhanced.

In response to such conversations, I initially intended to jettison the books entirely. But having stumbled so badly twice in selecting appropriate books, I decided there might be an object lesson residing within these foibles. So I decided to turn my experience into an online inquiry-oriented simulation, creating a WebQuest called "*Shabanu*: To Use or Not to Use?" (www.tc.edu/faculty/crocco/webquestshabanu.htm). A WebQuest is a modality ideally suited to posing problems for student deliberation that admit of no easy answers.[1] In creating this WebQuest, I was sympathetic to an argument advanced by a Pakistani-American student with whom I had spoken (for more on this, see Crocco, 2003, 2006). She felt strongly that proscribing *Shabanu* in classrooms might result in no attention given to Pakistani women in a classroom. Thus, she argued that, despite its shortcomings, the novel should remain part of my course.

Her comments highlighted the difficulties in making decisions about such matters. Finding suitable material for middle and high school students in English about South Asian women is challenging. It is hardly surprising, therefore, that a quick perusal of the Internet reveals the widespread popularity of the novel *Shabanu*. Numerous teacher testimonials offer evidence of the book's appeal in bringing "multicultural" perspectives about women into classrooms. These testimonials—and the complaints of my teacher education students about the book—together created an authentic teaching dilemma I wanted my students to experience.

The WebQuest was designed to simulate a situation in which participants represented members of a school district's textbook selection committee charged with considering adoption of the novel for middle school students. As a way of getting into this topic, I provided a number of online teacher testimonials, followed by other examples of the negative responses to the novel by U.S. Muslim groups. In the end, students had to do several things: adopt a set of criteria for deciding whether they would recommend the book or not and develop a rationale justifying the decision that they conveyed to the school board. Over the years, students split in their decisions, indicative of the difficulties posed by the issue. Overall, most groups, however, did decide against use of *Shabanu*.

Besides simulations, another useful approach for teaching global content is semantic mapping. Semantic mapping provides a graphic representation, diagram, or picture of concepts related to a subject. Engaging in a semantic mapping exercise is based on the assumption that students come into classrooms with preconceived notions, which may interfere with learning of new content about a topic. If semantic mapping makes those misconceptions explicit, then teachers can tailor instruction toward correcting the misconceptions. I used semantic mapping in teaching about African women, a subject fraught with misconceptions of all sorts.

A great deal of misunderstanding pervades Americans' views of Africa. A fundamental mistake is considering Africa a country rather than a continent. More widespread, perhaps, is the "National Geographic" problem of Africa, all savannah and desert, exotic animals and "primitive" tribes, with no urban centers, industry, literature, or universities. The corollary to this one-dimensional view of Africa is to see all African women in terms of such travesties as genital cutting, rape (especially since the genocide in Darfur), and polygamy. Few will have heard the names of Ellen Johnson-Sirleaf, the Harvard-educated president of Liberia; Wangari Maathai, the 2004 Nobel Peace Prize winner for her "greenbelt" work in Kenya; or writers such as the Senegalese author, Mariama Bâ, who wrote *So Long a Letter* (1981), or the Nigerian author, Buchi Emecheta, who wrote *The Bride Price* (1989). In addition, exploring "ordinary" women's many contributions to local and regional agriculture and commerce is another critical dimension in teaching against both invisibility and stereotyping in teaching about Africa.

Teaching Multiple Perspectives through Primary Sources and Contrapuntal Literature

Novels such as the two mentioned above have been useful as a means of introducing multiple perspectives on the complex situation of women of the world. Over the years I have relied upon a variety of genres—novels, historical accounts, social science research, United Nations reports, and documentary film, among others—to bring content about women of the world into classroom discussions. Here I will highlight a few books that have worked particularly well, noting that the special issue of *Social Education* in which the Merryfield and Subedi framework first appeared includes several articles that offer extended discussions of recommended works for classroom use (see, in particular, Asher, 2003; Doughty, 2003; Rierson & Duty, 2003).

Julia Alvarez's *In the Time of the Butterflies* (1995) is the lyrically written, gripping story of four young sisters in the Dominican Republic who stand up to the dictator Trujillo during the 1950s and 1960s. The narrative is told from the standpoint of one of the sisters who are collectively known as "las mariposas," or "the butterflies." Alvarez, herself a Dominican, writes in the form of a flashback about these sisters' struggles against this repressive regime. Based on a true story, the novel provides a gateway into Latin American history and culture. Students investigate gender relations as well as political relations between the Dominican Republic and the United States during the Cold War. Among the activities used for considering the book, which was made into a commercial film, is a text-rendering exercise.[2] The exercise is used during our discussion of the novel with a passage in which Alvarez describes growing up female. I also have students chart the complicated chronology of the novel with the software program *Timeliner* that helps them sort out the historical timeline from the literary timeline used to structure the narrative.

Each approach highlights different aspects of the novel's contribution to building a portrait of women worldwide—in the one case, the voices of women reflecting on their socialization into their gender roles, and in the other case, the ways in which women's private lives are unavoidably political, caught up in the cross-currents of regional strong-man governments supported as anti-Communist by the U.S. government at this time, despite their repression of Dominican citizens. One of the options for the final project is to create a WebQuest based on the novel for secondary classrooms, which will allow users to pursue many fascinating aspects of this history in an inquiry-oriented format that draws on relevant online resources.

The text-rendering exercise contrasts nicely with two other class readings about growing up female: the one-page story, "Girl," written by Jamaica Kincaid (1978/2006), and the book, *Girls: A History of Growing Up Female in the United States* by Penny Colman (2000). In class, students are asked to write their own "Girl" stories (or "Boy" stories) that recollect their own experiences of being socialized female or male, just as the admonitions to "fold the laundry" and "wash the dishes" were meted out to Kincaid as a young girl. In this context, issues of sexuality often arise. One student from Guam decided to explore socialization to sexual identity in more depth through a WebQuest she designed on the ways in which sexuality is conceptualized outside the United States. This wonderful project, called "Can we count past two?", was described briefly in an article I wrote with Judith Cramer about the digital technology approaches used in "Women of the World" (2005) for *Social Education.*

Another important topic in considering the lives of women of the world is work. In an effort to ensure that the course deals with women of different social classes, we look at how work is defined, distributed, and valued in various societies. We borrow a group exercise created by the former Upper Midwest Women's History Center. The "What is Work?" exercise asks participants to start by defining the concept, which is not as easy as it sounds. Students then consider a checklist of everyday activities for many women, considering whether each is work. This Activities Survey includes items such as the following: "feeding his baby brother his breakfast," "doing homework assignments in math," "helping an elderly neighbor with her groceries," "washing and ironing clothes," "raking the yard," and "working as a cashier at a local store." The list includes over 20 items; students put a plus sign by activities considered work; a minus sign by those not seen as work, and a question mark near those that the group disputes. This exercise reminds students of the "invisible" nature of a great deal of women's daily living— the routine yet essential work done by women that Peggy McIntosh (1987) calls "the making and mending of the social fabric" (p. 3). The volume of such work serves as a potent reminder to those who need to be educated on why more women have not been famous artists, musicians, captains of industry, and political leaders.

Once this exercise is done, students research women's work worldwide, either in statistical (United Nations, 2005; National Council for Research on Women, 2006; Seager, 2003) or narrative (Ehrenreich & Hochschild, 2004) form. Among the topics I ask them to investigate are the following: the degree to which women's work is counted in gross national product tallies, the "double day" phenomenon, and barriers to access for women in entering the paid labor force, such as availability of childcare and family leave policies.

Analyzing Norms, Beliefs, and Values as They Shape Their Worldviews

Getting at the norms shaping any society's gender roles brings us back to discussion of ethnocentrism and cultural relativism. Once again, I draw upon a strategy introduced by the Upper Midwest Women's History Center, which suggests posing this question: "How do I teach respect and understanding of other cultures while discussing customs and conditions that have a negative impact on girls and women?" This statement captures the ongoing challenge of my course and a difficult intellectual problem for Western feminism. As noted previously, Asher and Crocco (2001) advocate for finding a "middle ground" in respecting other cultures while supporting universal human rights for women. In my class, I have included topics such as veiling and seclusion, genital cutting, and the worldwide sex trade, but, over time, have deemphasized these "hot button" issues in response to an evolving understanding of the problems posed by such emphases. Gradually, I have tried to emphasize the strengths of women worldwide while acknowledging their continued subjugation in many places. For example, we examine the gender-balanced system of local governance in India called the *panchiyatji raj*, the numerous nongovernmental organizations worldwide focused on women's issues; the Grameen Bank, established in Bangladesh to give women micro-credit; or the many African women's collectives, established to provide support for commerce. I also include discussion about American women, their struggles against domestic violence, and the continuing problems of "work–life" balance for American women. I want to ensure that students do not take away the view that gender-based problems exist only outside the United States.

Central to consideration of the human rights movement worldwide is the history of the United Nations (UN). We examine Eleanor Roosevelt's contribution to the establishment and promulgation of the *Universal Declaration of Human Rights* (Glendon, 2004). We also review U.N. documents supporting development of human rights for women since 1949, especially those dealing with security issues (Reardon, 2003). In investigating women's status worldwide, students are encouraged to turn to the U.N.'s Cyber-SchoolBus, an online resource (www.un.org/cyberschoolbus.org), as well as various online newspapers in English, which provide competing perspectives on topics of the day (www.onlinenewspapers.com).

We consider the views of those outside the West who identify with and advocate for women but do not share the perspectives of Western feminists on many matters (Bulbeck, 1998). Bulbeck's volume takes up the "postcolonial critique of Western feminism" (1998, p. 14), highlighted in the Asher and Crocco (2001) article, looking specifically at tensions around the individual and the community, mothers and wives, sexual identities, and the international traffic in women. Another avenue into such considerations is our review of the Beijing conference on women's issues in 1995 and other international women's meetings over the last 20 years.[3]

In a threaded discussion online one year, I posed the following problem for discussion:

Put yourself in the role of a Human Rights Watch representative assigned to monitor women's rights in Southeast Asia. You have uncovered widespread sex tourism in this region among girls as young as 10. These girls are "encouraged" by their parents to take up this role in order to support themselves and their families. How do you respond? Do you see this as a violation of human rights for women? Or is this an instance of a culture's having a different viewpoint from our own about sexuality, childhood, and work?

In the end, helping students recognize that their own stances on women's issues are imbricated with their own norms, beliefs, and values remains a challenging aspect of the course. Even though I place consideration of U.S. women toward the end of the course, addressing ethnocentrism and decentering Western women, as encouraged by Merryfield and Subedi (2003), remains challenging, something I struggle with each year. When more than one student from outside the United States enrolls in the class, especially if she or he is comfortable in articulating their perspectives forthrightly, this aim is closer to being accomplished. Still, not all students from outside the United States wish to serve as cultural spokespersons for their homelands. I understand this and don't try to force the issue. Nevertheless, it is all too easy, I have found, to slip into a monocultural way of seeing women's issues.

I try to get at the problem of recognizing our own historicity and cultural specificity, what feminist scholars call "situatedness," through an oral history assignment that I know students can use when they are teaching in their own classrooms. Each student must interview two women of different generations, preferably family members. I provide a one-class introduction to doing oral history, an approach that is more art than science and one that has been used successfully in many K–16 classrooms. The students' task involves doing background historical research on women of the eras during which their interview subjects lived and creating a set of questions about their life histories.

Typically, what they find is that the stories they uncover can only partially be explained by the larger sociological and historical context. They gain insights into the degree to which women's stories can be quite divergent— from one another and from the generalized historical record, which tends to focus on the larger trends from which their subjects' lives often deviate markedly. In the years in which we have had women from outside the United States in class, sharing the oral histories has been an even richer exercise than it typically is. We have heard stories of women from Norway, Ethiopia, Japan, China, Singapore, Vietnam, Canada, and Korea, and drawn many parallels and noted many differences across nations and generations.

Teaching about Interactions of Power, Prejudice, Injustice, and Worldview

Not far from the surface of our discussions are always considerations of power. The works of Gerda Lerner on patriarchy (1987) and the development of feminist consciousness (1993) have been fruitful in analyzing women's situation. Lerner provides a carefully constructed set of definitions at the end of her book on patriarchy, which provides a conceptual framework for the course. She is sensitive to issues of class and female collusion in the subordination of women. She provides a set of criteria for analyzing the rise of feminist consciousness in the West that can be applied outside this geographic context. Although the students find these books difficult, Lerner offers a shared vocabulary for tackling many of the issues addressed in the course. A somewhat different social science–oriented resource for tracking women's participation in government and the economy is the book *Rising Tide: Gender Equality and Cultural Change around the World* (Inglehart & Norris, 2004). This study offers evidence explaining the structural prerequisites for women's advancement in gaining formal power in a society.

On a different level entirely, a story by Stan Karp (1996/97), a frequent contributor to *Rethinking Schools* magazine, provides an opportunity to talk about power dynamics in classrooms. Many individuals enrolled in the course each year are student teaching in the New York City schools, with over 1 million students and scores of languages and national origins. In this article, Karp tells the tale of his "culturally insensitive" reaction to Rafia, a Bengali student, when she shared with him the story of her future arranged marriage (pp. 6–7). Out of Karp's article, I fashioned a two-part exercise aimed at putting my students in his shoes. First, I present them with a brief excerpt from the article in which he describes how he is "horrified" by the idea of Rafia's arranged marriage:

> [M]y main reaction consisted in expressing my outrage that women were oppressed in this way in her culture. I told her I didn't think anyone had the right to tell her who to marry, and that it was much more important for her future to go to college than to please her parents....I somewhat flippantly told her she could stay at my house for a while if she decided to run away. (p. 1)

At the end of this excerpt, I pose this question: "If you were this teacher, what would you do?" Many students quickly distance themselves from Karp's ethnocentric reaction. Others admit that they could easily see themselves in Karp's position, even if they acknowledge his poor judgment in offering to take the student into his own home (problematic in a number of ways, they readily recognize).

After they have discussed this excerpt in small groups, I then circulate a second sheet. This passage chronicles a later encounter Karp had with another Muslim student who, like Rafia, shares a story about an arranged marriage. This time Karp responds differently, having learned a lesson, he says, about respect for traditional values, even when they conflict with his own. In this second case, Karp explains that he asked Jihana, another Bengali student, to write an essay about the subject of arranged marriage for the school's newspaper.

In her editorial, Jihana wrestles openly with her culture's traditions, considering them within the framework of women's rights as human rights. She also addresses the tensions for traditional women such as herself in living in the more "liberated" sexual culture of the United States. She believes this culture presents American women "with its own set of problems: higher levels of sexual assault, single teenage parenthood, divorce, and domestic violence" (1996/97, p. 7). Karp concludes by reflecting on his learning process and the development of "a deeper appreciation of the need to deal with issues of cultural difference with more humility and care" (p. 7).

In thinking about the place of immigrant women in New York City's schools, I came to the conclusion that my course had not taken up the intersections of power and privilege circulating across the first and third worlds, especially among women, adequately. In light of the profound effects of globalization on women, attending to this dimension seemed increasingly imperative. I decided to add the book *Global Woman: Nannies, Maids, and Sex Workers in the New Economy* by Barbara Ehrenreich and Arlie Russell Hochschild (2004) to the required readings. *Global Woman* tackles the feminization of a mobile worldwide workforce, from Vietnamese mail-order brides to the importing of Mexican nannies and housekeepers into southern California. All in all, the authors tell harrowing stories that strike close to home for many students, illuminating the inequities and injustices faced by women struggling to support themselves and their families. In many ways the book is a reminder of Lerner's conclusion that class trumps gender in helping to maintain patriarchal systems worldwide. Lerner argues that women of the upper classes have less gender solidarity and more class solidarity, thus undercutting women's ability historically to come together to demand an end to patriarchy.

Providing Students with Cross-Cultural Experiential Learning

As I have suggested, having a cross-cultural mix of students in this course improves the interactions immensely. Nevertheless, this is not something that can be banked upon, which is unfortunate because of the tremendous value added by a mix of cultures in this classroom. So, a few years ago, I decided that offering the class online might help address this issue.

During the summer of 2007, I taught the course for the first time online. Interestingly, out of a class of 11, two students were from Singapore; another was a first-generation Vietnamese American taking the class from home in San Francisco. This cross-cultural collection of students was extraordinarily powerful in stimulating dialogue about women's issues. Despite the many challenges of offering an online class, this experiment is one I will certainly repeat in the future, hoping to attend more effectively to this dimension of the Merryfield and Subedi (2003) framework. I think the emphasis they place on cross-cultural interactions in their many writings about global education is one that I need to attend to more fully in years ahead.

CONCLUSION

Given the constraints of different teaching contexts, I recognize that few teacher educators may be in a position to devote an entire course to teaching about women of the world. Nevertheless, many teacher educators do seem to find a way to bring attention to human rights into their courses, perhaps in foundations courses, social studies methods, student teaching seminars, or another offering. Including women's rights as a dimension of human rights is a strategy that can open up possibilities within social studies teacher education for introducing content concerning the world's women (see Crocco, 2007) and for discussion of how women outside the West view the notion of human rights (e.g., Oloka-Onyango & Tamale, 1995).

By way of conclusion, I offer here a set of general strategies for bringing gender into social studies education in a piece written (with Andrea Libresco) for the book *Gender in the Classroom* (Sadker & Silber, 2007). Our chapter, entitled "Citizenship Education for the 21st Century—A Gender Inclusive Approach to Social Studies" (Crocco & Libresco, 2007), outlines four essential equity questions for pre-service teacher education in the field:

- Who are our students?
- Whose story gets told in my social studies classroom?
- Which instructional and assessment approaches advance gender equity in social studies classrooms?
- What kinds of citizens do we want to be and what do we know and believe about the implications of the citizenship mandate for social studies education?

Taking these questions seriously means interrogating the work we do as teacher educators on a regular basis. As we reflect on these issues and offer pre-service, in-service, and doctoral students examples of good social studies practice in K–12 classrooms, it is certainly possible to recast some of those examples with content concerning the world's women. Plenty of material about the world's women is available in print and online. Requiring, for example, that lesson plans developed for methods courses by prospective teachers are balanced for gender as well as other dimensions of diversity can contribute to the social justice ethos felt so keenly by many social studies instructors these days.

As caring and competent teacher educators, we owe it to our students— new and old immigrant, white, black, and brown, male and female—to provide an education informed by postcolonial feminist discourses. Women are on the rise and on the move globally. We have a responsibility in teacher education to introduce their perspectives to teacher education students so that they can begin to grasp the complex and contradictory meanings of being a woman. And, in understanding the many ways of being a woman, they will better understand the world today, as the old order of margins and center rearranges itself.

ACKNOWLEDGMENTS

I wish to thank Nina Asher for offering helpful suggestions on an earlier draft of this chapter.

NOTES

1. For more information about WebQuests, see the Bernie Dodge website: http://www.webquest.org/index.php
2. Text-rendering is a read-aloud exercise in which the following instructions are given:
    1. First everyone reads the selection silently.
    2. Participants select a sentence that strikes them. Label it No. 1.
    3. Participants select a phrase that stands out for them. Label it No. 2.
    4. Participants select a word from the text. Label it No. 3.
    5. Participants select their own word suggested by the text. Label it No. 4.
    6. Remind the group that repetition is fine.
    7. In order, have participants read their Nos. 1, 2, 3, 4.
    8. Allow some silent time.
    9. Ask them what they have heard.
3. For a review of the decade of women's meetings worldwide leading up to the Beijing conference, which the UN called "the decade for women," see Zinsser (2002).

REFERENCES

Alvarez, J. (1995). *In the time of the butterflies.* New York: Plume.

Anderson, C. C., Nicklas, S. K., & Crawford, A. R. (1994). *Global understandings: A framework for teaching and learning.* Alexandria, VA: Association for Supervision and Curriculum Development.

Asher, N. (2003). At the intersections: A postcolonialist woman of color considers feminism. *Social Education, 67*(1), 47–51.

Asher, N., & Crocco, M. S. (2001). (En)gendering multicultural identities and representations in education. *Theory and Research in Social Education, 29*(1), 129–151.

Bâ, M. (1981). *So long a letter.* Portsmouth, NH: Heinemann.

Blackwell, P., Applegate, J., Earley, P. & Tarule, J. M. (2000). *Education reform and teacher education: The missing discourse of gender.* Washington, DC: American Association of Colleges for Teacher Education.

Bulbeck, C. (1998). *Re-orienting Western feminisms: Women's diversity in a postcolonial world.* Cambridge, UK: Cambridge University Press.

Bumiller, E. (1991). *May you be the mother of a hundred sons: A journey among the women of India.* New York: Ballantine Books.

Campbell, P., & Sanders, J. (1997). Uninformed but interested: Findings of a national survey on gender equity in preservice teacher education. *Journal of Teacher Education, 48*(1), 69–75.

Clark, R., Ayton, K., Frechette, N., & Keller, P. J. (2005). Women of the world, rewrite! Women in American World History high school textbooks from the 1960s, 1980s, and 1990s. *Social Education, 69*(1), 41–45.

Colman, P. (2000). *Girls: A history of growing up female in America.* New York: Scholastic.

Crocco, M. S. (2003). Teaching *Shabanu:* The challenges of using world literature in the social studies classroom. *Journal of Curriculum Studies, 37*(5), 561–582.

Crocco, M. S. (2006). Caught between invisibility and stereotyping: Teaching the novel *Shabanu. Social Education, 70*(4), 178–183.

Crocco, M .S. (2007). Speaking truth to power: Women's rights as human rights. *The Social Studies, 98*(6), 257–270.

Crocco, M. S., & Cramer, J. (2005). Women, WebQuests and controversial issues in the social studies. *Social Education, 69*(3), 143–146.

Crocco, M. S., & Libresco, A. (2007). Citizenship education for the 21st century—A gender inclusive approach to social studies. In D. Sadker & E. Silber (Eds.), *Gender in the classroom* (pp. 109–165). Mahwah, NJ: Erlbaum.

Doughty, J. (2003). Integrating history and literature to teach about women of West Africa. *Social Education, 67*(1), 17–22.

Ehrenreich, B., & Hochshild, A. (2004). *Global woman: Nannies, maids, and sex workers in the new economy.* New York: Holt.

Emecheta, B. (1989). *The bride price.* Oxford, UK: Oxford University Press.

Gaudelli, W. (2003). *World class.* Mahwah, NJ: Erlbaum.

Glendon, M. A. (2004). *A world made new: Eleanor Roosevelt and the Universal Declaration of Human Rights.* New York: Random House.

Inglehart, R., & Norris, P. (2004). *Rising tide: Gender equality and cultural change around the world.* Cambridge, UK: Cambridge University Press.

Jennings, T. (2007). Addressing diversity in US teacher education programs: A survey of elementary and secondary programs' priorities and challenges from across the United States. *Teaching and Teacher Education, 23*(8), 1258–1271.

Kailin, J. (1999). How white teachers perceive the problem of racism in their schools: A case study in liberal "Lakeview." *Teachers College Record, 100*(4), 724–750.

Karp, S. (1996/97). Arranged marriages, rearranged ideas. *Rethinking Schools, 11*(2), 6–7.

Kincaid, J. (2006). *Girl.* Retrieved February 22, 2006, from http://mysite.du.edu/~crowe/girl.htm. (Original work published in *The New Yorker,* June 26, 1978)

Kirkwood, T. F. (2002). Teaching about Japan: Global perspectives in teacher decision making, context, and practice. *Theory and Research in Social Education, 30*(1), 88–116.

Klein, S. (2007). *Handbook for achieving gender equity in education* (2nd ed.). Mahwah, NJ: Erlbaum.

Lerner, G. (1987). *The creation of patriarchy.* New York: Oxford University Press.

Lerner, G. (1993). *The creation of feminist consciousness.* New York: Oxford University Press.

Luibhéid, E. (2004). Heteronormativity and immigration scholarship: A call for change. *GLQ: A journal of lesbian and gay studies, 10*(2), 227–235.

Mader, C. (1994). Gender equity instruction in Michigan teacher education programs. *Dissertation Abstracts International, 55,* 1917A. (University Microfilms No. 9431288)

McIntosh, P. (1987). *Listening for all voices: Gender balancing the school curriculum.* Summit, NJ: Oak Knoll School.

Merryfield, M. M. (1994). *Teacher education in global and international education.* Washington, DC: American Association of Colleges for Teacher Education.

Merryfield, M. M. (2000). Why aren't teachers being prepared to teach for diversity, equity, and global interconnectedness?: A study of lived experiences in the making of multicultural and global educators. *Teaching and Teacher Education, 16,* 529–443.

Merryfield, M. M. (2002). Rethinking our framework for understanding the world. *Theory and Research in Social Education, 30*(1), 148–152.

Merryfield, M. M., & Subedi, B. (2003). A global education framework for teaching about the world's women. *Social Education, 67*(1), 10–16.

Najmabadi, A. (2006). Beyond the Americas: Are gender and sexuality useful categories of historical analysis? *Journal of Women's History, 18*(1), 11–21.

Narayan, U. (1997). *Dislocating cultures: Identities, traditions, and third-world feminism.* New York: Routledge.

National Council for Research on Women. (2006). *Gains and gaps: A look at the world's women.* New York: Author.

Oloka-Onyango, J., & Tamale, S. (1995). "The personal is political," or why women's rights are indeed human rights: An African perspective on international feminism. *Human Rights Quarterly, 17*(4), 691–731.

Olsen, L. (1998). *Made in America: Immigrant students in our public schools.* New York: The New Press.

Paley, V. (2000). *White teacher.* Cambridge, MA: Harvard University Press.

Pryor, S., & Mader, C. (1998). *Perspectives on gender equity instruction in teacher education programs.* Paper presented at the annual meeting of the American Association of Colleges for Teacher Education, New Orleans, LA. (ERIC Document Reproduction Service No. ED 420624).

Reardon, B. (2003). Women organizations working for human rights and peace. *Social Education, 67*(1), 58–63.

Rierson, S., & Duty, L. (2003). Conscientizacoa: Latina women, American students, and empowerment in the social studies classroom. *Social Education, 67*(1), 33–38.

Sadker, D., & Silber, E. (Eds.). (2007). *Gender in the classroom: Foundations, skills, methods, and strategies across the curriculum.* New York: Erlbaum.

Said, E. (1979). *Orientalism.* New York: Vintage.

Schneider, A. I. (2003a). *Internationalizing teacher education: What can be done? A research report on the undergraduate training of secondary school teachers: A summary for AACTE.* Retrieved on February 11, 2008, from www.aacte.org.

Schneider, A.I. (2003b). *The state of teacher training for K–12 international education.* Retrieved on February 11, 2008, from www.duke.edu/web/cis/global challenges.

Seager, J. (2003). *The state of women in the world atlas* (3rd ed.). New York: Penguin.

Staples, S. F. (1989). *Shabanu: Daughter of the wind.* New York: Knopf.

Subedi, B. (2007). Recognizing respondents' ways of being and knowing: Lessons un/learned in researching Asian immigrant and Asian-American teachers. *International Journal of Qualitative Studies in Education (QSE), 20*(1), 51–71.

Tye, B. B., & Tye, K.A. (1992). *Global education: A study of school change.* Albany: State University of New York Press.

United Nations. (2005). *The world's women 2005: Progress in statistics.* Available at http://unstats.un.org/unsd/demographic/products/indwm/wwpub.htm

Wiener, R. (2005). Teaching 9/11: What the textbooks say. Accessed February 23, 2008, at http://hnn.us/articles/15810.html.

Willinsky, J. (1999). *Learning to divide the world.* Minneapolis: University of Minnesota Press.

Wilson, A. H. (1993). *The meaning of international experience for schools.* Westport, CT: Praeger.

Zinsser, J. P. (2002). From Mexico City to Copenhagen to Nairobi: The United Nation's decade for women, 1975-1985. *Journal of World History, 69*(5), 139–168.

Zittleman, K., & Sadker, D. (2002). Gender bias in teacher education textbooks: New (and old) lessons. *Journal of Teacher Education, 53*(2), 168–180.

CHAPTER 3

"ICKITY-ACKITY OPEN SESAME"

Learning about the Middle East in Images

Özlem Sensoy
Simon Fraser University

I'm gonna go where the desert sun is/Go where I know the fun is
Go where the harem girls dance/Go where there's love and romance
Out on the burning sands, in some caravan/I'll find adventure, while I can
To say the least, go on, go east young man
Go east young man, go east young man/You'll feel like a sheik, so rich and grand
With dancing girls at your command/Go eat and drink and feast, go east young man

—"Go East, Young Man,"
Performed by Elvis Presley in the 1965 film, *Harum Scarum*[1]

INTRODUCTION

I remember when I first saw *Harum Scarum*. I was in my mid-teens. It was a Saturday afternoon. Having completed all my homework, I was ready to

Critical Global Perspectives, pages 39–55
Copyright © 2010 by Information Age Publishing

39

settle in for a Saturday afternoon matinee. I know it was a Saturday because the local television station used to run classic movies on Saturdays at 2:00 p.m. Fred and Ginger, Abbott and Costello, Lucy, and Elvis were familiar faces Saturday afternoons on Channel 12. This chapter is about "Elvis" and pop culture in general; but above all else, it is about the politics of visuals. How we (as an audience) look at, gaze upon, get familiar with, and learn about cultural and social others through visual representations. It deserves stating that schools are not the only places where knowledge about social groups is canonized and disseminated. Working from a familiar "expanding horizons" model in the standard Social (Studies) Education curriculum, students begin by studying themselves and their families, then their communities, city, province, state, region, nation, and (finally, when they are ready) the world.

While most canonized knowledge about the world is indeed transmitted formally in school curricula (most often explicitly via the Social Education/ Social Sciences), in this chapter I consider whether the school curricula are as powerful, as enduring, as organized and canonized an educator about the world as are the societal, media-based curricula. This suggestion is not new. Scholars in fields such as critical multicultural education (Banks, 1996; Cortés, 2001; Gay, 2000), cultural studies (Hall, 1997; Kellner, 1995), and critical pedagogy (Giroux, 1999; Steinberg & Kincheloe, 1997) have indicated how significant an educator about racial, ethnic, and other diversities popular culture and mass media can be, functioning as both a *curriculum* (reinforcing normative representations) as well as a "teaching machine" (Giroux, 1997), or a "cultural pedagogy" (Steinberg & Kincheloe, 1997) that is not simply a reflection of, but a producer of, culture.

This conceptualization of popular culture demands that we move away from the commonsense tendencies among teachers, educators, and parents to dismiss cartoons, movies, and other popular culture texts as "just" entertainment, and instead apply criticisms that we might of any educative text. And given the overwhelming power of mainstream corporate media to circulate their messages in a manner, format, and consistency that classroom texts rarely enjoy, media texts may in fact demand closer scrutiny than any other curricula with which students engage. Kellner and Share (2005) argue that, "[t]here is expanding recognition that media representations help construct our images and understanding of the world" (p. 370). In this chapter, I argue that by the time students "get to" studying the world (usually in upper elementary, and at length at the secondary levels), they have already received a lifetime of media-based schooling about the world. I consider the example of the Middle East, and trace just how such a cultural pedagogy can occur.

TV TEACHER

Despite the fact that I was born in the Middle East, Western-produced popular culture, and television in particular, had already organized the way I viewed the Middle East. I was schooled by cartoons like Bugs Bunny in *Ali Baba Bunny* (1957) in which the bumbling, diaper- and turban-wearing oaf Hassan, charged with guarding the gems of a nondescript Sultan, is easily tricked by a wish-granting Genie (Bugs in disguise) so he and Daffy can escape (Daffy with the riches, of course). Bugs's "ickity-ackity, hocus-pocus" karate/Genie dance is of special note. Then there was Mighty Mouse in *Aladdin's Lamp* (1947) and *The Sultan's Birthday* (1944). *The Sultan's Birthday* is another case of a bumbling oaf—this time a Sultan rather than a slave—who has more wealth than brains, a big belly, and a small sword. He gorges in a lavish birthday celebration, in which the belly-dancing seductress is his grand gift. She is, of course, also the grand prize the black cat marauders capture, and must be saved by our hero, Mighty Mouse. Even the buildings in the Middle East sway hypnotically.

It is important not to write off these kinds of representations as relics of a racist past, or as mere cartoons—just harmless fun. These characters and plots are intimately connected to mainstream narratives about good versus evil, industriousness versus sloth, modernity versus backwardness, intelligence versus stupidity. And the manner in which these particular character-types are cast reflects how characteristics (such as industriousness versus sloth) are thought to be distributed among particular cultural, racial, and ethnic groups in a globally situated visual and discursive vocabulary. It is easy to add to this list of pop culture representations of the Middle East (Shaheen, 2001). Think back to *I Dream of Jeannie* (1965–1970), popular movies such as *Harum Scarum* (1965), *Midnight Express* (1978), and *Not Without my Daughter* (1991), not to mention the endless news coverage of the Palestinian "terror" group the PLO, and the continuing discourses about a tribal, backward, terror-seeking region—all this prior to September 11, 2001.

The power of this early education was such that I, as a Turkish-acculturated-Sunni-Muslim-immigrant-ESL-Canadian, reliably avoided any discussion of the Middle East or Islam. Whenever the topic of the Middle East or of Islam comes up, even today, I participate through a fog of nervous anticipation, waiting for that moment when questions about the oppression of women, or the impoverished societies of the region, or backwardness of its people inevitably arise, and I have to answer for "my people." Most recently, I was at a dinner party when a well-meaning professor from another university boldly declared that she saw more diversity among the evangelical Christian community than there likely existed in all of Islam.

This background is important, because as authoritative as academic literature can be, I want to argue that the media-based curriculum is an even more powerful teaching machine about cultural and social others. What causes my anxiety, nervousness, and avoidance of these topics today is more a response to the informal, media-derived knowledge about the Middle East and Islam than it is about any school-based knowledge. Furthermore, I believe that the same visual vocabulary, and the ideas about the Middle East that it represents, is found in *both* media and school curricula (Sensoy, 2009). And thus by studying the visual representations of the Middle East, we are learning about the way knowledge about the Middle East is canonized in general.

In subtle ways, students "learn about physical appearances, gender differences and relations, meanings of race, experiences of different ethnic groups, the existence of different religions and belief systems, myriad variations of cultural practices, intergroup conflict and cooperation, and the multitude of languages spoken within the United States and around the world" via a media-based curriculum (Cortés, 2001, p. 19). If we apply the ideas of media-derived education, as expressed by the scholars discussed thus far, to the Islamic Middle East in particular, we can extract some very compelling histories about the ways in which those of us who may not have any personal relationships with people from that region have been educated to look upon, think about, and understand those who are (or are assumed to be) from *there*.

What is the relationship between Elvis educating the belly dancers of the fictional Middle Eastern country of Lunarkand, Jeannie serving her White Master in *I Dream of Jeannie*, Bugs's hocus pocus Genie worshipped by the stupid Hassan, and the countless, nameless veiled women standing around in nondescript corners of World History textbooks, as well as the countless men bending and leaning in ritualistic movements of prayer? How are the images of the Middle East imagined by the West? For the remainder of this chapter, I examine the ways in which the societal curriculum about Muslim women has historically been organized, and extract out the elements of popular knowledge this curriculum has reinforced. From there, I examine several principles relevant to issues of representation in regards to cultural others and that may be useful for educators teaching/researching about cultural differences.

WHO IS THE MIDDLE EASTERN WOMAN?

If I were to say to you: I am about to show you pictures of Muslim women, what would you expect to see? Take a moment to think about it…. Is she alone, or in a group? Is she speaking, or silent? Active, or passive? What is she wearing? What, if anything, is she doing? Does she work? Do you see her driving a car? Reading a book? If so, what is she reading? Richard Dyer (2002) has written extensively about the relationship between visuality, stereotypes, and the relations between how groups are represented and how that representation produces, as well as re-produces, certain ideas about them. He writes:

> How a group is represented, presented over again in cultural forms, how an image of a member of a group is taken as representative of that group, how that group is represented in the sense of spoken for and on behalf of (whether they represent, speak for themselves or not), these all have to do with how members of groups see themselves and others like themselves, how they see their place in society, their right to the rights a society claims to ensure its citizens. Equally, re-presentation, representativeness, representing have to do also with how others see members of a group and their place and rights, others who have the power to affect that place and those rights. How we are seen determines in part how we are treated; how we treat others is based on how we see them; such seeing comes from representation. (p. 1)

What Dyer argues is that how we look at and "see" a group, and how that group is repeatedly represented in various cultural forms, is intimately connected to how we understand members of that group, who they are, their place in a broader network of social relations. So how are Muslim Middle Eastern women *seen?* And what does that form of seeing reveal about how "we"—those who are in positions to produce and widely circulate those representations—view them?

There has been a long familiar narrative in popular culture about the Muslim woman: Long under the oppression of the backward Arab/Muslim male, the Muslim woman has had to endure the primitive conditions of her life, and backwards practices (such as veiling) that have resulted in the unequivocal limiting of her physical and psychological rights and freedoms. If she refuses to veil, she will be subjected to various degrees of humiliation, punishment, torture, and possibly death. All Arab/Muslim women are mistreated by violent Arab/Muslim men, and women in the Arab and Muslim world are in general being abused (Shaheen, 2001). This narrative, with minor variations, has been a dominant element of Western knowledge about the status of Muslim women since the 18th century (Kahf, 1999) and a prominent discourse in Hollywood representations of Muslim women (Kamal-Eldin, 1999; Shohat, 1990). Parallel to this story of mistreatment and abuse is a story of hypersexuality and eroticism associated with Arab and Muslim women (Kamal-Eldin, 1999; Steet, 2000). Images of Afghani women in *burqas* and belly-dancing seductresses coexist (characters like Jeannie from *I Dream of Jeannie*, and the harem girl mouse from *Mighty Mouse* cartoons), as well as "real-life" Middle Eastern women like Sharbat Gula (*National Geographic*'s "green-eyed girl"), each encapsulate this paradoxical narrative (see Lutz & Collins, 1991). They are both seductresses, glancing or gazing deeply, overtly and covertly sexual beings—while they are also in need of rescue, protection, or supervision.

In this way, mainstream narratives about "Muslim women as oppressed" also carry with them a powerful discourse of gaze that can be described as "myopic" (Sensoy & DiAngelo, 2006). This myopic gaze is triggered by particular markers that reinforce the narrow plot about Muslim women's lives. These markers have no inherent meaning; they are signs that require interpretation (Hall, 1997). For example, a photograph of a veiled woman contains an iconic representation of the veil. The image (or the word "veil") *stands in for* the actual, three-dimensional thing, as well as for concepts associated with it. Thus the visual image triggers a series of concepts that render its meaning within a particular cultural context. In the case of the veil, the ethnic appearance of the person wearing it, its color, and the religious iconography that may surround it all trigger different sets of cultural concepts. For example, from a normative Western perspective, a black veil might trigger concepts such as religious fundamentalism, mourning, or seclusion. But a black veil on a white woman (such as Mother Theresa) might trigger concepts such as sacrifice, Catholicism, and social justice. A white veil might trigger concepts about marriage, virginity, and "true" love. A veil along with a bared midriff might evoke ideas about seduction, eroticism, and entertainment. Note through these examples that the veil is a highly gendered marker.

Odalisque: Woman of Algiers by Renoir (1870), National Gallery of Art, Washington, D.C.[2]

By this manner of looking, it is the eroticized, sexualized body that is most prominent. The theme that women's bodies must be on display for the pleasure and gaze of men is a product from the Victorian era and

Orientalist ways of looking. It is, of course, not exclusively so that Muslim or Middle Eastern women were (or are) the only targets of a narrow, sexualized narrative (McClintock, 1995). What is relevant is that just as a veil stands in for a set of concepts (such as "true love"), we must consider the ways in which character-types such as the oppressed/seductress Muslim woman also play a part initiating a particular set of social discourses. We might speculate along the lines of character and plot. What ideas and concepts does she stand in for? What concepts about the West and the East does she represent?

Odalisque with Red Culottes by Matisse (1921), Musée Nazional d'Art Modern Centre Georges Pompidou, Paris.[3]

Paintings like these by Renoir, Matisse, and by Ingres and Gérôme are representative of a European fascination with harems, the odalisque, bathing, and otherwise exposed women of the Middle East. As with cartoons, the temptation may be to assign these as benchmarks in a particular period of human, artistic, or creative history. Many white European male painters and sculptors, artists, and authors were fascinated by the Orient. There were many paintings of this type by a multitude of European painters. A quick search of the Internet will give you the full scope. It is interesting that so much of this fascination is about unveiling, revealing, making bare and visible and accessible a body that is often presented as publically hidden, veiled, and confined.

Paintings like these are not simply paintings of imaginary or nameless women. Their work, and the authority that institutions and experts give them, *sanction* a particular way of looking at the Middle Eastern woman's body. Ingres, one of the major portrait painters of the 19th century, was painting Western women like this:

Portrait of Madame Moitessier by Ingres (1851), National Gallery of Art, Washington, D.C.[4]

And women of the Orient like this:

The Turkish Bath by Ingres (1862), Musée du Louvre, Paris.[5]

And there was the painter Jean-Léon Gérôme whose painting from 1880, titled *The Serpent Charmer,* was made famous when printed on the cover of Edward Said's book *Orientalism* (1979). Gérôme spent time in Turkey and in Egypt, and this is how he represented Middle Eastern women:

The Dance of the Almeh (*The Belly Dancer*) by Gérôme (1863), Dayton Art Institute, Ohio.[6]

The relevance of this history of representation lies in at least two realms. First, the contemporary discourses about oppression in the Middle East, backwardness of Islam, and general cultural decay of the region are part of a historically rooted, institutionally sanctioned, expert-authenticated way of looking and knowing. Although these paintings were created during the period of colonization, they do not lose their relevance to today's ways of looking. Tradition has power. It has the power of authority, it has the power of expertise (both academic and professional), and it has the power of normalizing a particular way of looking, making it common and unremarkable.

Second, as these representations enter into contemporary discourse, they are co-opted by marketplace-multiculturalism in which diversity (in the form of costumes, food, or dance) become currency in an increasingly competitive market. Britney Spears popularly co-opted the harem seductress character in her infamous performance at the MTV Music Video Awards in 2001 in which she performed a snake-charmer dance.

Britney Spears, "I'm a Slave 4-U," MTV Video Music Awards performance, 2001.[7]

And now a new generation of children are being socialized in the ways of the Oriental, exotic, sexual, snake-charming woman. The *Bratz* franchise, a very popular doll line for girls "with a passion for fashion," has a line of popular dolls called *Genie Magic*, accompanied by a movie (2006) and an audio CD (2006) by the same name.

Bratz *Genie Magic* doll.[8]

Bratz operates on an international stage, with a very significant presence in retail giants such as Wal-Mart and Toys-R-Us in countries around the world. The official website for Bratz facilitates chat across an international (including Belgium, Canada, France, Mexico, the United Kingdom, and the United States) network of "girlz who want to be Bratz." So how can we (and perhaps most significantly, how can children) differentiate those "ways of looking" that are sanctioned by experts like famous painters who are studied in universities from "ways of looking" that are in the movies, on the covers of books, postcards, and magazines, and other forms of pop culture? And furthermore, how can both of these ways of looking be distinguished from textbook-based and other school-based ways of looking and knowing?

STUDYING REPRESENTATION IN THE SOCIAL EDUCATION CURRICULUM

In this final section of the chapter, I consider ways in which to engage with the concept of representation in social education, and explore strategies for critical readings of media-based texts in the school curriculum. *Representation* refers to self- and other-generated images and knowledges about cultural and social groups. What stories are told? How are they told? Who tells whose stories? Whose interests are served? And how does group and individual resistance (or reclaiming of identity) affect social representation?[9] Because much of this resistance occurs in a space relegated as "outside" the mainstream, understanding representation invites us to examine the separation of "high culture" and "low" or "popular culture," to examine representations characterized as "good" and positive, and compared to those that are "bad" and negative.

Studying representation in classroom settings can be organized in the following way:

- Studying the *accuracy* of a representation
- Studying the *context* of a representation
- Studying the *motivations* for a representation

The Accuracy

One method of addressing issues of representation is by examining the accuracy of the portrayal of a group in any particular setting (textbooks, newspapers, movies, etc.). Thus, the study would include the measure of accuracy or inaccuracy—how right, true, or real—any particular representation is. For example, in studying the representation of Arabs in the Disney film *Aladdin* (or of indigenous peoples in the Disney film *Pocahontas*), we might ask students to consider the accuracy of those representations as a starting point:

- Is the representation of Arab peoples' dress and practices right for the time and place?
- How true is the representation of the life of royalty in ancient Arabia?

Such measures can be useful because it is important to note distortions and examine the reasons for such distortions by mass media or textbook-based representations. This discussion could be extended to ask compara-tive questions about similarities and differences among accounts: the movie account, as well as other accounts supplied by textbooks and other sources.

However, limiting the study of representation to this level creates chal-lenges because it can lead to essentializing or stereotyping group character-istics. Thus, the danger of this exploration of accuracy becomes establish-ing "the" correct interpretation of what was right at a particular time, and applying that to all cases.

In the case of studying Muslim Middle Eastern women, there are several compelling discussions that could be had in relation to what counts as accurate representation. The most interesting is around the character of the 'jinn—Ge-nie or Jeannie. The 'jinn are just one category of mythical characters from the Islamic tradition (they appear in the Qur'an, and the most popular *alf layla wa layla* known as *The Thousand and One Nights*). 'jinn are not wish-granting do-gooders. They are spirits of smokeless fire who are tricksters, and in some traditions, to be feared. In their discussion of the importance of developing students' understanding of all the abstract concepts that are so much a part of the social studies (concepts such as justice, democracy, culture), Myers and Case (2008) point out how "Learning a concept involves more than simple transmission of a label or a definition. It is centrally connected with recogniz-ing the range of application or scope of the concept" (p. 52). Thus, explor-ing the accuracy of representations in pop culture contexts can offer students a concrete set of examples as they explore the limits of an application. For example, why is it that the definition of 'jinn that I offer above is different from the range of "genies" we see in popular culture representations? In this brief account, you might already imagine the danger of essentialism that can quickly creep in to this type of definition-making. But it is just these types of complexities and limits that students must be prepared and able to engage with as they build their *understanding* (not simply their recall) of concepts.

The Context

The study of representation can proceed on from this study of the truth of an image (its accuracy) to the study of the *context* of the image (the time, audience, and setting for which and in which it was produced). To examine the context of an image invites us to explore how various groups make meaning of any particular representation, and how that representation reflects or challenges dominant ideas in society. There is a famous example given by sociologist Stuart Hall (1999) that illustrates the point well. It is the example of the ball. We may all agree that a ball is a spherical object, and if we were to simply study the accuracy of a representation (say, a photograph), we might all say "Yes, that is an accurate picture of a ball," or, "No, that picture looks more like a balloon than a ball." However, Hall suggests that the ball has no *meaning* until it is in the context of a *discourse* about the ball. Thus a football gains its meaning as a football only when the rules of the game are simultaneously in place around it. That is, when it (the object) is given a context (the rules of a particular game).

In a similar way, earlier I offered a discussion about the relationship between the meaning and context of an object like a veil and what it "means" in the social context in which it is represented. In parts of the Middle East and West and Southeast Asia, it may mean just another item of clothing women wear (like high heels or purses), something quite unremarkable. However, in parts of Europe, the United States, or Canada, it may mean other things. So the *context* of the representation is part of what gives meaning to the objects. Clark (2008) argues that we give more attention to visual resources in social education in order to gain a richer understanding of a particular historical moment, and that can become an opportunity for practicing critical engagement. Popular culture's visuality offers a rich site for exploring the contexts within which visual representations are read, and how new contexts can create new meanings.

The Motivation

To study the motivations for a representation means to incorporate knowledge about the production of the image in its analysis.

- Who produces any particular representation? For whose consumption?
- What motivations might any group have for putting forward particular representations?

In the context of the Muslim Middle Eastern women in the images in this chapter, we may ask questions about the motivations for depicting baths and bedrooms. Setting aside the accuracy (i.e., Could male painters have set up their easels, sat in the corner making notes, drawings, and painting women bathing or lounging? Would *you* let a painter set up shop in your bathroom?), there is the question of motivation. Both Gérôme's motivation to paint *The Serpent Charmer*, and Said's publisher's to reproduce it on the cover of his book, *Orientalism*. Regarding motivations and using images in the social education classroom, Clark (2008) writes that "Students should discuss why artists do not always represent events as they actually happened" (p. 291). This opens the door for an exploration of the social and political contexts and motivations for particular representations. For instance, in a discussion of staged photographs, Clark examines the photographs of Edward S. Curtis in which he staged Native peoples using wigs, costumes, and other props in order to preserve traditional images of them.

This discussion can be taken to other realms. For example, students can study the (in)famous photographs of "looters" in the post–Hurricane Katrina depiction of citizens. The representation (in text and image) of white and black survivors was contextualized differently, often representing black survivors as opportunists and deviant. Similarly, the toppling of Saddam Hussein's statue in Baghdad's Fardus Square can be used to further discuss the discourse on motivation. The two photographs of the incident: one closeup and the other, a wide-angle shot, offers a very different *picture* of what took place at the Square, and invites discussions on why one photograph might have been more widely circulated than the other. For instance, the close up photo gives the impression of a large crowd being present during the toppling of the statue. The second photo with its wide angle reveals how small the crowd was in reality. The first photo, which was widely circulated in Western countries, served to create a myth on how the general Iraqi public responded to the destruction of the statue.

CONCLUSION

Educators across all subject areas engage students, in some way, in the study of "otherness"—other societies, other cultures, other practices. Yet often they do so with incomplete understanding, or insufficient tools, for examining a culture in thoughtful, nonethnocentric ways. To study cultural or social "others" is no easy task. In fact, as schools become increasingly pluralistic, and the formal and societal curricula continue on relatively mainstream, Eurocentric, and white, the work of teachers becomes more challenging. Educators often are unclear on what to look or aim for in the study of other peoples, and that can unwittingly settle on approaches and content that reinforces the exotic, quaint, or romantic view about the other. This may lead to the superficial, trivial, or stereotypical studies of cultural others, thus reinforcing problematic patterns of stereotypes.

The way that I was seen, and I believe the way that younger Muslim youth are often seen (wherever they fall on the spectrum between secular and orthodox Islam), is greatly shaped by the historically organized and current media-based images about the Middle East and Islam. Just as 'jinns are out of this world characters, along with textbook images, one can see how much of the popular discourse about the Muslim Middle East is an intergalactic discourse. It is a world of women who are both mysterious and inaccessible (as we are repeatedly reminded through the veils and layers of distance between a rational West, and an irrational, mysterious East), while it is simultaneously there for the gaze and pleasures of the West, and in particular Western men.

What I have examined in this discussion is the relationship between the traditions, sanction, and normalcy of this way of looking at Muslim women in particular, and the Middle East in general, and contemporary ways of looking, thinking about, and representing Muslim women's bodies, and the Middle East in general. History cannot be separated from the present. Tradition has power. Ideological incompatibility between that which is East and that which is West is an enduring narrative that is reinforced by a history of images that perpetuate popular knowledge about religious fervor, absence of technology, and oppression of women.

One's way of looking is not simply "my" (i.e., "one's own") unique way of seeing the world. That seeing, looking, and knowing is fundamentally shaped and determined by the traditions of representations, and ways of looking within which one has been socialized. Representations that are out there (or *not* there) do not negate the framework of knowing and the history of sanctioned looking that has determined our relationship to one another, especially in the absence of meaningful relationships with one another. Popular culture representations offer a unique and readily accessible site in which to examine a key concept in the social studies, representation. By engaging seriously with popular culture representations of cultural others, students can begin to understand both themselves and the world in all its complexity. Our local problems are quickly becoming shared problems: shared in the sense of collective knowledge about events around the globe, and also shared in terms of a collective call to act. In order to prepare young people to live in this world in ways that are not imposing and menacing, but kind, compassionate, and well informed, we must practice not simply identifying what we have in common, but identifying the differences between us that matter.

NOTES

1. Written by Bill Giant, Bernie Baum, & Florence Kaye for the soundtrack *Harum Scarum* (released in 1965).
2. Retrieved May 3, 2008, from http://www.renoir.org.yu/gallery.asp?id=104.
3. Retrieved May 4, 2008, from http://www.henri-matisse.net/paintings/co.html.

4. Retrieved May 6, 2009, from http://www.ibiblio.org/wm/paint/auth/ingres/ingres.mme-moitessier.jpg.
5. Retrieved May 13, 2008, from http://www.wga.hu/index1.html.
6. Retrieved May 10, 2009, from http://www.opaintings.com/artists/gerome/reproduction/2721/the-dance-of-the-almeh-the-belly-dancer.html.
7. Retrieved May 18, 2008, from http://www.gobritney.com/displayimage.php?pid=4996&fullsize=1
and also http://www.gobritney.com/displayimage.php?pid=5127&fullsize=1.
8. Retrieved May 19, 2008, from http://z.about.com/d/toys/1/5/R/9/Genie.jpg.
9. This discussion of representation is elaborated upon in Sensoy (2010).

REFERENCES

Banks, J. A. (1996). The canon debate, knowledge construction, and multicultural education. In J. A. Banks (Ed.), *Multicultural education, transformative knowledge, and action* (pp. 3–29). New York: Teachers College Press.

Bratz. (2006). *Genie Magic* [Audio CD]. Hip-O Records.

Bratz. (2006). *Genie Magic* [DVD]. 20th Century Fox Home Entertainment.

Clark, P. (2008). Training the eye of the beholder: Using visual resources with elementary students. In R. Case & P. Clark (Eds.), *The anthology of social studies: Issues and strategies for elementary teachers* (pp. 290–305). Vancouver: Pacific Educational Press.

Cortés, C. E. (2001). Knowledge construction and popular culture: The media as multicultural education. In. J. A. Banks & C. A. M. Banks (Eds.), *Handbook of research on multicultural education* (pp. 169–183). San Francisco: Jossey-Bass.

Dyer, R. (2002). *The matter of images: Essays on representations.* New York: Routledge.

Gay, G. (2000). *Culturally responsive teaching: Theory, research, and practice.* New York: Teachers College Press.

Giroux, H. (1999). *The mouse that roared: Disney and the end of innocence.* Lanham, MD: Rowman & Littlefield.

Giroux, H. (1997). Are Disney movies good for your kids? In S. R. Steinberg & J. L. Kincheloe (Eds.), *Kinderculture: The corporate construction of childhood* (pp. 164–180). Boulder, CO: Westview Press.

Hall, S. (Ed.). (1997). *Representation: Cultural representations and signifying practices.* London: Open University.

Kahf, M. (1999). *Western representations of the Muslim woman: From termagant to odalisque.* Austin: University of Texas Press.

Kamal-Eldin, T. (1999). *Hollywood harems* [Video recording]. New York: Women Make Movies.

Kellner, D. (1995). *Media culture: Cultural studies, identity and politics between the modern and the postmodern.* London: Routledge.

Kellner, D., & Share, J. (2005). Toward critical media literacy: Core concepts, debates, organizations, and policy. *Discourse: Studies in the Cultural Politics of Education, 26*(3), 369–386.

Lutz, C., & J. Collins (1991). The photograph as an intersection of gazes: The example of *National Geographic. Visual Anthropology Review, 7*(1), 134–149.

McClintock, A. (1995). *Imperial leather: Race, gender, and sexuality in the colonial contest.* New York: Routledge.

Myers, J., & Case, R. (2008). Beyond mere definition: Teaching for conceptual understanding in elementary social studies. In R. Case & P. Clark (Eds.), *The anthology of social studies: Issues and strategies for elementary teachers* (pp. 48–59). Vancouver: Pacific Educational Press.

Said, E. (1979). *Orientalism.* New York: Pantheon Books.

Sensoy, Ö. (2009). Where the heck is the "Muslim world" anyways? In Ö. Sensoy & C. D. Stonebanks (Eds.), *Muslim voices in school: Narratives of identity and pluralism* (pp. 71–85). Boston: Sense Publishers.

Sensoy, Ö. (2010). *Learning to teach about culture and society.* Vancouver: Critical Thinking Consortium.

Sensoy, Ö., & DiAngelo, R. J. (2006). "I wouldn't want to be a woman in the Middle East": White female student teachers and the narrative of the oppressed Muslim woman. *Radical Pedagogy, 8*(1).

Shaheen, J. G. (2001). *Reel bad Arabs: How Hollywood vilifies a people.* New York: Olive Branch Press.

Shohat, E. (1990, January/February). Gender in Hollywood's Orient. *Middle East Report, 162,* 40–42.

Steet, L. (2000). *Veils and daggers: A century of National Geographic's representations of the Arab world.* Philadelphia: Temple University Press.

Steinberg, S. R., & Kincheloe, J. L. (Eds.). (1997). *Kinderculture: The corporate construction of childhood.* Boulder, CO: Westview Press.

CHAPTER 4

POWER, SPACE, AND GEOGRAPHIES OF DIFFERENCE

Mapping the World with a Critical Global Perspective

Todd W. Kenreich
Towson University

A map of the world that does not include Utopia is not worth even glancing at.
—Oscar Wilde (1891)

Our representations of the world say a great deal about ourselves and the way we view others. With the advent of color photography in the 1930s, *National Geographic*'s signature images of indigenous peoples have exoticized difference as they sparked the imagination of readers (Lutz & Collins, 1993; Steet, 2000). On television in the United States, the long-running series *Survivor* has taken audiences from Marquesas to the Amazon, from Kenya to Fiji. In each place, the program producers have reinforced stereotypes by marginalizing indigenous peoples and their cultures. Today, GoogleEarth provides us with yet another window to the world. Its satellite imagery has

Critical Global Perspectives, pages 57–75
Copyright © 2010 by Information Age Publishing
All rights of reproduction in any form reserved.

begun to transform our spatial understanding of global issues. In Sudan, even Khartoum's restrictions on the domestic and foreign press cannot hide the evidence of the Janjaweed's wholesale destruction of villages in Darfur. In this case, a new geographic tool can help to raise awareness of genocide as a global issue that demands political action.

Geography has much to contribute to the development of a critical global perspective. Tuan (1991) broadly defined the field of geography as "the study of Earth as the home of people" (p. 99). Geography's focus on spatial patterns and processes provides a unique lens for viewing the world's cultures, systems, and issues. This chapter traces the evolution of the geographic thought from the late nineteenth century to recent work from critical perspectives. New epistemological assumptions have transformed the discipline into fertile ground for global educators, in which discourses on place and space are seen as highly contested. Spatial processes unfold within the context of broader systemic struggles for power and privilege. Tuan (1977) observed that "what begins as undifferentiated space becomes a place as we get to know it better and endow it with value" (p. 6). Endowing a place with value is inherently a political act. As such, any place becomes an unstable construct that can only be partially understood as a reflection of existing power relations. To provide a context for critical geography and its relationship to global education, this chapter begins with an introduction to geographic thought and its major traditions. Next, I examine two issues that illustrate geography's analytic tools to interrogate inequality in local and global contexts. First, I analyze the systematic displacement of Native North American peoples as well as the racial segregation of urban landscapes in the United States. Second, I explore the social geographies of women as a barometer of patriarchy in India and the United States. Throughout the chapter, an argument is made for the vital role of geography in the development of critical global perspectives.

SHIFTS IN GEOGRAPHIC THOUGHT

Since its inception as a modern academic discipline in the late 19th century, geography has struggled with its identity. Over the course of the 20th century, three main traditions developed within geography: environmental, regional, and spatial (Taaffe, 1974). The first tradition focused on the relationship between humans and the environment. Originally, "environment" referred to the biophysical environment—namely, landforms, climate, soil, and vegetation. Early work in this tradition suffered from a bias toward environmental determinism. For example, in his now infamous work, *Climate and Civilization*, Ellsworth Huntington (1911) causally linked the degree of "civilization" of a people to levels of climatic elements, such as temperature and precipitation. As he saw it, a mild climate like that of Europe was an essential condition for the development of advanced civilizations. In contrast, hotter climates prevented the growth of civilization. From his writing, the stereotypes of lazy people from hot climates and industrious people from temperate climates gained further circulation. Such a conclusion conveniently supported the early 20th-century British imperial order. The political boundaries drawn by European nations in Africa stand as a sober reminder of the complicity of geography with colonial power.

Over time, the definition of the term "environment" expanded. By the 1950s, "environment" included natural, human-made, and even psychological environments. Interest in the environmental tradition continued as more geographers turned their attention to environmental problems such as acid rain and desertification. In contrast to the environmental tradition, the regional tradition viewed geography as the study of areal differentiation: how areas of the world's surface differ within various locations. With its roots in the 1920s, the regional tradition gathered momentum in the 1950s and 1960s. Areas were differentiated by examining a range of physical, social, and economic phenomena. For geographers in the regional tradition, searching for how areas differed from each other was more important than strictly searching for a relationship between humans and the environment. The earlier generation of regional geographers was chiefly concerned with classification and description of regions. For instance, the Köppen climate classification system was emblematic of the attention given to areal differentiation, thus placing emphasis on differences on surfaces. In such classifications, regions were formally mapped, had limited descriptive analysis, and the relationship between humans and landscape was not highlighted. Houston's (1959) work about the plain of Valencia represented the early attention to region as a description. Drawing on municipal records and maps, Houston described in rich detail the organic growth of Valencia as a leading Spanish city. For Houston, it was inconceivable to attempt to separate the spatial configuration of the Valencian landscape from the substance of the broader landscape itself—its flora and fauna, irrigated fields, roads, buildings, and indeed its people. Houston's work placed emphasis on analyzing the functional elements in the study of a region in the sense that it showed the interrelationships between physical landscape and the overall environment.

The spatial tradition focused, instead, on the spatial distribution of phenomena. Space can be defined as "... a realm without meaning, a 'fact of life' which, like time, produces the coordinates of life" (Cresswell, 2004, p. 10). The organizing concept of this tradition is the explicit causal role of terrestrial space. The spatial distribution of phenomena is implicitly considered within the regional and environmental traditions, but the spatial tradition is distinct from the other two in that it pays attention to the *explicit* rather than the implicit role of space. Schaefer (1953) argued that "geography must pay attention to the spatial arrangement of phenomena in an area and not so much to the phenomena themselves" (p. 574). As a result, the spatial tradition employed quantitative methods such as locational analysis in order to empirically uncover and explain the causal role of space. This effort aimed to generate scientific laws directly linked to spatial patterns of fundamental and underlying processes. Geographers used quantitative data to create spatial models of various phenomena, including patterns of deforestation in sub-Saharan Africa. Such an approach, in the social sciences, often placed emphasis on the need to empirically observe an objective reality or truth. Sack (1974) termed the divorce of space and substance as spatial separatism. Later, this dichotomy would be challenged by critical geographers. The next section highlights the development of critical geography.

THE RISE OF CRITICAL GEOGRAPHY

Over the last four decades, social sciences have encountered a series of new epistemologies. Unlike the natural sciences, social sciences are now marked by deep-rooted disagreement between scholars about "the nature of legitimate scientific problems and methods" (Kuhn, 1970, p. viii). Several epistemologies have emerged that call positivism into question. Positivism aims to understand the world while postpositivism seeks to change it. Critical geography is an umbrella term for a diverse and fluid field of human geography that embraces "emancipatory politics within and beyond the discipline,...the promotion of progressive social change, and...the development of a broad range of critical theories and their application" (Painter, 2000, p. 126). Three epistemological frameworks have shaped research in critical geography: Marxism, feminism, and poststructuralism.

Marxist theory foregrounds the role of economic structures in constraining human activities. Researchers have examined the dynamics of class formation and struggles over space (Harvey, 1972, 1982; Massey, 1984; Sheppard & Barnes, 1990; Smith, 1990). The seeds of critical geography were sown when Harvey (1972) boldly called geographers to spend less time measuring uneven distributions of human and natural resources and to spend more time questioning the fundamental assumptions of the discipline of geography. How does a democratic capitalist society shape epistemology? How might a commitment to social justice reconfigure epistemology? Harvey advocated for new geographic "concepts and categories, theories and arguments...in the process of bringing about a humanizing social change" (p. 11).

Feminism focuses on the role of patriarchy in human relations. For feminist geographers, the vast majority of geographic research reflects patriarchal assumptions of the male scholars who conducted the research (Rose, 1993). New lines of research focused on the body, economy, and society as spatial evidence of patriarchy at work (Duncan, 1996; McDowell, 1993; Pratt & Hanson, 1994; Rose, 1993; Sharp, 2005; Women and Geography Study Group, 1997). Borrowing from Marxist and feminist approaches, Massey (1984) pioneered early work on the role of gender in the spatial division of labor.

Poststructuralists such as Foucault (1984) have in part triggered a "crisis of representation" by critiquing conventional notions of reason through deconstruction. This technique decenters meaning to uncover its inherent contradictions and instability. Deconstruction exposes how power relations inform the continual negotiation of meaning. Soja (1989) explained that ". . . [i]t is now space more than time that hides things from us . . . the demystification of spatiality and its veiled instrumentality of power is the key to making practical, political, and theoretical sense of the contemporary era" (p. 61). Poststructuralists claim that every representation contains multiple, hidden, and even contradictory meanings (Gregory, 1994; Soja, 1989, 1996). As such, maps—visual representations of geographic space—are not innocent (Crampton, 2001; Monmonier, 1991). Drawing on postcolonial theorists such as Said (1978) and Spivak (1988), Blunt and Wills (2000) have examined the complicity of cartographers in the establishment of empire. They envision postcolonial studies in geography as a means to problematize and transform relations between colonized and colonizing peoples.

Poststructural contributions to geography have triggered a shift from region as description to region as explanation for human geographers. For example, in reaction to what Sack (1974) called spatial separatism, Johnston (1991) called for renewed attention to the role of the local milieu in structuring how people address problems. Milieu has variously been labeled as "region," "place," and "locality." The intention, though, was not to revive a notion of environmental determinism but instead to suggest that place is a context that enables and constrains social activities (Johnston, 1991). Taken as a whole, the major strands of critical geography offer fresh perspectives for global educators. What follows are a description of the aims of global education and an argument for the role of geography in global education.

GEOGRAPHY AND GLOBAL EDUCATION

In the United States, popular awareness of globalization has increased (Barber, 1996; Friedman, 2005). At the same time, global education has galvanized support as a legitimate field of inquiry (Fujikane, 2003; Gaudelli, 2003; Tye, 1999). This section theorizes global education and the role geography plays in developing a critical global perspective. Over the last three decades, numerous appeals have been made for a K–12 global education curriculum that focuses on student understanding of global interdependence, multiple perspectives, and the connection between local and global issues (Alger & Harf, 1986; L. F. Anderson, 1979, 1990; Becker, 1979; Case, 1993; Collins, Czarra, & Smith, 1998; Hanvey, 1976; Kniep, 1986; Merryfield & Wilson, 2005; Pike & Selby, 1988). In short, the purpose of global education is to prepare all students for participation in the global society as well as in their local communities.

As a broad educational movement, global education includes specific curricular content. Its content emphasizes perspective consciousness (Alger & Harf, 1986; Collins et al., 1998; Hanvey, 1976; Kniep, 1986; Merryfield & Wilson, 2005, Pike & Selby, 1988), global interdependence (Alger & Harf, 1986; Becker, 1979; Collins et al., 1998; Hanvey, 1976; Kniep, 1986; Merryfield & Wilson, 2005; Pike & Selby, 1988), and connections between local and global issues (Alger, 1974; Alger & Harf, 1986; C. C. Anderson, 1990; L. F. Anderson, 1979; Collins et al., 1998; Hanvey, 1976; Merryfield & Wilson, 2005; Pike & Selby, 1988). In addition to these three themes of global education, a perceptual dimension of global education, according to Case (1993), suggests that open-mindedness, anticipation of complexity, resistance to stereotyping, and empathy are the perceptual components that complement the content of global education. A description of the three main themes of global education follows.

Perspective consciousness is a critical awareness of multiple perspectives that are culturally mediated (Alger & Harf, 1986; Collins et al., 1998; Hanvey, 1976; Kniep, 1986; Merryfield & Subedi, 2001; Merryfield & Wilson, 2005; Pike & Selby, 1988). For example, a contemporary issue such as AIDS should not be viewed from one monolithic perspective. Instead, AIDS should be understood from multiple perspectives—such as a West African, a European, an East Asian, an African American, the World Health Organization, and a gay perspective. Recognizing that diversity exists within and among perspectives, students learn to be skeptical of essentialist claims and reject Eurocentrist views (Merryfield & Subedi, 2001). Ultimately, students determine for themselves the congruence and incongruence of multiple perspectives.

Global interdependence is another theme that is often addressed within the field of global education. Global interdependence is the concept that the world and its people are interrelated by various systems: economic, political, cultural, technological, and ecological (Alger & Harf, 1986; Becker, 1979; Collins et al., 1998; Hanvey, 1976; Kniep, 1986; Merryfield & Wilson, 2005; Pike & Selby, 1988). This theme may explore the role of diverse transnational institutions such as Oil and Petroleum Exporting Countries (OPEC) or the United Nations. It also may address broader issues connected to world religions and specific issues such as U.S. foreign policies in the Middle East, Asia, and Africa.

The connection between local and global issues is a third prominent theme addressed within the scholarship of global education (Alger & Harf, 1986; C. C. Anderson, 1990; L. F. Anderson, 1979; Collins et al., 1998; Hanvey, 1976; Merryfield & Wilson, 2005; Pike & Selby, 1988). This theme challenges the human tendency to view global issues as a remote or secondary issue and critiques the perspectives that serve narrow national interests or policies. It argues that contemporary issues affect people differently in various global locales, whether in the United States or in the global context. As a result, global education challenges students to understand the dynamic relationship between local and global issues. Of the three global education areas, the local–global intersection theme has the most potential to empower students for participation in both the global and local communities. This theme supports a critical global perspective when it pays special attention to issues of difference, power, inequality, and social justice (Merryfield & Subedi, 2001).

Despite the many calls for global education, teachers are not well prepared to teach from a global perspective (Torney-Purta, 1982; Tucker & Cistone, 1991). This is not surprising given the general public's lack of basic knowledge about world geography, world cultures, global systems, and issues. For example, from a national study of 18- to 24-year-olds in the United States, the National Geographic Education Foundation (2006) concluded that young adults possess a limited understanding of the world beyond our nation's borders. According to the study, despite 3 years of media coverage of U.S. military intervention in Iraq, more than 60% of participants were unable to identify Iraq's location on a blank outline map of world nations (p. 6). More than 50% of participants did not know that Sudan is an African nation. Approximately 20% of participants placed Sudan on the continent of Asia, and another 10% placed it in Europe (p. 8). This is particularly important because the genocide in Darfur—located in western Sudan—has been described as the worst humanitarian crisis of the 21st century. Any understanding of global issues or conflicts must begin with knowledge of the geography, history, and politics of the region.

Geography's contribution to global education lies in its attention to the spatial patterns and processes that shape our identities, our communities, and our world. For far too long, global educators have examined change over time and marginalized change across space. We live in a time–space continuum, but our collective obsession with history and memory means that we have short-circuited our understanding of the social construction of space. Renewed attention to the reciprocal roles of space and social relations is essential for developing a critical global perspective. The spatial dimensions of global systems and issues are paradoxically visible as well as veiled. Soja (1989) reminded us that space masks power, yet with closer examination we can see that space is inherently shaped by power. For example, the urban location of a large industrial plant may seem benign until a closer examination reveals that the location was likely chosen because the local residents of the neighborhood lacked the political power to challenge the plant's construction. We need not set aside historical knowledge, but geographic knowledge and skills can powerfully illuminate salient and interconnected issues from a variety of scales. Through this exploration, we can develop what Hanvey (1976) described as a deeper awareness of human choices and a more robust sense of individual and collective agency. Imagining alternative futures and communities requires students to courageously situate human choice as an inherently ethical decision in a context where information is partial, ambiguous, and often contradictory.

GEOGRAPHIC CONCEPTS AND TOOLS FOR GLOBAL EDUCATION

Geography offers global educators a heuristic set of concepts and tools for understanding and changing the world. The description below highlights the two key concepts: scale and region. The geographic concepts of scale and region can be used to understand diverse phenomena such as the movement of indigenous peoples, the segregation of cities, and even the social geography of women. Lastly, I address the relevance of remote sensing and geographic information systems as technological tools and their promising applications. Increasingly, social scientists from a number of disciplines draw on geography to highlight the spatial dimension of their work. Global educators trained in other disciplines will find that these concepts and tools can assist in interdisciplinary approaches to the curriculum.

Scale: Degree of Magnitude

In human geography, scale or scale of analysis is developed in regards to describing the relationship between time and space, and ways in which one conceptualizes a scale clearly shapes one's frame of analysis. The traditional approach to theorizing scale defined time and space as being narrow and fixed according to absolute frames of reference. For example, too often the boundary of a nation-state became the centerpiece or the scale to theorize transnational issues. For instance, such an approach to scale did not consider how environmental issues needed to be analyzed on the transnational context since issues such as pollution were not only national concerns but also global issues. Furthermore, human subjects may respond to a researcher's scale of analysis in different ways: the ways in which a researcher may show the relationship between time and space. For instance, indigenous people who live in New Zealand may contest the ways in which nonindigenous researchers have defined the relationship between land and people via the use of various scales within maps and graphs. This helps us understand how methodology is tied to the researcher's determination of the scale of analysis. Poststructuralists problematize the notion of scale as continuously shifting and thus difficult to hold constant for research on human subjects. Still, the importance of scale as a concept for geographers lies in its ability to sharpen our attention to particular patterns and processes and is attentive to how marginalized people may view the researcher's analysis differently.

Region: A Differentiated Area

A region is an area with a common set of characteristics that distinguish it from other areas near and far. A formal region possesses established boundaries, such as the city of Tokyo. The Pacific Rim, though, is a functional region where the area is defined by its function and the activities that take place within it are multilayered and culturally, socially and politically heterogeneous. The utility of the concept of region persists in modern geography. Although critical human geographers have shifted the emphasis from description to explanation within regional geography, the notion of region as a manifestation of areal differentiation is relevant. As long as the world comes unsorted to geographers, one role of geographers is to make sense of the world. The core concept of region enables geographers to interpret the world.

New Tools

Critical global educators have come to recognize that new geographic tools are changing the way we view the world and its people. For instance, a new generation of geographers has harnessed rapid technological developments in relation to remote sensing. Remote sensing refers to the collection of information from great distances and over broad areas by means of instruments mounted on aircraft or satellites (Strahler & Strahler, 1994). Geographers use remote sensing to describe and analyze the physical, chemical, biological, and cultural characteristics of the Earth's surface. Since 1972, the National Aeronautic and Space Administration has launched six earth-observing satellites, known as Landsats. Advances in image processing have permitted researchers to more easily manipulate the digital images from remote sensors such as Landsats. Such technology offers critical ways of understanding space.

Another rapidly expanding technological development is a geographic information system (GIS). A GIS is a "computer system capable of assembling, storing, manipulating, and displaying geographically referenced information" (USGS, 1992). A GIS allows the user to create a spatial data set that can be compared with various data sets, particularly in relation to making projections. For example, many urban planners currently use GIS software to analyze census data in order to forecast demographic trends. Such forecasting can inform decisions about the location and distribution of social services. GIS can enable students to explore global issues from a variety of scales (Kenreich, 2003). The next section introduces three examples of geographic topics that can be used to develop critical global perspectives: the movement of indigenous peoples, racial and ethnic segregation of urban spaces, and the social geographies of women.

MOVEMENT OF INDIGENOUS PEOPLES

Critical global educators can examine indigenous peoples from a variety of scales in various regions. Any study of the movement of indigenous peoples reveals deep connections among ethnicity, place, and power. The movement of Native North American peoples can best be understood as a geography of genocide. The U.S. federal government's systematic displacement of Native American peoples stands as a stark reminder of the unequal power relations that shape where people live. The political and military campaigns to remove Native American peoples to reservations demonstrate a pattern of repeated and flagrant violations of human rights. During this struggle, land became a contested and highly prized commodity where alleged property rights by white settlers and government assertions of eminent domain trumped the human rights of those who were displaced. After decades of broken treaties and broken promises, Native American peoples have had some success in petitioning the government for a redress of grievances. For example, the Lakotas asserted land rights to the Black Hills in South Dakota, lost the land rights claim, but won a multimillion-dollar award for the loss of potential revenue from land and water use (Churchill, 2002). Ultimately, the Lakotas rejected the award on the principle that no amount of money can replace the loss of one's homeland. This response is consistent with the sentiment of Lakota leader Tensunke Witko, who observed in 1875 that "one does not sell the earth upon which people walk." His words provide a window into a worldview that resisted the commoditization of land. The Anglo-European understanding of individual property rights runs up against a much older indigenous conception of land as sacred and communal. Global educators can use the geography of Native North American peoples as evidence of one nation's attempt to displace its indigenous people. Case studies of the Ainu in Japan and of the Aborigines in Australia can provide comparative perspectives of those who have been forced to the geographic margins of society.

RACIAL AND ETHNIC SEGREGATION OF URBAN SPACES

For critical global educators, urban segregation is an issue of great interest. Urban geographers have studied the nature and development of cities for decades. Drawing on the early work of the Chicago School, U.S. cities were viewed as central business districts surrounded by tidy concentric zones of various land uses. Today, though, cities are seen as contested spaces with overlapping and blurred boundaries. Soja (1989) characterized Los Angeles as "a metro-sea of fragmented yet homogenized communities, cultures, and economies confusingly arranged into a contingently ordered spatial division of labor and power" (p. 244). He further argued that Los Angeles remained "so fragmented and filled with whimsy and pastiche . . . [that] the hard edges of the capitalist, racist, and patriarchal landscape seem to disappear, melt into air" (p. 246). The challenge, then, for critical geographers is to deconstruct the urban landscape and generate geographies of difference and resistance. Spatial perspectives on the issue of segregation provide a powerful illustration of geography's value for developing critical global perspectives.

Patterns of ethnic segregation in urban residences reflect processes of discrimination, disadvantage, and individual choice (Johnston, Poulsen, & Forrest, 2007). Discrimination chiefly denies access to specific areas for members of a targeted group by law or other measures. Racially restrictive housing covenants and municipal segregation ordinances, for example, excluded specific groups of people from property rights. In 1911, Baltimore was the first U.S. city to enact such an ordinance separating "whites and Negroes" (Jones-Correa, 2000). Despite a legal challenge to the ordinance in 1914, a Maryland court upheld the ordinance. A number of cities throughout the U.S. passed similar ordinances in the 1910s and 1920s. Unlike the public ordinances, the housing covenants were private agreements. The covenant was typically an appendix to the property deed. Here is an example of a covenant on property in a Seattle neighborhood:

> No person or persons of Asiatic, African or Negro blood, lineage or extraction shall be permitted to occupy a portion of said property, or any building thereon, except, domestic servants to be actually and in good faith employed by White occupant of such premises. (Seattle Civil Rights and Labor History Project, 2008)

In 1926, the Supreme Court upheld housing covenants as legally enforceable, and this in part paved the way for a nationwide proliferation of covenants. Two decades later, the Supreme Court reversed course and struck down covenants. Despite the court's decision, the practice widely continued until federal legislation in 1968 banned covenants and made racial discrimination in the transfer, sale, or rental of property illegal. Since then, thousands of housing-related hate crimes have been perpetrated in order to police the racial boundaries of neighborhoods (Crump, 2004).

Given the historical and legal record, it is not surprising to see that the process of discrimination has a spatial context and expression. Disadvantage further shapes patterns of segregation through three spatially structured processes: the labor market, housing market, and school systems (Johnston et al., 2007). The geographies of job, housing, and educational opportunities are dynamically intertwined and mutually reinforcing. Simply put, one cannot afford to live in a community with high-quality schools unless one possesses the right type of job. Yet, job opportunities are contingent on one's education and social network.

While discrimination and disadvantage shape segregation patterns, individual choice remains a factor. Voluntary "self-segregation" reflects individuals'—especially recent immigrants—desire to maintain their cultural identity through a strong community. In a five-nation study of ethnic segregation in urban residences, the degree of segregation in U.S. cities is substantially higher than that of cities elsewhere (Johnston et al., 2007). In particular, blacks are more likely than any other group to live in segregated communities (p. 733). The authors of the study point out that European and Asian immigrants have long viewed urban ethnic enclaves as temporary steps toward cultural assimilation in the United States. For many blacks, though, discrimination and disadvantage reinforced their social and spatial isolation. As a result, segregation has spatially concentrated poverty in urban ghettoes (Massey, 1990). However, the aim of cultural and spatial assimilation is not universally embraced. In the 1960s, the Black Power Movement rejected assimilationist rhetoric and celebrated the ghetto as a site of political engagement and resistance (Tyner, 2006). Like the urban ghetto, various geographic places are inextricably bound to the discourse of race. The geography of whiteness in Vermont (Vanderbeck, 2006) raises questions about the meanings of assimilation when whites embrace spatial isolation.

Patterns of residential segregation persist, but emerging race relations in integrated workplaces may begin to change this. Ellis, Wright, and Parks (2004) studied patterns of racial segregation in the workplace and in residential communities in metropolitan Los Angeles. They found lower levels of racial segregation in the workplace than those found in residential communities. They argued that less segregated workplaces may be a factor in the rise of interracial partners and families. They anticipate that residential segregation may decline as interracial families make new decisions about where to live.

How does this recent scholarship in geography contribute to the development of a critical global perspective? Global educators can draw on this body of work to explore issues of power and oppression in a spatial context. In the first example, the movement of Native North Americans reflects a coordinated campaign to uproot people from their land. In the second example, racial and ethnic segregation is at once a global and local phenomenon. One approach is a comparative case study of racial segregation of local public spaces in the United States and that within contemporary South Africa (Smith, 2002). Another approach is to explore segregation of immigrant communities in the United States. Consider New York's Chinatown. Geography can help us deeply understand the physical and human characteristics of Chinatown. Why is Chinatown located where it is? What are its geographic boundaries? Who lives and works in Chinatown? What is the meaning of Chinatown? How do people perceive Chinatown as a place? How does New York's Chinatown relate to the global Chinese diaspora? How does Chinatown's landscape reflect unequal power relations? What political efforts seek to promote and preserve Chinatown as a distinct neighborhood? How does Chinatown in New York compare with San Francisco's Chinatown or Manila's Chinatown? Regional patterns of segregation can be compared domestically and internationally. In addition, GIS maps of census data provide critical representations of the uneven distribution of people by race, ethnicity, and income. Global educators can use such maps as a tool to interrogate larger systems of power and privilege.

SOCIAL GEOGRAPHY OF WOMEN

Critical global educators recognize that geography not only helps us examine ethnic and race relations but also gender relations and the social standing of women. Recent explorations of the spatial terrain of women's lived experiences include Indian women (Patel, 2006), Pakistani women (Besio, 2006; Halvorson, 2005), lesbian women (Cieri, 2003), and adolescent girls (Wridt, 1999) in the United States. This section highlights two studies. The first examines the experiences of women working at transnational call centers in India, and the second turns our attention to the movement of adolescent girls in the United States. Employing a feminist theoretical framework, Patel (2006) explored women's access and mobility in an urban nightscape. Patel, a geographer, described herself as ABCD (American-born confused Desi), an acronym that refers to the identity confusion that may arise from being born Indian American in the United

States. For feminist geographers, a woman's access to and physical mobility in public spaces reflect larger power relations between men and women. Patel begins with the observation that it is generally considered "improper and unsafe" (p. 11) in India for women to be outside of the home at night-time. Despite this cultural expectation, as Patel argued, there has been a rapid rise in the number of women working the night shift at call centers. For women, the jobs are relatively high-paying—by Indian standards—in the information technology sector. The jobs are seen as an alternative to domestic work and, for some, as a stepping-stone to more skilled work in information technology. Through observations and interviews, she found that call center workers encounter high levels of surveillance within and outside of workplaces. For example, the employer provided transportation from home to work. At the call center, video cameras and computer software constantly monitor the employees' every move or work activities. The employer used this surveillance regime in part to reassure relatives of female workers that their daughters or sisters were safe and were supervised while away from home at night.

For employment, the prospective workers had to participate in specialized training that amounted to cultural code-switching. Because the call centers primarily catered to British and American multinational corporations, the employees were required to "neutralize" their accent while making phone calls. In addition, the work setting in this study included American office décor such as artwork from an American artist and even Disney-themed items. The employees were required to wear Western-style clothes. In some sense, the entire operation represented a reengineering of the employees' cultural identity. Saying "Good Afternoon" with a Standard American English accent at 3:00 A.M. in Mumbai is an attempt to veil the fact that the employee was an Indian national, calling from India in the middle of the night. Patel noted that women's work in call centers illustrates new social geographies for women in India. Greater access and mobility at night have been met with higher levels of scrutiny and surveillance. Yet, the expanding physical and temporal mobility of women can spark a renegotiation of gender relations and indeed a reconstitution of a woman's place in society.

Another example of research on gender and social geography is Wridt's (1999) study of the social geographies of adolescent girls and boys in the United States. In this study, each participant recorded her or his daily movements from home to school and beyond. The data from the journals were displayed by maps. A map of the boys' movements contrasted sharply with a map of the girls' movements. The area of the social geography of the boys was larger than that of the girls. This study invites questions about power and privilege. Why do the boys inhabit a larger social geography? Do parents more tightly control the social space of their daughters? Do boys advocate for greater space and movement? Do parents more often allow boys rather than girls to venture out unsupervised? A next step for critical global educators is to consider how the social geography of adolescents in other parts of the world could be compared to that of the United States.

How does this recent scholarship in geography contribute to the development of a critical global perspective? Critical global educators can explore the social geography of women at varying scales. Patel's study in India and Wridt's study in the United States lend themselves to comparison with Halvorson's (2005) study of Muslim girls in northern Pakistan. Through interviews with women in a rural mountain village, Halvorson finds that childhood for girls is marked by unequal access to public spaces where health care, nutrition, education, and employment opportunities are available. The social geography of girls is centered on the home. Not surprisingly, the mobility of women and girls in different cultures is constrained by a unique constellation of legal, economic, religious, and social structures. Mapping the spatial structures of patriarchy can help students understand the dynamic interplay between society and space.

CONCLUSION

Discussions on the geographies of difference contribute to the field of global education by emphasizing the highly complex and layered relations that exist between society and space. Geographic concepts and tools enable us to theorize race, class, gender, sexuality, and other constructs of difference from a spatial perspective. In this chapter, the exploration of the spatial landscapes of race and gender demonstrates that geography contributes toward a more critical understanding of what constitutes a global perspective. Geography is uniquely positioned as a bridge between the natural and social sciences. Global issues such as nuclear proliferation, renewable energy, and hunger can be more deeply understood with a spatial perspective from varying scales: individual, community, region, nation, and world. Each scale produces a new kinetic geography of the problem, its causes, and possible solutions. The geographic concept of scale is an essential component of a critical global perspective. Too often, though, the media and our elected officials define scale as a fixed entity or system for public policy issues. Too often, within mainstream discourses, scale begins and ends with our national borders. As Subedi explained in the introductory chapter, the nation-state has become the de facto unit of analysis in the school curriculum and in our wider public policy discourse. Despite considerable evidence of the transnational scope of many public issues, a provincial *weltanschauung* narrows the discourse and paralyzes civic action. This worldview ultimately short-changes creative and innovative ways to address the issues of the day.

Instead, a critical global perspective is an antidote to such provincialism. The juxtaposition of local and global scales opens up the curriculum and indeed the public discourse.

With a critical global perspective, students have the capacity to generate a greater quantity and quality of solutions to the world's pressing issues. Here, curriculum knowledge shifts from the reproduction of existing power relations to a transformative approach where power, difference, and resistance become central. Awareness of human choices helps students identify local sites of resistance to oppressive structures. Through an emphasis on individual and group agency, students can imagine a better world based on creative decision making at multiple scales. In the end, developing a critical global perspective is nothing less than an act of courage. Global educators must boldly position themselves and their students as advocates for a more just and sustainable world.

REFERENCES

Alger, C. F., & Harf, J. E. (1986). Global education: Why? For whom? About what? In R. Freeman (Ed.), *Promising practices in global education: A handbook with case studies* (pp. 1–13). New York: National Council on Foreign Language and International Studies.

Anderson, C. C. (1990). Global education and the community. In K. A. Tye (Ed.), *Global education: From thought to action* (pp. 125–141). Alexandria, VA: Association for Supervision and Curriculum Development.

Anderson, L. F. (1979). *Schooling for citizenship in a global age: An exploration of the meaning and significance of global education.* Bloomington, IN: Social Studies Development Center.

Anderson, L. F. (1990). A rationale for global education. In K. A. Tye (Ed.), *Global education: From thought to action* (pp. 13–34). Alexandria, VA: Association for Supervision and Curriculum Development.

Barber, B. (1996). *Jihad vs. McWorld: How globalism and tribalism are reshaping the world.* New York: Ballatine Books.

Becker, J. M. (1979). *Schooling for a global age.* New York: McGraw-Hill.

Besio, K. (2006). Chutes and ladders: Negotiating gender and privilege in a village in northern Pakistan. *ACME: An International E-Journal for Critical Geographies,* 5(2), 258–278. Retrieved March 3, 3009, from http://www.acme-journal.org/vol5/KBe.pdf

Blunt, A., & Wills, J. (2000), *Dissident geographies: An introduction to radical ideas and practice.* Harlow, UK: Pearson Education.

Case, R. (1993). Key elements of global perspective. *Social Education,* 57(6), 318–325.

Cieri, M. (2003). Between being and looking: Queer tourism promotion and lesbian social space in greater Philadelphia. *ACME: An International E-Journal for Critical Geographies,* 2(2), 147–166. Retrieved April 17, 2008, from http://www.acme-journal.org/vol2/Cieri.pdf

Churchill, W. (2002). *Struggle for the land: Native North American resistance to genocide, ecocide, and colonization.* San Francisco: City Light Books.

Collins, H. T., Czarra, F. R., & Smith, A. F. (1998). Guidelines for global and international studies education: Challenges, cultures, and connections. *Social Education, 62*(5), 311–317.

Crampton, J. W. (2001). Maps as social constructions: Power, communication and visualization. *Progress in Human Geography, 25,* 235–252.

Cresswell, T. (2004). *Place: A short introduction.* Malden, MA: Blackwell.

Crump, J. R. (2004). Producing and enforcing the geography of hate. In C. Flint (Ed.), *Spaces of hate: Geographies of discrimination and intolerance in the U.S.* (pp. 227–244). New York: Routledge.

Duncan, N. (1996). *BodySpace: Destabilizing geographies of gender and sexuality.* New York: Routledge.

Ellis, M., Wright, R., & Parks, V. (2004). Work together, live apart? Geographies of racial and ethnic segregation at home and at work. *Annals of the Association of American Geographers, 94*(3), 620–637.

Foucault, M. (1984). Space, knowledge and power. In P. Rabinow (Ed.), *The Foucault reader* (pp. 239–256). New York: Pantheon Books.

Friedman, T. (2005). *The world is flat: A brief history of the twenty-first century.* New York: Farrar, Strauss & Giroux.

Fujikane, H. (2003). Approaches to global education in the United States, the United Kingdom, and Japan. *International Review of Education, 49*(1–2), 133–152.

Gaudelli, W. (2003). *World class: Teaching and learning in global times.* Mahwah, NJ: Erlbaum.

Gregory, D. (1994). *Geographical imaginations.* Cambridge, MA: Blackwell.

Halvorson, S. (2005). Growing up in Gilgit: Exploring the nature of girlhood in northern Pakistan. In G. Walid-Falah & C. Nagel (Eds.), *The geographies of Muslim women: Gender, religion, space* (pp. 19–41). New York: Guilford Press.

Hanvey, R. (1976). *An attainable global perspective.* Denver, CO: Center for Teaching International Relations.

Harvey, D. (1972). Revolutionary and counter revolutionary theory in geography and the problem of ghetto formation. *Antipode 4,* 1–13.

Harvey, D. (1982). *The limits to capital.* Oxford, UK: Blackwell.

Houston, J. M. (1959). Land use and society in the plain of Valencia. In R. Miller & J.W. Watson (Eds.), *Geographical essays in honor of Alan G. Ogilvie* (pp. 166–194). London: Nelson.

Huntington, E. (1911). *Climate and civilization.* New York: Wiley.

Johnston, R. J. (1991). *A question of place.* Oxford, UK: Blackwell.

Johnston, R. J., Poulsen, M., & Forrest, J. (2007). The geography of ethnic residential segregation: A comparative study of five countries. *Annals of the Association of American Geographers, 97*(4), 713–738.

Jones-Correa, M. (2000). The origins and diffusion of racial restrictive covenants. *Political Science Quarterly, 115*(4), 541–568.

Kenreich, T. W. (2003). Beyond state capitals: Making the case for teaching geography. *International Social Studies Forum, 1*(4), 168–170.

Kniep, W. (1986). Defining a global education by its content. *Social Education, 50*(10), 437–466.

Kuhn, T. (1970). *The structure of scientific revolutions.* Chicago: University of Chicago Press.

Lutz, C. A., & Collins, J. L. (1993). *Reading National Geographic.* Chicago: University of Chicago Press.

Massey, D. B. (1984). *Spatial divisions of labour: Social structures and the geography of production.* London: Macmillan.

Massey, D. S. (1990). American apartheid: Segregation and the making of the underclass. *American Journal of Sociology, 96*(2), 329–357.

McDowell, L. (1993). Space, place, and gender relations. Part 1: Feminist empiricism and the geography of social relations. *Progress in Human Geography, 17,* 157–179.

Merryfield, M., & Subedi, B. (2001). Decolonizing the mind for world-centered global education. In E. W. Ross (Ed.), *The social studies curriculum: Purposes, problems, and possibilities* (pp. 277–290). Albany: State University of New York Press.

Merryfield, M. M., & Wilson, A. (2005). *Social studies and the world: Teaching global perspectives.* Silver Spring, MD: National Council for the Social Studies.

Monmonier, M. (1991). *How to lie with maps.* Chicago: University of Chicago Press.

National Geographic Education Foundation. (2006). *National geographic-roper public affairs 2006 geographic literacy study.* Washington, DC: Author. Retrieved June 12, 2008, from http://www.nationalgeographic.com/roper2006/pdf/FINAL-Report2006GeogLitsurvey.pdf

Painter, J. (2000). Critical human geography. In R. J. Johnston, D. Gregory, G. Pratt, & M. Watts (Eds.), *The Dictionary of Human Geography* (pp. 126–128). Malden, MA: Blackwell.

Patel, R. (2006). Working the night shift: Gender and the global economy. *ACME: An International E-Journal for Critical Geographies, 5*(1), 9–27. Retrieved April 8, 2008, from http://www.acme-journal.org/vol5/Patel.pdf

Pike, G., & Selby, D. (1988). *Global teacher, global learner.* London: Hodder & Stoughton.

Pratt, G., & Hanson, S. (1994). Geography and the construction of difference. *Gender, Place and Culture, 1,* 5–29.

Rose, G. (1993). *Feminism and geography: The limits of geographical knowledge.* Minneapolis: University of Minnesota Press.

Sack, R. D. (1974). The spatial separatist theme in geography. *Economic Geography, 50,* 1–19.

Said, E. (1978). *Orientalism.* New York: Pantheon Books.

Schaefer, F. K. (1953). Exceptionalism in geography: A methodological examination. *Annual of the Association of American Geographers, 43,* 226–249.

Seattle Civil Rights and Labor History Project. (2008). *Racial restrictive covenants.* Seattle: University of Washington. Retrieved January 6, 2008, from http://depts.washington.edu/civilr/covenants.htm

Sharp, J. (2005). Geography and gender: Feminist methodologies in collaboration and in the field. *Progress in Human Geography, 29*(3), 304–309.

Sheppard, E., & Barnes, T. (1990). *The capitalist space-economy: Geographical analysis after Ricardo, Marx, and Sraffa.* London: Unwin & Hyman.

Smith, D. M. (2002). Social justice and the South African city. In J. Eade & C. Mele (Eds.), *Understanding the city* (pp. 66–81). Oxford, UK: Blackwell.

Smith, N. (1990). *Uneven development: Nature, capital, and the production of space.* Oxford, UK: Blackwell.

Soja, E. (1989). *Postmodern geographies: The reassertion of space in critical social theory.* London: Verso.

Soja, E. (1996). *Thirdspace: Journeys to Los Angeles and other real-and-imagined spaces.* Cambridge, MA: Blackwell.

Spivak, G. (1988). Can the subaltern speak? In C. Nelson & L. Grossberg (Eds.), *Marxism and the interpretation of culture* (pp. 271–313). Urbana: University of Illinois Press.

Steet, L. (2000). *Veils and daggers: A century of National Geographic's representation of the Arab world.* Philadelphia: Temple University Press.

Strahler, A. N., & Strahler, A. H. (1994). *Elements of physical geography.* New York: Wiley.

Taaffe, E. J. (1974). The spatial view in context. *Annuals of the Association of American Geographers, 64*(1), 1–16.

Torney-Purta, J. (1982). The global awareness survey: Implications for teacher education. *Theory into Practice, 21*(3), 200–205.

Tuan, Y.-F. (1977). *Space and place: The perspective of experience.* Minnesota: University of Minnesota Press.

Tuan, Y.-F. (1991). A view of geography. *Geographical Review, 81*(1), 99–107.

Tucker, J. L., & Cistone, P. J. (1991). Global prespectives for teachers: An urgent priority. *Journal of Teacher Education, 42*(1), 3–10.

Tye, K. A. (1999). *Global education: A worldwide movement.* Orange, CA: Interdependence Press.

Tyner, J. A. (2006). "Defend the ghetto": Space and the urban politics of the black panther party. *Annals of the Association of American Geographers, 96*(1), 105–118.

United States Geological Society. (1992). *Geographic information systems.* Washington, DC: Author.

Vanderbeck, R. M. (2006). Vermont and the imaginative geographies of American whiteness. *Annals of the Association of American Geographers, 96*(3), 641–659.

Women and Geography Study Group of the Royal Geographical Society with the Institute of British Geographers. (1997). *Feminist geographies: Explorations in diversity and difference.* Reading, MA: Addison-Wesley.

Wridt, P. (1999). The worlds of girls and boys: Geographic experience and informal learning. *Journal of Geography, 98*(6), 253–264.

CHAPTER 5

DECONSTRUCTING EURO-CENTRIC MYTHS ABOUT MUSLIM WOMEN

Reflections of a Saudi Educator

Amani Hamdan

Muslim women are seen through Western eyes, according to Sabbagh (1996), as "docile, male dominated, speechless, veiled, secluded and un-identifiable beings" (p. 11). Fernea (1998) suggested how it is not uncommon for Muslim women to be represented as "oppressed prisoners of religious dogma" (p. 391) within much of the mainstream circles in Western societies. This is mostly because "The Western world has contributed to this perception by centering on the place of women in its depiction of Islam as repressive and backward" (Amiri, 2001, p. 27). I agree with Ahmed (1999) that the "misconception that Muslim women are helpless prisoners in the homes needs to be corrected" (p. 156). People who claim that Muslim women are oppressed subjects and that Muslim women need to be rescued (from their religion/culture) impose their own notions of freedom on Muslim women.

Critical Global Perspectives, pages 77–101
Copyright © 2010 by Information Age Publishing

What I would like to counter in this chapter is the discourse that represents Muslim women as subjects who lack freedom, and also the perspective that Muslim women's oppression is somehow connected to their religious affiliation (Islam), which is believed to oppress women. For many Muslim women around the world, the term "freedom" is culturally mediated and may convey multiple meanings. Freedom may mean the desire or the need to participate in social, political, and cultural life in the societies they live within. Freedom, to Muslim women, may mean gaining freedom from repressive societal practices or in regards to male-dominated politics and laws. It may also mean the freedom to wear or not to wear *hijab*, not being discriminated upon because of one's religious affiliations, and the freedom to practice their spiritual beliefs without restrictions. For many people in Canada and in the United States, freedom may mean "free" to politically participate or vote, not being forced by their governments to follow certain regulations, or being free to move without restrictions. Of course, Muslim women globally have their own interpretations on what constitutes freedom and may resist Western (or local) conceptions of freedom.

This chapter argues for the need to critique mainstream Western stereotypes about Muslim women, particularly the misinformation about how Muslim women are oppressed by Islam and also how Muslim women cannot speak for themselves in regard to their personal freedom. This topic is critically important when we are teaching about global perspectives or global citizenship and, in general, teaching about differences in schools. I ask that we consider: Who is defining the meaning of freedom and oppression? What might be the politics behind representing Muslim women as oppressed subjects? I am particularly interested in examining how the interconnected discourses on *hijab* (known as the "veil" in Western societies), marriage, and education are simplistically evoked in mainstream and academic circles to illustrate how Muslim women are oppressed by their religion or culture—a myth that is widespread in Canada as well as in the United States. I argue that we consider the diverse experiences and identities of Muslim women and resist homogenizing the identity of "Muslim women." In this chapter, I also offer a critique of Islamic extremists' perspectives on gender issues, particularly how they claim to speak for Muslim women, the Arab world, and Islam. Extremist Muslims, in particular the male scholars, do not represent the majority of Muslims nor are they considered credible sources on Islamic teachings. However, Muslim extremists' patriarchal interpretation of the *Quran*, including Prophet Mohammed's (PBUH)[1] narrations, has widely dominated the Muslim world for the last century. Today, progressive Muslim scholars, both males and females, are reinterpreting the Islamic sacred texts. I argue that the re/interpretations provided by the progressive Muslim scholars open new spaces to understand religious and cultures issues pertaining to Muslim women (see Alghamdi, 2005).

This topic is significant in the field of global education since various scholars have argued for the need to incorporate a more diverse global curriculum in U.S. classrooms (Crocco, 2005; Merryfield & Subedi, 2001). I believe that global education holds the potential for breaking misconceptions about cultural issues. Similarly, "global education can also help in restructuring attitudes and behaviours around a new perspective without diminishing the strengths of [different] cultures" (Tucker, 1990, p. 117). Diaz, Massialas, and Xanthopoulos (1999) urged social studies educators to incorporate transformative knowledge into global education, thereby challenging the dominant Western knowledge embedded within school curriculum. Conversations about Muslim identities within schools are shaped by societal discourses, and teachers will undoubtedly interact with Muslim girls in classrooms and schools. Research demonstrates that Muslim students face challenges in negotiating the mainstream culture of schools (Zine, 2001). There is widespread anti-Muslim and Islamophobic sentiment in schools that needs to be critiqued so that all students can learn to value and respect differences (Rizvi, 2004). Rarely are students taught to critique stereotypes and the need to value complexities when learning about global issues (Case, 1993).

I bring my experiences and insights into this chapter since I am an "insider" as well as an "outsider" in regard to discussions about Muslim women's identities. I may be considered an "insider" since I am a Muslim woman who was born in Saudi Arabia and one who currently lives in Canada. I am intimately connected to Muslim immigrant communities and I am (partially) knowledgeable about how Islamic spirituality shapes people's lives and cultures. In many ways, I am also an "outsider" in Saudi society since I have not lived in Saudi Arabia for almost 10 years. I am also an outsider within Canadian Muslim communities since I know only about Muslim communities that I have lived within or those I have affiliated with. I have come to realize that what constitutes Muslim or Arab identity is misunderstood, and often willfully misrepresented in societies/schools. I agree with Dangor (2001) that

> Muslims are perceived by many as a monolithic community with a uniform world view—a homogenous group unified by the common symbols of Islam. This is an oversimplification of a complex and highly diverse people, marked by social diversities and cultural pluralism. In the world of Islam, there are conflicting views about a multitude of issues, ranging from the nature of the state to essence of spirituality. (p. 109)

My interest in writing this chapter stemmed from the experiences or encounters that I have had with people who assume that women like me are oppressed because of our Muslim affiliations. Such perceptions are fueled by the sentiment that Islam oppresses women. As a way to critique the mainstream representation of Muslim women as being oppressed, I explore three dominant discourses that have often become a vehicle to claim that Muslim women are "different" and are subjugated by their religion/culture. The three discourses are (1) women are oppressed because they wear *hijab*, (2) women are oppressed because they are married within Islamic marriages, and (3) women are oppressed because Islam does not allow women to be educated.

EXAMINING MISCONCEPTIONS ABOUT THE OTHER

I have found post-colonial theory useful because it addresses the relationship between knowledge and power in local/global context (Subedi & Daza, 2008). Post-colonial theory offers ways of understanding how imperialism has shaped the way we have come to know the world and provides multiple, competing perspectives on the politics of knowledge production (see Willinsky, 1998). This is particularly significant in relation to critiquing the academic knowledge about the Middle East and how Islam has been represented in scholarly or academic discourses (Said, 1978). Utilizing post-colonial lenses, Merryfield (2001a) indicated that the topic of imperialism cannot be separated from the ways in which we think about the idea of global. Calling for the need to decolonize dominant perspectives, Merryfield argued for the urgent need to read the world from marginalized people's viewpoints. In particular, Merryfield utilizes Said's concept of contrapuntal perspectives as a way to challenge dominant narratives on history and culture (Said, 1993). It is through the use of contrapuntal perspectives that educators can learn to recognize viewpoints that are complex, including how oppressed subjects provide radical reinterpretation of global issues. Thus, the incorporation of contrapuntal perspectives within "[global education] brings to the center of the curriculum the voices of people past and present who are silenced because they had little or no power to be heard" (Merryfield, 2001b, p. 187). I also agree with Merryfield (2001a) that: "If global education is to be truly global, it is critical that students learn from the experiences, ideas, and knowledge of people who are poor, oppressed, or in opposition to people in power" (p. 182).

Henry (1993) argued that a more complicated understanding of histories and cultures enable us to confront Eurocentric perspectives and the Western legacy of colonialism. Thus, a critical approach to global education is "a journey towards wholeness that requires seeing the world as neither Black nor White, but in its full spectrum" (Henry, 1993, p. 214). A more critical understanding of historical and contemporary global issues invites us to work toward social change and toward a more just society (hooks, 1994; McCarthy & Crichlow,1993; Ngugi, 1993). Said (1978), in his ground-breaking work *Orientalism*, argued how colonial representations shaped the ways the cultures of the Middle East were portrayed as exotic in Western academic and popular writings. Said (1993) further argued that "in our time, direct colonialism has largely ended; imperialism, as we shall see, lingers where it has always been, in a kind of general cultural sphere as well as in specific political, ideological, economic, and social practices" (p. 8). Therefore, educators have much more work to do toward creating social change that will lessen the power of stereotypes and exotic conceptualizations in our collective consciousness.

Arab feminist scholars have utilized post-colonial theory to examine how Muslim women have been represented within various historical and contemporary Western writings. It is worth considering how, as Mehdid (1993) explained:

> The prevailing images of Arab Muslim women in the occidental world seems to shift between dual paradigms, either between the images of salient beast of burden, or that of a capricious princess, the half naked ... or the shapeless figure of woman behind the veil. (p. 21)

Thus, contemporary representations of Muslim women in textbooks and media contain stereotypes and cultural essentialisms. Historically, according to Ahmed (1992) and Kandiyoti (1991), various dominant narratives have been used to discredit and essentialize Islam and Arab cultures. Women were often positioned within Western narratives as being submissive and oppressed, thus the "proof of the inferiority of Islam" (Esposito, cited in Hashim, 1999, p. 8). The Arab feminist post-colonial perspective critiques the dominant representation of Muslim women and its essentialist perspective about Islam and the Arab world. I argue that discussions about Muslim women, whether in the historical or within contemporary contexts, have been situated between Western colonialists—currently imperialist—who seeks to "liberate" the "exotic" women (from Islam) and the Islamic religious extremists who have manipulated women's issues to fulfill extremists' own political agenda (see Alghamdi, 2005).

Being and Becoming a Reflexive Muslim Woman

My experiences living in Saudi Arabia as well as in Canada have influenced how I think and write about Muslim women. As an Arab Muslim feminist, I am reflexive of my identity and see the value of examining perspectives of various Muslim women who have very different views on issues ranging from the wearing of *hijab* to women's role in politics. Reflexivity signifies the value of critically examining one's views in all aspects of the writing process, including a willingness to pay attention to the effects of our involvement with Others. The act of being critically reflexive is no longer seen as being self-serving or solipsistic but as a way of coming to terms with one's knowing(s) or not knowing(s). Being critically reflexive "helps us to recognise that, we ourselves, are a part of the world, rather than apart from the world" (Usher, 1996, p. 35).

Growing up in Saudi Arabia, my family supported and encouraged me to have my own voice and suggested that I develop my own identity. I was taught to value my gender identity and to recognize patriarchal structures in society, both in Saudi Arabia and now in Canada. Of course, this is not to suggest that all women in Saudi Arabia have the experiences I have had. Many women have been discriminated against and have not been allowed to continue schooling at an early age. Others have been forced by their fathers and brothers to get married at 17 or 18 years of age. These acts are not reflective of Islamic teachings, yet they take place within certain families. We ought to critique the perspective that there is a specific (or more) cultural or religious basis for gender marginalization within the Arab societies.

GENDER AND ISLAM

In the context of the United States and Canada, "while Muslims make up one of the fastest-growing religious groups, largely because of immigration, they are among those least understood" (Jonah, 1998, p. 22). I find it important to differentiate between the normative teachings of Islam and the diverse cultural practices among Muslims. One of the criticisms levelled against Islam is that it treats women unjustly. However, Islamic teachings have always recognized the prominent role that women have played historically and "Islam is praised for its historically liberating role for women" (Farhad, 2000, p. 30). In the past, women in Islamic societies have reached political status unparalleled in most Western nation-states (Jawad, 1998).

The gender discrimination that takes place in the Middle East, and many cases that are widely circulated in the Western media, are often perpetuated via the edicts of religious extremists, and they do not reflect the actual teachings of Islam. I believe that Islamic teachings promote women's education, career opportunities, and full social participation. Clearly, extremists, who disregard and refuse to believe that women ought to have equal rights as men, promote rigid ideas about how Muslim women should be treated. Islamic texts advocate that men should treat women (and vice versa) with respect and honor. As we have witnessed in recent years, for example in countries such as Afghanistan, women have been oppressed by extremists who claim that "god" speaks to them (only). Although extremists claim that they know the "true" interpretation of Islamic teachings, their actions and policies have suppressed women's voices, often violently.

Despite the positive treatment of Muslim women in Islamic texts, Muslim women are often represented as being oppressed and intellectually naive in Western academic discourses. Many Westerners' perception of Muslim women is that of silent, submissive people who are covered with black tents (Glaser & Napoleon, 1998). Such a racist belief discounts the diverse ways Muslim women across many countries/cultures negotiate life experiences and identities. Clearly, women in the Islamic world cover a wide spectrum of ethnicities and cultures. The Muslim population worldwide is approximately one billion, with the majority living in East and South Asia; most Muslims live within Indonesia, Pakistan, and Bangladesh. And, not all Arabs are Muslims and not all Muslims are Arabs.

Gender and the Politics of the Hijab

Perhaps no aspect of women's lives in Islamic societies arouses as much immediate, visceral reaction in Western societies as the *hijab* (known as the "veil" in Western societies), which Muslim women are often criticized for wearing (Talvi, 2000). For me, the *hijab* is not a psychological or cultural "prison" as it is falsely assumed. I wear the *hijab* because of my own choices and it signifies my affiliation with Muslim values of respect and integrity. For me, the wearing of the *hijab* has been a conscious decision to re/claim an Arab feminist identity. "To veil or not to veil" is an ongoing debate among Muslims—male and female, orthodox and progressive—as well as between Muslims and non-Muslims. Sadly, it is through the debate over the *hijab*[2] that most people in the Western world come to (mis)understand Arab Muslim women. Stewart (1990) argues that by "wearing the *hijab* they [Muslim women] externalize their identity as a visible discourse" (p. 46) and produce their identity as Muslim women. The social action of wearing the *hijab* is a means through which Muslim women construct a narrative space and wearing the *hijab* allows women to depersonalize and desexualize the body (Cayer, 1996, p. 14). For instance, the *hijab* is a strategy to contest imposed gender and dominant ideologies, and to alter the view on what it means to be both a Muslim woman and a Canadian subject (Ginsburg & Tsing, 1990).

The looks of pity, ignorance, and anger I see in the eyes of some Canadians toward the *hijab* often troubles me. I am asked, "Are you forced to put on a *hijab*?" or "Does your husband force you to put this on?" I respond by explaining that, "*hijab* is part of my identity, and I wear it of my own choosing." In Western societies, people often assume that women wear *hijab* to "hide" their oppressed status or identity. Thus, for many people in the West, *hijab* is a symbol of the oppression of Muslim women. Some Muslim immigrant women in Canada wear the *hijab* because their father or spouse or their family may require them to do so; others see it as an economic issue that allows them to resist consumerism.

Muslim women's motivations, as mentioned above, for covering their hair vary dramatically. For instance, the *hijab* is worn by many Arab Muslim and also Asian and African Muslim women in North America as a form of resistance: to challenge stereotypical identities about Muslim women. Many Muslim women I have come across argue that *hijab* is an affirmation of a woman's dignity and many women perceive *hijab* as a symbol of their identity as a Muslim woman (Hoodfar & McDonough, 2005). "Some Muslim women veil to express their strongly held convictions about gender difference, others are motivated to do so more as a means of critiquing Western colonialism in the Middle East" (Read & Bartkowski, 2000, p. 396). The notion that the *hijab* liberates women from the male gaze and helps them be in charge of their own bodies is an argument that many Muslim women have made in recent years (Ruby, 2004). Fernea (1998) rightly concluded that "*hijab* means different things to different people within [Muslim] society, and it means different things to Westerners than it does to Middle Easterners" (p. 122).[3] Furthermore,

> Some women view the *hijab* as a powerful statement about their identity. They are proud to be Muslim and they want the world to know it . . . the *hijab* is her rebellion and resistance against the "commercialization" of women's bodies that is so prevalent in the West. (Abdo, 2002, p. 232)

Personally, I have never questioned my decision to wear the *hijab*. Like Hirschmann (1998), I believe that "Muslim women not only participate voluntarily in veiling, but defend it as well, indeed claiming that it as a mark of agency, cultural membership, and resistance" (p. 346). I started researching the discourse of *hijab* after I came to the realization that, in most Western academic writings, *hijab* was represented as a symbol of Muslim women's oppression (see Alghamdi, 2005). Yet, rarely did I find in academic writings, particularly within educational research, how *hijab* has been "a tool of women's agency in that it allows women to negotiate the structures of patriarchal custom to gain what they want, to assert their independence, and to claim their own identity" (Hirschmann, 1998, p. 359).

The *hijab* makes it easy to identify a Muslim woman, and thus it may stigmatize her in societies in which the *hijab* is equated with oppression and cultural backwardness. When I was conducting research, I met an immigrant Muslim woman who shared the following story in the context of Canadian society:

> I get mistreated by some people. . . . My faith has actually given me rights, and someone is actually trying to force me to think that it does not. So they are oppressing me.

I asked her to clarify what she had meant by "they." She paused and then continued:

> Anyone making me feel guilty. Or the ones who are treating me differently than my faith.... Islam does not treat me unjustly. The issue of *hijab*, for example, and then the mistreatment afterwards.... Like if you're feeling sorry for me because I am a Muslim woman, why are you mistreating me? If you're feeling that I'm oppressed by my own religion, why are you looking at me as if I'm somehow diseased...not smart enough. If you don't think I'm a free woman, and you want to liberate me, why are you treating me that way? Shouldn't you be doing something that makes me actually be interested in what you're saying and treat me better so I would know the difference so I would join you...?

The *hijab* has become a politically and culturally contested marker or symbol and has come to symbolize everything from Islamic fundamentalism, freedom of religious expression, and women's subordination, and to women's empowerment and equality (Ahmed, 1992; Bullock, 2002; Hoodfar, 1993; Mernissi, 1987). Sadly, within much of the Western academic writings, *hijab* often becomes a symbol through which "Islam is often represented as a religion which denigrates women and limits their freedom" (Hashim, 1999, p. 7). Yet many women, including those I have interviewed, have found *hijab* to be a safe symbol/space or attire, which allows women to resist marginalization, including the objectification of their bodies. Although women are forced to cover themselves within certain societies because of religious extremists' order, the wearing of *hijab* is also a matter of personal choice for women in many countries (Fernea, 1998). Many Muslim women refer to the following passage in *Quran* in which *Allah* calls: "*the believing women to draw their outer garments around them (when they go out or are among men). That is better in order that they may be known (to be Muslims)*" (*Quran* 33:59).

In the last decade, there have been widespread controversies in France over Muslim girls wearing *hijab* to school, including students being expelled from schools (Singh & Basil, 1999). In September 1998, François Bayrou, the French Minister of Culture, went as far as to issue a decree calling for the *hijab* to be banned in public schools.[4] Many French educators considered *hijab* as an "ostentatious religious symbol" (Pike & Selby, 2000, p. 217). This is because the *hijab* was often perceived as a threat to the French secular identity and it was assumed that the banning of *hijab* would serve "as a bulwark against Islamic fundamentalism and also 'American-style' multiculturalism" (Ezekiel, 2006, p. 2). In spaces such as schools and workplaces in France, Muslim women who wore *hijab* often found themselves being the object of curiosity as well as resentment.

In recent years, several incidents have taken place in Canada that demonstrates how *hijab* has become a political and a cultural issue. Although laws are written in some regions to protect women from discriminations, Muslim women often find themselves being victims of racism. For instance, in 2001, Quebec City passed a bylaw barring women from wearing the *hijab* in public. Clearly, "it is appalling to think that a Muslim woman could be subjected to possible police interrogation, required by law to explain herself for practicing her religion" (Spooner, 2001, p. 1). In 2007, five Muslim girls from a Montreal tae kwon do team were barred from competing in a tournament in Québec because the girls wore *hijabs*. A spokesperson for the Fédération de Tae Kwondo du Québec stated that World Tae Kwon Do Federation rules were merely being enforced (Stastna, 2007). In Ontario, Asmahan Mansour, a young soccer player, was ejected from a soccer game by a referee who ruled that the *hijab* was a safety concern for players. Québec's soccer federation noted that the referee was enforcing the rules of the Federation Internationale de Football Association (FIFA), even though the actual ruling allowed the wearing of headgear that was not deemed dangerous to participants. The Muslim Council of Montreal noted that the refusal to allow Mansour to play with her *hijab* would discourage many young Muslims from participating in sports, particularly within settings where Muslims and non-Muslims interacted (Scott, 2007).

Clearly, Muslim women's observance of the *hijab* does not hinder their physical activity and Muslim women can clearly negotiate sports and their gender/spiritual identities. Read and Bartkowski (2000), in a study about Muslim women's interpretation of the *hijab*, concluded that

> Muslim women were able to counterpose their own choices and fashion. Their identities are malleable and inclusive enough to navigate through controversy surrounding the veil and Muslim women's issues in general, and the social context within which the women are situated seems to provide them with resources that facilitate their innovation. (p. 411)

Hijab became a controversial issue in the Montreal school system in September 1998, when Emilie Ouimet, a 13-year-old Muslim girl, was sent home since *hijab* was not considered to be a proper school dress code. The Quebec Human Rights Commission, a social-rights organization, indicated that the dress codes of public schools that banned the wearing of the *hijab* were discriminatory (Cane, 1995). It seemed for mainstream people that Emilie was

> making a radical statement about her violent political ideas. To others, she is the symbol of absolute subjugation and is in dire need of rescue. For them, having such women as part of the North American landscape is frightening. She is "the veiled woman," belonging in a foreign place, an actor on an exotic stage. (Mustafa, n.d.)

Similarly, in November 1998, in the same school system, 15-year-old Dania was officially told to leave the school if she continued to wear *hijab* even though the new dress code had been introduced after Dania had enrolled in the school system. Muslim groups in Montreal protested and argued that the two incidents involving Emilie and Dania were biased and racist. Radwan Yousef, the principal of a Muslim school in Montreal, asked: "If women are putting on a bikini and people are not harassing them, then why should they bother a woman who covers her head?" (cited in Pike & Selby, 2000, p. 217). In both Emilie's and Dania's cases, the schools' responses mirrored Western societies' biased understanding about Islam, and the school policies marginalized the cultural identities Muslim students negotiated in everyday settings.

Mainstream people are not cognizant of the fact that "Women who dress in the *hijab* may be seen as submissively attired, but they may be enjoying tremendous personal freedom. Independence is a state of mind and a manner of living one's life, not the style of the dress" (Husain, 2001, p. 4). I have come to realize that people are quite often surprised to find out that Muslim women desire to cover their hair because of their spiritual beliefs. Again, this is because of the stereotype that Muslim women are imprisoned behind a veil of powerlessness (Al-Hegelan, 1980). Or people may hold the belief that the *hijab* represents the "dark" side of Islam, which is equated with fundamentalism, violence, and the subjugation of women. In contrast, many Muslims believe *hijab* to be the "code of modesty and chastity prescribed by *sharia*, Islam's religious law" (Pike & Selby, 2000, p. 216).

Women's wearing of *hijab* also complicates mainstream gender discourses and generates anxiety within mainstream feminist thinking over what counts as "normal" gender values. I would argue that the practice of criticizing Muslim women for wearing *hijab* allows European Canadians or European Americans to reassert gender/cultural superiority. Ahmed (1982) faulted Western feminists for being complicit in perpetuating the "backward" image of Islam, thus positioning Western women as being advanced and modern. Weber (2001) indicated how "Western feminists attached ever-greater significance to the veil as a symbol of 'tradition' holding Muslim women back" (p. 141). Weber explained how, for many years, the International Alliance of Women (IAW) viewed veiling as a sign of Muslim women's oppression; and proclaimed how, in order for Muslim women to be equal to their Western sisters, they needed to unveil. According to Rydh (1947), the unveiling of Muslim women constituted a necessary first step toward Muslim women's liberation. Rydh believed that European women

first and foremost they must help their sisters out of the veil. It can never be repeated too often that the veil is no mere fashion. It is a wall, which materially and spiritually is debarring its bearer from the developing intercourse and opportunity to co-operate with the men in a world crying for co-operation. (cited in Weber, 2001, p. 142)

Of course, as indicated above, there are historical reasons to why *hijab* is misrepresented in contemporary North American contexts. Ahmed (1982) traced how British officials justified colonialism by noting how the veil was a symbol of Islamic cultural inferiority. Ahmed suggested that colonialists used women's presumed oppression (since they wore the veil) to validate their imperialist belief on the need to save the Other. And, the colonialists often referred to Islam as being oppressive to women since women wore the veil. The insistence of IAW feminists that Muslim women "be freed" from their veils often became the justification for colonial expansion (Weber, 2001). Thus,

> The unwillingness of the Western feminists to the reality of vast inequality among nations was grounded, at least in part, in the fundamental orientalist assumption of Western superiority, an assumption that ultimately implicated Western feminist in the imperialist projects. (Weber, 2001, p. 148)

Weber further argued that "Despite their sympathy for, and occasional identification with, their Middle Eastern sisters, Western feminists never regarded themselves as equals" (p. 151). And,

> feminists in the West envisioned one model for feminist movement and they saw themselves as the natural vanguard who will bring aid and enlightenment to their more "oppressed" sisters in the East. Moreover, their [Western feminists'] unwavering conviction that they had nothing to learn from (and everything to teach) Middle Eastern women blinded Western feminists to the possibility of alternate bases for, and expressions of, feminism in cultures unlike their own. (p. 152)

It is through stereotypes that many Western feminists have sought to "establish the superiority of Western women's lives and Western culture" (Sabbagh, 1996, p. 13). In the Western hegemonic discourses, not only was Muslim women's status used to demonize Islam but these discourses also manipulated images about Muslims and the Arab world. Such representations often portrayed Muslims as being anti-Western, uncivilized, backward, uneducated, illiterate, violent, and rife with men who constantly subordinated women (Ahmed, 1999; Cayer, 1996; Said, 1978). Such racist images of Muslims, particular in relation to Arab Muslim women, have historically been "considered Common Knowledge" (Nader, cited in Hoodfar, 1993, p. 8) in Western societies. Moreover, historically, Western feminists' scholarship about Muslim women either oversimplified (i.e., mistakenly conflated cultural and religious issues) women's lives or demonized women as being helpless subjects. Read and Bartkowski (2000) argued that "caricatures that portray Muslim women as submissive and backward have become more pervasive within recent years" (p. 396). Currently, there is a debate among Muslim women about the political and cultural significance of *hijab* (El-Solh & Mabro, 1994). Many Muslim women believe that *hijab* is a way to secure personal liberty or freedom from the sexual gaze that objectifies women. Thus, the *hijab* becomes a way to protect women from men's sexual surveillance. On the other hand, some argue that the *hijab* provides only the illusion of protection and serves to absolve men from the responsibility of controlling their practices (Parker, 1996). For instance, some Muslim feminists oppose the wearing of the *hijab*, contending that it represents a tradition of oppression and servility (see Mernissi, 1991).

GENDER AND MARRIAGE

Similar to the discourse of *hijab*, the topic of marriage, as represented in Western writings, is another space in which Muslim women's identities are misrepresented, particularly in relation to how the concept of "arranged marriage" is constructed. While many Muslim communities encourage arranged marriages, Western cultures consider the practice of arranged marriages to be bizarre and view it as a primitive custom. Thus, "As most young Western couples select their own marriage partners, the arranged marriage appears to be odd and out-dated to them" (Ahmed, 1999, p. 154). The irony is that many Westerners do not limit themselves to one marriage, and have sex outside of marriage; and, in many cases, couples often live together and have children before getting married. Of course, such practices are not thought to be exotic or traditional. But, on the other hand, the practice of arranged marriage, in which families and/or communities are involved in finding suitable partners, is seen as an archaic practice. Islamic religious texts do not indicate that arrangements between various families need to be made for couples to get married; however, arranged marriages are a common practice, especially in societies where segregation between the two sexes is common, such as in Saudi Arabia. It is a common practice for families and community members to make suggestions and recommendations for their sons and daughters, and marriages take place as long as both parties are agreeable to the marriage. In many Arab or Muslim societies where men and women are less segregated, as in communities in Egypt or Jordan, arranged marriages are less common in comparison to Saudi Arabia.

Too often, arranged marriage is represented as being a marriage that is forced upon women: not recognizing how an arranged marriage can be different from a forced marriage. The *Quran* grants women the right to choose their spouse, as well as the right to refuse an unwanted marriage proposal. Sadly, the misconception is that virtually every Muslim woman has been forced into a marriage. Within many Muslim communities, marriage obligations and responsibilities are noted as being equal between a man and a woman. The *Quran* entitles women to contract their marriage, retain control of wealth, and receive and share inheritance. If we are to examine the history of Islam, we notice how various legal schools of thought were established and, within the framework of the *Sharia*,[5] norms and laws were formulated to meet women's needs, especially when domestic, childbearing roles rendered women dependent upon men (Badawi, 1995; Jawad, 1998). The following are two passages from the *Quran*[6] that emphasize the need to value gender equality.

> Each human being shall face the consequences of his or her deeds. And their Lord has accepted of them and answered them: Never will I suffer to lose the work of any of you, be he/she male or female: you are members one of another. (*Quran* 3:195)

> If any do deeds of righteousness, be they male or female, and have faith, they will enter paradise and not the least injustice will be done to them. (*Quran* 4:124)

For me, the passages suggest that a marriage ought to be a space where human beings find tranquility and affection with each other. The passages also indicate that both woman and man are created from the same soul and are equal. Clearly, men and women ought not to be part of hierarchical relationships in which men dominate women. Sadly, if we are to examine historical and contemporary conditions in the world, we see (because of patriarchal practices), women's rights have been constantly violated and issues or concerns in regard to women's rights have not been taken seriously.

Another misconception of Islamic marriage is that it encourages violence and domestic abuse. Not surprisingly, when Islam is misrepresented as being a violent religion, the marriage is also constructed as a violent relationship. Of course, domestic abuse, or in general violence against women, takes place not only in the Arab/Muslim world but also within European Canadian or European American (or Christian) communities. Yet, it is assumed that Muslim women are oppressed and abused by their husbands because of the family's affiliation with Islam (Hekmat, 1997). We should not forget that in some family contexts women may not have equal rights or that they may be abused. Too often, Western scholars (or media outlets) focus on individual cases of domestic abuse to claim how all women are abused within the Arab world or within Muslim communities. Such a view claims that domestic abuse takes place more within Muslim communities in comparison to non-Muslim communities.

The Discourse of Polygamy

A question that often comes up in my interactions with people, and that is connected to the discourse of marriage, is the practice of polygamy. I am often asked, "Is this a religion where a man marries four women?" The above-noted question is connected to the stereotypical representation of Muslim woman who is thought to be a slave to male sexual indulgence. I have responded by asking people where they had received the information and what they imagine when they hear about a polygamous family in the United States. Would they generalize that this is a representative family in the United States or Canada? It is certainly worth considering how media often represents polygamy as if it was an Islamic tenet or a pillar of Islam. Too often, the assumption is that Islam, as a religion, is believed to encourage polygamy; and when women wear *hijab*, according to this belief, they attempt to hide their polygamous lifestyle. This perception of women as being involved in polygamy (and women approving of such practices) cannot be divorced from how concepts such as sexuality/marriage is understood within mainstream circles in the United States and Canada. This is because, too often, the framework of understanding the Other has operated through stereotypical discourses on marriage and sexuality. In Western societies, mass media aggressively exploits women and girls as being objects of male desire. Thus, Western views of sexuality become the prism to interpret the supposed sexual/marital deviancy within Muslim communities.

I have asked people to consider whether having an extramarital affair would be considered a polygamous practice. People are often astonished by this comparison. Many people I have interacted with are ignorant of the fact that polygamy has existed in many civilizations and cultures. Clearly, when we hear about a Christian woman being part of a polygamous relationship, we should not interpret this as a Christian religious practice. Similarly, when we hear about a Muslim woman being married into (or takes part into) a polygamous relationship, then this must not be interpreted as an Islamic teaching or practice. However, when Arab or Muslim relationships are discussed in the North American mass media, they receive more attention and it is often assumed that such practices take place in all Muslim communities.

The question of social justice for women must be placed as a critical global issue since discrimination against women takes place in many forms, including through misogyny, sexism, racism, and so on. In Canada, laws have been written to protect women from oppression and discrimination, yet many women experience violence in their marriages and everyday experiences. Open critical dialogue, in relation to gender biases, will help us understand how domestic violence takes place in all communities. The assumption that arranged marriages are forced and that only Muslim women are victims of domestic abuse is misleading since this view fails to recognize how similar forms of violence take place in non-Muslim communities. In North America, most people are not willing to question their presuppositions about what constitutes polygamy since this forces people to critique their prior beliefs. I have come to realize that people are resistant to recognizing cultural complexities, particularly viewpoints that invite them to unlearn their biases about Islam or Muslim women.

THE MYTH THAT ISLAM DOES NOT PROMOTE WOMEN'S EDUCATION

The discourse on education also shapes how Muslim women are represented in mainstream circles. This is based on the gross misconception that Islam discourages women from pursuing education to safeguard male domination, thus ensuring male superiority. A typical Euro-centric statement claims that "it is questionable if Islam has improved the situation of women" (Galletti, 1991, p. 1). It is often assumed that because of their lack of education (and that they are not properly educated) that Muslim women have been robed (and veiled) and that they are languishing in the harems under the harsh rule of a polygamous husband (Walther, 1999). It is also alleged that "Muslims attach greater importance to the education of males" (Khan, 1990, p. 1), a viewpoint that further creates the stereotype of Islam promoting or sanctioning female illiteracy. In other worlds, the belief is that "both women and the teachings of Islam are presented in certain ways that safeguard male and class privilege by keeping women illiterate and powerless" (Nayyar, 1994, p. 58).

The misunderstandings about educational issues pertaining to women are widespread because Islamic extremists' viewpoints are often printed or promoted in mainstream media outlets to demonstrate how Islam promotes violence. Rarely are perspectives of those who resist extremists are covered in the Western media. Extremists believe that Muslim women should be limited to learning of extremists' interpretation of Islamic teachings. This is because "Female education is often criticized by conservative religious leaders as a threat to the purity of the Islamic family" (Dupree, 1992, p. 1). My reading of Islamic texts has led me to believe that *Quran* strongly encourages the education of women in religious, economic, political, and social domains and points out how men and women are to be educated in equal terms. For me, the verses from *Quran* advocate that men and women need to gain knowledge in equal terms and that "the search of knowledge is a duty for every Muslim male and female" or that one must "seek knowledge from the cradle to the grave" are the prophet Mohammed's (peace be upon him) sayings. The belief that Islam denies women the right to educate themselves is a fiction of the Western imagination.

Sadly, in some Muslim countries (and globally), because of patriarchal practices, women's educational rights have been marginalized and women have yet to fully enter fields such as engineering, law, and medicine (Jawad, 1998). For instance, the simple fact that women face restrictions on driving in Saudi Arabia restricts their mobility and access to higher education institutions. It must be understood that the restriction to drive a vehicle is not an Islamic law. The restriction on driving was enforced by extremists in specific regions of the world to control women's mobility, and Muslim women have reclaimed some of their rights over the past five or six decades in spite of extremists' opposition. However, education continues to be a contentious issue between Muslim women and extremists who believe that women's essential role is to be (only) a good mother and a good wife. For example, extremists have argued that, even after formal education was introduced as one of women's rights in Saudi society during the 1950s, women were to be only educated in subject areas that prepared them for essential "home" role. Historically, in Saudi Arabia, women have not had access to living in residence halls in colleges and the vocational education that women received was restricted to subject areas such as tailoring (sewing, etc.) and dress design. Women were not admitted in universities to study medicine until 1975 and the admission to a dentistry program was not open until the early 1980s. To this day, women have had difficulties in getting admitted into programs in fields such as geology, engineering (except for interior design), and law and political science; however, many changes have taken place in the past decade and Saudi women have been able to challenge and raise their voices to advocate changes. When I share such cases, readers may assume that Saudi women are unfortunate or less advanced in regard to what they perceive as "better" Western lifestyles. However, such a perception is misleading since it ignores the context of Saudi women's experiences and the tremendous achievements made by Saudi women in the fields of literature, medicine, and various scientific fields.

Although there are some merits to women and men being separated in educational settings, the current restrictive elementary and secondary schooling system in Saudi Arabia has not allocated enough resources for girls' education. In all-female schools, there were fewer women teachers and limited educational resources. It is worth emphasizing again that the historical and contemporary restrictive practices on education are not reflective of Islamic teachings. I would argue that, as in the global context, patriarchal practices have marginalized girls' or women's education. Equal educational opportunities for men and women are included in the tenets of Islam, which extremists have refused to support. It is by educating themselves that Muslim women are affiliating with their spiritual/cultural beliefs and redefining the meaning of being mothers, agents of social change, and Muslim subjects. Today, Muslim women in some Islamic countries are gaining more access to educational systems and workplaces but not necessarily the access to social or political freedom. Sadly, Muslim women in many Middle Eastern, African, or Asian countries are restricted from practicing political freedom. In North America and Europe, Muslim women continue to suffer bitter racism and discriminations and find their voices being constantly silenced. Western values of freedom (individual freedom, etc.) often become attractive for young Muslim women who are desperate or eager for immediate freedom, but who often lose their cultural identities in the process. For example, young Muslim women may abandon their faith and embrace the Western lifestyle without recognizing that by doing so they are abandoning an important part of their identity. Many women and men become victims of Western consumerism and fail to see the importance of refraining from practices that are contrary to Islamic teachings, such as consuming alcohol or dropping out of school. On the other hand, after being victims of bitter racism in Western countries, some women and men withdraw into their own ethnic/cultural communities. And, from my own experiences, I have come to recognize that there are many young Muslim women who are "educated, privileged, and engaged and are struggling to improve the status of women" (Cooke, 2001, p. ix) within their communities. I believe that, whenever possible, Muslim women ought to be active members in the larger Western society they live within and, at the same time, be part of their religious/cultural communities. Muslim women need to take up issues of political advocacy and social justice (Bullock, 2005, p. xv). By making their voices heard, Muslim women can help the mainstream society unlearn their prejudices and biased understandings about Arab societies and Islam.

Unfortunately, Muslim extremists have limited Muslim women's educational and social freedoms in many parts of the Islamic world. The Taliban regime in Afghanistan is an example of how extremists oppress and suppress Muslim women in the name of Islam. Muslim feminists continue to argue that the values and practices endorsed by Islamic extremists are not only harmful to women (and men) but that they are also detrimental to the formation of civil societies (El-Solh & Mabro, 1994). A myth that is prevalent in Western societies is that Arab women are not supposed to publicly participate in political or administrative positions. This assumption is based on the idea that Islam, as a religion, restricts the role of women in public affairs.

I would argue that historical and contemporary restrictive practices in regard to women's education has been perpetuated by age-old traditions that have no basis in the *Quran* (Al-Leil, 1996). There is a general misperception in the West that there is an association between the secondary role of Muslim women in societies and the physical and symbolic segregation of the sexes, whether in schools or in workplaces (Glaser & Napoleon, 1998). Educated and skilled Muslim women are limited by social pressure and traditional belief systems to pursue academic interests in fields such as teaching and nursing. Clearly, progressive gender equality is a global issue and I would argue that Islamic teachings uphold equality between women and men. Extremists fear that when women re/educate themselves and re/claim their rights, their hold on power will loosen.

CONCLUSION

The teaching about global perspectives cannot avoid how Islam and Muslim women are represented in various academic discourses. Global educators need to critique misrepresentations and stereotypes that dehumanize the lives of Muslim women and men. In Western societies, powerful people such as politicians, religious leaders, and individuals in the entertainment industry play a key role in perpetuating the misinformation about Muslim women. According to stereotypical Western beliefs, Muslim women are downtrodden, submissive slaves forced into the veil and who are incapable of entering the civilized world simply because they are Muslim women (Aslam, 1995). Clearly, there is an urgent need to critique such portrayals since they distort the diverse experiences and identities of women. Similarly, the misrepresentations about Muslim women are also perpetuated by Islamic extremists who, claiming to be the true followers of Islam, desire to maintain their hold on power and continue to deprive women of their political and cultural rights. As I have argued, extremists misrepresent Islam, and Muslim extremists' claim that Muslim women's search for freedom has been influenced by Western ideologies is misleading. In classroom contexts, educators must be wary of the perspectives shared by mainstream Westerners as well as Islamic extremists who desire to locate Muslim women as marginal subjects.

The mass media in Western societies has quite often silenced Muslim women's voices. Unfortunately, this has helped sanction the misinformation about the complex role gender plays in the global context. Nowadays, topics such as the *hijab*, marriage, and education are often invoked whenever there are conflicts in the Middle East or whenever Muslims are suspected of wrongdoings in Western societies. Many Westerners are intelligent enough to realize that the actions of an individual Muslim are not representative of Islam or a country or a cultural community. Unfortunately, media often depicts extremists' voices as being the mainstream perspective within the Middle East. Moreover, inaccurate media coverage of Islam or the Arab world is often circulated as the "truth" in Western societies and Western reporters often advertently or inadvertently represent Muslims as being terrorists and as promoting violence. Too often, Islam is represented as a monolith religion, one that is unyielding to the forces of democracy, modernity, and intellectualism (Said, 1993). Such a misleading representation of Islam hinders the genuine dialogue that can take place among societies.

Although women's political freedom has been marginalized in many parts of the Arab world, this can be attributed to age-old traditions rather than to the teachings of Islam. The status of women as effective participants in various societies is reemerging and gaining strength. Despite barriers, Muslim women such as Benazir Bhutto of Pakistan, Khaleda Zia of Bangladesh, and Sukarnoputri Megawati of Indonesia reached the highest political position in their countries. These three Muslim women made significant impact in regards to gender issues even though they governed for a relatively short period of time. Moreover, the Muslim female leaders became role models for many women around the world. Although women have gained more rights over time in the Arab world, they have not been granted equal political, economic, and cultural status as men in many nation-states. I do agree that this is a global issue since women, in the global context, continue to be marginalized in various cultural and educational arenas. In recent years, women have taken a greater role in shaping policies that positively influences the lives of marginalized women.

Because of the changes in the global information system and how knowledge is exchanged, our generation of Muslim feminists have had better access to knowledge. We are now more conscious of how extremists have negatively interpreted Islamic rituals in various countries (Afghanistan, etc.) and how the extremists have imposed their own notions of spiritual truths. My generation is more aware of the changes taking place all over the world, including within the global feminist movements. The new generation of women is in a better position to understand and make social changes and to stand up for women's rights. Although Muslim women are marginalized in societies, as I have argued, women are quite capable of resisting dominant practices.

Global educators can play a key role in critiquing the misrepresentations of Islam and Arab communities in their classrooms, particularly in relation to how Muslim women are constructed in media and various educational outlets. Similarly, educators need to recognize how Muslim girls may often find themselves as being read as the Other and may find it difficult to negotiate their identities in classrooms. Since school curriculum often emphasizes mainstream knowledge, many Muslim or Arab students may critique the knowledge they come across in textbooks or during classroom discussions about Islam or the Arab world. And students may also find what they have learned in schools to be contradictory to what they have learned within their cultural communities. This contradiction can cause deep conflicts and can negatively affect the psychological development of Muslim girls and boys. Schools need to promote more candid discussion on religious or cultural differences since, as Pike and Selby (1988) suggested, "Students should have the appreciation of others and be willing to find the beliefs and practices of other cultural and social groups of value and interest, and be prepared to learn from them" (p. 68).

NOTES

1. PBUH is short for Peace Be Upon Him, and the statement is often uttered after one mentions the Prophet Mohammed's name.
2. *Hijab* is different from the veil (full covering of face) or *neqab* (the covering of the face except for the eyes). Yet, *hijab* is often referred to as the veil in Western writings.
3. For more details, see Walbridge (1997) and Abu-Lughod (1986).
4. For more on the topic, see Hamdan (2007).
5. *Sharia* is the Islamic Law, which is partly informed by the *Quran* and the Prophet's narrations and practices but has been largely influenced by conservative male interpretations of the sacred texts.
6. *Quran* is considered the sacred book for Muslims.

REFERENCES

Abdo, D. (2002). Uncovering the harem in the classroom. *Women's Studies Quarterly, 30*(1/2), 227–238.

Abu-Lughod, L. (1986). *Veiled sentiments.* Berkeley: University of California Press.

Ahmed, L. (1999). *A border passage: From Cairo to America–a woman's journey.* New York, NY: Farrar, Strauss & Giroux.

Ahmed, L. (1992). *Women and gender in Islam: Historical roots of modern debate.* New Haven, CT: Yale University Press.

Ahmed, L. (1982). Feminism and feminist movements in the Middle East, a preliminary exploration: Turkey, Egypt, Algeria, People's Democratic Republic of Yemen. *Women's Studies International Forum, 5*(2), 153–168.

Alghamdi, A. (2005). *Quilted narratives of Arab Muslim women's tapestry: Intersecting educational experiences and gender perceptions.* Unpublished manuscript, University of Western Ontario, London, ON, Canada.

Al-Hegelan, N. (1980). *Women in the Arab world. Arab women's potential and prospects.* Retrieved February 12, 2001, from http://www.thefuturesite.com/ethnic/arab.html

Al-Leil, H. (1996). Muslim women between tradition and modernity: The Islamic perspective. *Journal of Muslim Minority Affairs, 16*, 99–111.

Amiri, R. (2001, November 27). Muslim women as symbols and pawns. *New York Times*, p. A21.

Aslam, S. (1995). *Challenging the western concepts of Muslim women.* Retrieved December 21, 2001, from http://www.netiran.com/htdocs/clipings/social/950400xxSo006.ht.

Badawi, J. (1995). *Gender equity in Islam: Basic principles.* Plainfield, IN: American Trust Publications.

Bullock, K. (Ed.). (2005). *Muslim women activists in North America: Speaking for ourselves.* Austin: University of Texas Press.

Bullock, K. (2002). *Rethinking Muslim women and the veil: Challenging historical and modern stereotypes.* London: International Institute of Islamic Thought.

Cane, B. (1995, November). Veiled threats in Quebec. *Maclean's Magazine,* p. 47.

Case, R. (1993). Key elements of a global perspective. *Social Education, 57*(6), 318–325.

Cooke, M. (2001). *Women claim Islam: Creating Islamic feminism through literature.* New York: Routledge.

Crocco, M.S. (2005). *Social Studies and the press: Keeping the beast at bay?* Greenwich, CT: Information Age.

Cayer, C. (1996). *Hijab, narrative and production of gender among second generation, Indo-Pakistani, Muslim women in greater Toronto.* Unpublished master's thesis, York University, Toronto.

Dangor, S. (2001). Historical perspective, current literature and an opinion survey among Muslim women in contemporary South Africa: A Case Study. *Journal of Muslim Minority Affairs, 21*(1), 109–129.

Diaz, C., Massialas, B., & Xanthopoulos, J. (1999). *Global perspectives for educators.* Boston: Allyn & Bacon.

Dupree, N. H. (1992). The present role of Afghan refugee women and children. *Studies and Evaluation Papers No. 7,* 1–23

Ezekiel, J. (2006). French dressing: Race, gender, and the hijab story. *Feminist Studies, 32*(2), 256–278.

El-Solh, C., & Mabro, J. (1994). Muslim women's choices: Religious belief and social reality. In C. El-Solh & J. Mabro (Eds.), *Muslim women's choices: Religious belief and social reality* (pp 1–32). Providence, RI: Berg.

Farhad, K. (2000). Gender, Islam, and politics. *Social Research, 67,* 453–475.

Fernea, E. (1998). *In search of Islamic feminism: One woman's global journey.* New York: Anchor Books Doubleday.

Galletti, M. (1991). Women in the Arab-Islamic world. *Inchiesta, 21*(93), 1–8.

Ginsburg, F., & Tsing, A. (1990). *Uncertain terms: Negotiating gender in American culture.* Boston: Beacon Press.

Glaser, I., & Napoleon, J. (1998). *Partners or prisoners: Christian thinking about women in Islam.* Carlisle, UK: Solway Gallery.

Hamdan, A. (2007). The issue of hijab in France: Reflections and analysis. *Muslim World Journal of Human Rights, 4*(2), 4.

Hashim, I. (1999). Reconciling Islam and feminism. *Gender and Development, 7*(1), 7–14.

Hekmat, A. (1997). *Women and the Quran: The status of women in Islam.* New York: Prometheus Books.

Henry, A. (1993). Missing: Black self-representations in Canadian educational research. *Canadian Journal of Education, 18*(3), 206–222.

Hirschmann, N. (1998). Western feminism, eastern veiling, and the question of free agency. *Constellations, 5*(3), 345–368.

hooks, b. (1994). *Teaching to transgress: Education as the practice of freedom.* New York: Routledge.

Hoodfar, H. (1993). The veil in their minds and on our heads: The persistence of colonial images of Muslim women. *Resources for Feminist Research, 22*(3/4), 5–18.

Hoodfar, H., & McDonough, S. (2005). Muslims in Canada: From ethnic groups to religious community. In P. Bramadat & D. Seljak (Eds.), *Religion and ethnicity in Canada* (pp. 133–152). Toronto: Pearson Longman.

Husain, A. (2001). *Hijab: Suppression or liberation.* Retrieved January 17, 2002, from http://www.geocitics.com/athenes/Pathenon/4482/article31.htm

Jawad, H. (1998). *The rights of women in Islam: An authentic approach.* London: Macmillan Press.

Jonah, B. (1998, July). The Muslim mainstream. *U.S News & World Report,* pp. 22–26.

Kandiyoti, D. (1991). Introduction. In D. Kandiyoti (Ed.), *Women, Islam, and the state* (pp. 1–21). Philadelphia: Temple University Press.

Khan, Q. (1990). *Status of women in Islam.* New Delhi: Sterling Publisher Private Limited.

McCarthy, C., & Crichlow, W. (1993). Introduction: Theories of identity, theories of representation, theories of race. In C. McCarthy & W. Crichlow (Eds.), *Race, identity and representation in education* (pp. xii–xxix). New York: Routledge.

Mehdid, M. (1993). The Western invention of Arab womanhood: The 'oriental' female. In H. Afshar (Ed.), *Women in the Middle East: Perceptions, realities, and struggles for liberation* (pp. 18–58). Palgrave, UK: Macmillan.

Mernissi, F. (1987). *Beyond the veil: Male-female dynamics in modern Muslim society.* Bloomington: Indiana University Press.

Mernissi, F. (1991). *The veil and the male elite: A feminist interpretation of women's rights in Islam.* Reading, MA: Addison-Wesley.

Merryfield, M. M. (2001a). Moving the center of global education: From imperial world views that divide the world to double consciousness, contrapuntal pedagogy, hybridity, and cross-cultural competence. In W. Stanley (Ed.), *Critical issues in social studies research for the 21st century* (pp. 179–208) Greenwich, CT: Information Age.

Merryfield, M. M. (2001b). *Teacher education in global and international education* (No. NCRTL-RR- 94-3). (ERIC Document Reproduction Service No. ED 346 082)

Merryfield, M. M., & Subedi, B. (2001). Decolonising the mind for world-centered global education. In E. W. Ross (Ed.), *The social studies curriculum: Purposes, problems, and possibilities* (pp. 277–290). Albany: State University of New York Press.

Mustafa, S. (n.d.). The fear of *hijab.* Retrieved July 13, 2007, from http://www.themodernreligion.com/women/hijab-fear.html

Nayyar, J. (1994). Gender identity and Muslim women: Tool of oppression turned into empowerment. *Convergence, 27*(2/3), 58.

Ngugi wa Thiong'o (1993). *Moving the centre: The struggle for cultural freedom.* London: James Curry.

Parker, K. (1996). *The ongoing debate. Women, Islam, and hijab.* Retrieved December 1, 2001, from http://www.emory.edu/English/Bahri/Viel.html.

Pike, G., & Selby, D. (1988). *Global teacher and global learner.* London: Hodder & Stoughton.

Pike, G., & Selby, D. (2000). In the global classroom, book 2. Toronto: Pippin.

Read, J., & Bartkowski, J. (2000). To veil or not to veil? A Case study of identity negotiation among Muslim women in Austin, Texas. *Gender and Society, 14*(3), 395–417.

Rizvi, F. (2004). Debating globalization and education after September 11.*Comparative Education, 40*(2), 157–171.

Ruby, T. (2004). *Immigrant Muslim women and the hijab: Sites of struggle in crafting and negotiating identities in Canada.* Saskatchewan, Canada: University of Saskatchewan.

Rydh, H. (1947). *Amongst the women of Iraq, Jus Suffragii, 41*(12), 167.

Sabbagh, S. (Ed.). (1996). *Arab women: Between defiance and restraint.* New York: Olive Branch Press.

Said, E. (1978). *Orientalism.* New York: Pantheon Books.

Said, E. (1993). *Culture and imperialism.* New York: Alfred A Knopf.

Scott, J. (2007). Hijab red card sparks uproar in Quebec: No tempest over turbans but hassle over hijab & a Canadian mask on an alarming global trend toward fear-mongering and racism? Retrieved January 9, 2008, from http://www.saltspringnews.com/index.php?name=News&file=article&sid=15807.

Singh, B., & Basil, R. (1999). Responses of liberal democratic societies to claims from ethnic minorities to community rights. *Educational Studies, 25*(2), 187–196.

Spooner, M. (2001, March 2). Scarf ban attacks our freedoms. *Ottawa Citizen,* p. A15.

Stastna, K. (2007). Hijab…again—Muslim girls barred from martial arts tournaments. Retrieved January 9, 2008, from http://www.religionnewsblog.com/17967/hijabs

Stewart, K. (1990). Backtalking the wilderness: "Appalachian" en-gendering. In F. Ginsburg & A. Tsing (Eds.), *Uncertain terms: Negotiating gender in American culture* (pp. 43–58). Boston: Beacon Press.

Subedi, B., Daza, S. L. (2008). The possibilities of postcolonial praxis in education. *Race Ethnicity and Education. 11*(1), 1–10

Talvi, S. (2000). The veil and its meaning. *The Progressive, 64,* 41–43.

Tucker, J. (1990). Global education partnerships between schools and universities. In K. Tye (Ed.), *Global education: From thought to action* (pp. 109–124). Alexandria, VA: Association for Supervision and Curriculum Development.

Usher, R. (1996). Textuality and reflexivity in educational research. In R. Usher & D. Scott (Eds.), *Understanding educational research* (pp. 52–73). London: Routledge.

Walbridge, L. (1997). *Without forgetting the imam: Lebanese Shi'ism in an American community.* Detroit, MI: Wayne State University Press.

Walther, W. (1999). *Women in Islam: From medieval to modern times.* Princeton, NJ: Markus Wiener Publishing.

Weber, C. (2001). Unveiling Scheherazade: Feminist orientalism in the international alliance of women 1911–1950. *Feminist Studies, 27*(1), 125–157.

Willinsky, J. (1998). *Learning to divide the world: Education at empire's end.* Minneapolis: University of Minnesota Press.

Zine, J. (2001). Muslim youth in Canadian schools: Education and the politics of religious identity. *Anthropology and Education Quarterly, 32*(4), 399–423.

CHAPTER 6

THE CURRICULUM OF GLOBALIZATION

Considerations for International and Global Education in the 21st Century

John P. Myers
University of Pittsburgh

Educators from across different sectors have increasingly called for a new form of international education to prepare youth to live and work in the global age. Globalization is the principal reason behind these calls. Presently, it is the most powerful concept for explaining the functioning of the world system and the process of development of a global society. The concept of globalization encompasses a range of processes affecting different spheres of life, which include culture and politics in addition to economics. As a result, these calls come from diverse sectors and interests across society with their own purposes and goals. Making sense of this discourse is important for educators as they set out to enact contemporary practices of international education that are relevant to current world conditions.

Critical Global Perspectives, pages 103–120
Copyright © 2010 by Information Age Publishing
103

International educators in the United States have long lamented adolescents' lack of knowledge about the rest of the world. Recent reports have highlighted their lack of knowledge of geography (National Geographic/ Roper, 2002), foreign languages, and international current events (Stewart, 2007) in comparison with students from various nation-states. The contemporary phase of globalization, however, suggests that students need new knowledge and skills to flourish in the 21st century. Eminent global education scholar James Becker (2002) noted that globalization marks a change in the way we understand the nature of international education. In particular, he called for the reconsideration of the kinds of political values and governance that are needed in light of heightened interdependence. Becker further argued that although globalization has "made us all internationalists," the U.S. populace remains largely ambivalent and uncommitted to international institutions and ideals (Becker, 2002, p. 55).

National and state social studies standards have only recently begun to address globalization as a curriculum topic. Nonetheless, in most cases, coverage of globalization remains partial and does not meet the goals of recent national efforts for international education to prepare students for the global economy and international civic responsibility. Typically, expectations either lack specificity and depth of coverage, or ignore the topic entirely. For example, the Pennsylvania Standards for History do not explicitly mention globalization and were graded a '3' on a scale of 1–10 (with 10 the best score) in terms of coherency and inclusion of content for "Modern Contexts" in world history (Mead, 2006). This situation is not unique to the topic of globalization; the social studies curriculum in general is disconnected from the contemporary academic scholarship (see Hess, 2005). The relevant national standards, the National Social Studies Standards and the National World History Standards, address globalization more comprehensively. The World History Standards in particular pay attention to the historical development and evolution of the globalization. However, both are voluntary standards that only provide broad guidelines for teachers.

In this chapter, I make the case that the topic of globalization has not yet entered the U.S. social studies vocabulary in sufficient complexity and depth than is warranted. The educational community's attention to globalization has thus far focused primarily on the concept as a macro-level process (e.g., Stromquist, 2002) that influences educational provision and the labor market (Tikly, 2001) rather than as a curricular topic. Instead, most of the existing research emphasizes the process by which educational systems are converging, particularly in terms of policy and higher education. In this chapter, I examine the influence of globalization on the constitution of knowledge and learning and its implications for history and social studies education. To this end, I draw on critical globalization studies to take into account the extensive contemporary globalization scholarship. In the following sections, I outline three implications for education related to broad trends in the literature: (1) globalization and learning, (2) the myths of globalization, and (3) approaches to teaching about globalization. I then assess the implications of these trends for social studies education.

GLOBALIZATION AND LEARNING

As the primary conceptual lens for explaining the functioning of the world system, globalization also has important and long-reaching implications for learning about the world. However, because globalization is not a central topic in the social studies curriculum, individuals are likely to learn about it through the media, which often presents inaccurate portrayals and popular myths. This situation is an indication of the inability of educational institutions to keep pace with the rapid changes of our global era (Gardner, 2004).

Teaching and learning about globalization present distinctive problems for educators. One of the primary implications for learning is the expansion of knowledge and access to such knowledge. Held, McGrew, Goldblatt, and Perraton (1999) defined globalization as a

> process (or set of processes) which embodies a transformation in the spatial organization of social relations and transactions—assessed in terms of their extensity, intensity, velocity and impact—generating transcontinental or inter-regional flows and networks of activity. (p. 16)

This definition points to several of the key implications of globalization for learning: 1) accessing knowledge and information, including and most relevant for education, the flow of information across the world (see also Castells, 1996); 2) the intangible and complex nature of the meaning of globalization; and 3) the contestation over the meaning of globalization, especially in terms of its effects across the world.

Accessing Knowledge and Information in the Global Age

Understanding how the world functions in the 21st century increasingly requires an interdisciplinary approach to using knowledge. The processes of globalization have led to the rapid expansion of knowledge about the world and increasing complexity of social problems, such as poverty (Held & McGrew, 2003). At the base of these changes is a revolution in information and communications technology (ICT) and the deepening of economic, political, and social interdependence among peoples and nations (Larson, 2002; Mansilla & Gardner, 2007). For example, Boulding (1995) pointed out some of the most important and dramatic changes that have occurred in the existing social system. She was an early observer of the implications of global civic culture for engaging with the world:

> The emerging civic culture implies the existence of reflective human beings who are making choices. It also implies a willingness to immerse oneself in empirical realities, to find out how things are for many different kinds of people. (p. xxiv)

The notion of a civic culture that is global in scale points to the necessity to understand issues that have global reach and their interconnected nature.

The unprecedented access to information provided by technological innovations puts a premium on the skills of managing and making sense of information. Gardner's (2007a) concept of "minds of the future" captures some of the ways that knowledge is changing in light of globalization. He identified and described five such minds: disciplined, synthesizing, creating, respectful, and ethical. In particular, his concept of the "synthesizing mind" captures these changes. Gardner (2007b) argues that there is a pressing need for the ability to combine information from across disciplines or sources into a coherent whole that can be explained comprehensibly to a range of audiences. This ability is significant because there is an overwhelming amount of information that is accessible through sources such as the Internet. The problem, then, is to be able to sort through, identify, and interpret the available information. Although Gardner claims that synthesizing is the most important cognitive skill for the future, he observes that it has not been identified as a critical topic to be taught in schools and is not yet part of the curriculum.

Giving Meaning to an Intangible Concept

Another issue in relation to conceptualizing globalization is the tendency to perceive globalization as an omnipresent and monolithic phenomenon. Globalization, as a set of different processes, is not always closely connected and can have diametrically opposed effects in various regions of the world. Mansilla and Gardner's (2007) framework for the application of globalization as a curricular topic helps to address this issue. Noting that one of the central challenges for teaching about globalization is its vagueness and the perception that it shapes everything and is everywhere, they proposed a conceptual map based on four topics (p. 52):

1. *Economic integration:* The benefits and costs caused by the emergence of the global economy and the implications for peoples and nations.
2. *Environmental stewardship:* Issues concerning the world environment and its health impact on human populations.
3. *Cultural encounters:* The increased and more intense contact between diverse peoples caused by technological changes and the exchange of cultural products.
4. *Governance and citizenship:* The emergence of global political institutions and the extension of citizenship rights and responsibilities to a world scale.

This map provides an analysis of the ubiquitous phenomenon and helps educators to distinguish between its different elements as curriculum topics, which can be challenging in light of the partial and sometimes inaccurate understandings of globalization that are disseminated through the media.

Contesting the Meanings of Globalization

Globalization is a highly contested concept in the public arena and in academic disciplines, especially in terms of its effects. In the public arena, knowledge of globalization is driven primarily by the media, which generally reflect mainstream views portraying it as beneficial. Survey research reflects this situation by showing that the U.S. public is largely ambivalent toward globalization and typically holds erroneous understandings of the phenomenon (Pew Research Center, 2007; Scheve & Slaughter, 2006). On the one hand, there is a widespread view that the U.S. is leading economic globalization for its own benefit and that it is advantageous for consumers and companies. However, at the same time there are concerns that too much globalization undermines the national economy by outsourcing domestic jobs and that immigration weakens national identity. The *19-Nation Poll on Global Issues* (Globescan, 2004) showed that, overall, 65% of the U.S. population viewed globalization as having a positive influence on their family's interests. This positive outlook is shared in other countries that play prominent roles in the global economy, such as Brazil (72%), China (60%) and India (73%), although many less developed countries did not share this view.

Scholars in sociology, political science, international development, philosophy, and education continue to debate the effects of globalization on topics such as national sovereignty, the distribution of income, and the governance and provision of education. The range of claims made about globalization has led scholars in the social sciences to refer to it as an essentially contested concept (e.g., "democracy" or "liberalism") that is given different meanings by group interests (Strand, Mueller, & McArthur, 2005). As a result, one challenge to introducing the topic in the curriculum is to provide an overview of these debates. Indeed, one of the central problems of teaching controversial issues in schools is that a limited range of primarily mainstream perspectives is typically presented (Camicia, 2007). Furthermore, it is important to distinguish between the legitimate academic discourse and the various ideological positions that underlie myths of globalization.

CONFRONTING THE MYTHS OF GLOBALIZATION

Critical globalization studies provided insight into the ways that knowledge of globalization is related to location and power. A central aim of critical globalization studies is to link the discourse or the knowledge about globalization with issues of global justice. Such an approach employs a critical perspective in examining how globalization operates in various locales. Critical theories of globalization were formulated to critique the dominant message disseminated about globalization by political and business leaders, particularly in the media. These theorists aimed to assess what knowledge about globalization was meaningful in order to analyze and reconstruct dominant messages. Scholars in this area "seek to provide people with a better understanding of how dominant beliefs about globalization fashion their realities and how these ideas can be changed to bring about more equitable social arrangements" (Steger, 2004, p. 11). This focus on the ideological meanings ascribed to globalization facilitates an analysis of the discourse from a democratic and justice-oriented vantage point.

A central concern of critical globalization studies is the relationship of knowledge about globalization with global justice (Appelbaum & Robinson, 2005). Therefore, this field is not antiglobalist but seeks to align the study of globalization with the democratization of its processes. One of the basic principles of critical globalization studies is the understanding that the historical forms of globalization have produced negative consequences for some groups as well as for the environment. Reconstructing existing knowledge of globalization thus concerns an analysis of how globalization could function in more democratic terms (Mittelman, 2004). In this regard, the study of globalization is also significant for the contemporary exercise of citizenship. Although globalization has created an explosion of knowledge, this knowledge is poorly diffused, which puts democracy at risk by limiting open access to information about society that is needed to ensure transparency in governance (Holzner & Holzner, 2006).

One of the major barriers to confronting globalization as a curricular topic is to overcome the popular myths that have been spread about its meaning, scope, and effects. Critical globalization theorists argue that public knowledge of globalization is connected closely with political agendas and ideologies that control the ways that the topic is portrayed or spoken about in the media (Mittelman, 2004). Steger (2004) further described how "a critical theory of globalization interrogates ideological valorizations of asymmetrical power relations that benefit the few and increase the suffering of the many" (p. 11). The focus, then, is on reforming the ways that practices of globalization have produced detrimental consequences for some groups of people by democratizing the processes and practices of globalization.

Popular myths about globalization have become widespread through the media, such as that globalization is an inevitable process or creating a borderless world. These myths persist because their repetition in the media cause them to take on a life of their own even when exposed as inaccurate, a phenomenon recently popularized as "truthiness" (Manjoo, 2008). In what follows, I outline three common myths of the effects of globalization: (1) as a borderless world, (2) as a global village, and (3) as an inevitable process.

One of the most common popular beliefs about globalization is that it is creating a world without national borders. There is a substantial body of research that globalization is weakening the sovereignty of nation-states in several respects. Global markets disrupt the sovereignty of nation-states because they operate beyond the territory and control of a single nation. Technology has facilitated the movement of information and capital across borders. Globalization has also raised challenges to the traditional understanding of citizenship as bounded to, and limited by, the nation-state. A supranational form of civic affiliation and responsibility is emerging based on shifting allegiances and solidarities within and outside of the nation-state (Held, 2002). As well, the proliferation of problems that are beyond the control of a single nation have led to the emergence of global political actors and global civil society, which indicate a lessening of the role of the nation-state in international politics. Climate change and other environmental problems are examples of problems that cannot be solved unilaterally because the resources involved are spread across multiple nations. Also, the current economic crisis illustrates the interconnectedness of national economies in ways that have not previously occurred. Nevertheless, national sovereignty based on territory remains as a powerful principle in international politics and nation-states still grant citizenship and regulate migration (Mittelman, 2004).

Another effect of globalization has been to increase contact between diverse peoples across the world and the recognition of a world community. Consequentially, a second popular myth of globalization is that this cultural mixing has fashioned the world into a "global village." Yet the scholarship suggests that this term is simplistic and presents a very different picture of the world (Tomlinson, 2003). In contrast, the effect of globalization on world cultures is an uneven process. Not all cultural groups are included in the global village. Moreover, various communities have being undermined by a flood of foreign commercial goods and Western businesses while others have not sufficiently industrialized to be included. In addition, globalization is not a single process but is comprised of local and regional manifestations of global culture that either adapt or reject the dominant Western account.

A third popular myth, and perhaps the most pervasive, is that globalization is an inevitable and uniform process. Historians of globalization (e.g., Mazlish, 2006) have pointed out the ways that the world has been globalizing for centuries and shown how and why this process has accelerated and reversed at times. A key insight of this work is that globalization is a human-made process that can be shaped, altered, and remade. Resistance to aspects of globalization, particularly its neoliberal practices, has attempted to shape the speed and form of globalization by democratizing it and mitigating its harmful effects. Such resistance has occurred within Western nations and especially from less developed countries, in which the public often views globalization as a form of economic and cultural imperialism (Newlands, 2002). Scholars have shown the ways that the practices of globalization have been both resisted and adapted to local settings across the world.

APPROACHES TO TEACHING ABOUT GLOBALIZATION

Drawing on issues discussed in the previous section, I outline existing curriculum approaches to international education that can inform the integration of globalization in the social studies curriculum. I focus on three approaches: global history, global civics, and 21st century skills. Each of these areas is informed by the globalization scholarship and makes distinct contributions that help to bring the social studies curriculum in line with contemporary scholarship and world realities.

Global History

Global history, a distinct branch of world history, focuses specifically on the historical roots and development of present-day globalization. This emerging field within the globalization scholarship holds considerable promise for integrating international education in public schools (Dunn, 2008). Its unique contribution is to provide a historical perspective to the study of globalization, which has typically been portrayed as an ahistorical, modern phenomenon that emerged during the second half of the 20th century.

The emphasis on national history for patriotism in U.S. schooling, however, presents a formidable barrier to the extension of world and global history in secondary education. One of the traditional purposes of history education has been to transmit citizenship and to build national identity through a common and prescriptive "nation-building story" (VanSledright, 2008, p. 109). In fact, the nation-state has served as the common unit for history and remains the primary focus in history education research (e.g., Wineburg, Mosborg, Porat, & Duncan, 2007). One reason is that history education emerged within a national educational framework that developed prior to globalization scholarship. However, due to the extent of the modern phase of globalization, some historians have argued that an increased focus should be placed on world history in order "to narrate the world's pasts in an age of globality" (Geyer & Bright, 2000, pp. 565–566). Bender (2006), for example, makes the case that history's political purpose is to "encourage and sustain a cosmopolitan citizenry, at once proud nationals and humble citizens of the world" (p. 14).

Historians are increasingly critical of the national frame for historical scholarship and many have shifted toward regional and world approaches in response to globalization (Hopkins, 2002; Manning, 2003; Schissler & Soysal, 2005). These historians argue that at least since the 1500s nations have been interconnected to such a degree that they have experienced a single global history (Bender, 2006). World history, then, can be understood as "the story of connections within the global human community" that "ranges in scale from individual family tales to migrations of peoples to narratives encompassing all humanity" (Manning, 2003, p. 3).

Underlying the argument of world historians is the insight that the modern academic field of history arose in step with the development of nation-states and the use of history to legitimize the (often oppressive) authority of nations. World history, then, has challenged the dominant historical narrative based on the nation-state. Scholars in this area have incorporated the globalization scholarship as well as social science analytical frameworks, such as world systems theory and postcolonial theory, to the study of historical topics in order to locate them within global patterns of change. The premise is that many historical issues of the human experience and of the world, such as poverty or human slavery, can best be understood in a global perspective and cannot be limited to borders of a single country.

However, the case for a global frame has been particularly difficult to make for history education in the United States due to the entrenched exceptionalist view that portrays it as having a historical trajectory that is unique and primarily independent from other countries. Stearns (2006), a leading world historian who has worked to develop the field in schools, described this situation as follows:

> A number of educators, and even more patrons and observers of education, are convinced that world history threatens the values and knowledge they find central to a well-conceived history program. For them, the two central pillars of such a program involve, first, a special emphasis on American history, usually conceived (at least implicitly) along lines of American exceptionalism, and second, an appropriate dose of Western civilization. (para. 3)

Despite the increase in world history course titles in secondary education, which has been particularly notable since the 1990s, history education remains focused on Western civilization (Stearns, 2006).

Global Civics

By effectively shrinking distances between peoples across the world, globalization has made global citizenship a more real possibility than ever before (Dower & Williams, 2002). As Dower (2002) suggested, global citizenship promotes human flourishing and basic rights while at the same time respecting diversity of belief and practice between societies and individuals:

> This is the idea of there being a responsibility to promote the conditions of human flourishing and basic rights but at the same time there also being a responsibility to respect diversity of belief and practice within and between societies. This is the idea of a multicultural world based on *solidarity* between people for creating the conditions for flourishing within it. (p. 157)

Due to globalization, individuals are more likely to hold multiple civic identities that include their ethnic group or background, nationality or nationalities, and the human race. Global citizenship is closely linked with the emergence of global civil society, which comprises the political and institutional setting in which people can act as citizens (Tarrow, 2005). However, it is important to note that the practice of global citizenship also reflects broader social inequalities of gender, race, and class. Some critics have charged that global citizenship is a primarily Western idea and that it is only accessible to individuals with the resources for international mobility.

The global dimension of citizenship should be understood as a complement to and an extension of national citizenship rather than a replacement. For example, Held (2002) maintains that the change in the locus of citizenship in the nation-state toward a cosmopolitan form would allow for multiple citizenships. He did not call for the creation of a world government but suggested that there is a need for an international democratic law and a cosmopolitan "community of all democratic communities" (Held, 1995, p. 232). In this sense, cosmopolitan democracy is defined as "a model of political organization in which citizens, wherever they are located in the world, have a voice, input and political representation in international affairs, in parallel with and independently of their own governments" (Archibugi & Held, 1995, p. 13).

Nevertheless, the suggestion that U.S. citizens should hold any identification beyond the nation-state, or a "post-national" understanding of society in which nation-state sovereignty is in flux, remains highly controversial and weakly implemented in the school system (Myers, 2006). A global dimension to citizenship has been dismissed outright by some critics, who point out that a world government does not exist and that without such an institution any thought of global citizenship is baseless (Ravitch, 2002). Behind this opposition is a strong faith in American exceptionalism and the sanctity of national sovereignty. Such a position, however, is tied to an outdated understanding of citizenship that ignores current world realities and scholarship.

Global citizenship broadly refers to the moral or ethical responsibility to the well-being of the entire human race and planet, grounded in solidarity and respect among different peoples (see Dower & Williams, 2002). The goal, then, is to create a better world by resolving problems that are global in scope and with local effects. Educational efforts can contribute to this goal by teaching students to understand and make sense of persistent global social problems and by making topics such as human rights important topics in the curriculum (Myers, 2008). More specifically, global citizenship can be understood for educational purposes as having, respectively, moral, institutional, and political dimensions (Myers & Zaman, 2009):

1. Membership in a world community with shared identity and ethical responsibilities
2. Belief in human rights as a legal framework and in global institutions
3. Commitment with other global citizens to solve world problems

These dimensions highlight specific goals for global citizenship that can be incorporated in the social studies curriculum.

From this perspective, social studies education that addresses global citizenship should also be concerned with preparation for a "global dialogue" to deal with international conflict and world peace in addition to national problems through cross-cultural dialogue (Nussbaum, 2002). Although there are a variety of curricular and pedagogical approaches in civics education courses in the United States (Hahn, 1999), they largely remain "one-size-fits-all" and are based on a singular American creed of democracy (Junn, 2004, p. 255). Furthermore, U.S. public education is behind international nongovernmental organizations (e.g., OXFAM's Cool Planet program), intergovernmental organizations (e.g., the United Nations' Cyberschoolbus), and governmental organizations (e.g., the Peace Corps' Worldwise Schools) in shaping the educational discourse and practice on education for global citizenship.

Twenty-First Century Skills

A third approach for integrating globalization in the social studies curriculum is to focus on new cognitive skills needed to be successful in the 21st century. Although this approach is only recently beginning to garner attention in social studies education (see Yell & Box, 2008), it has been a prominent discourse in other educational fields. Much of the attention has been on the implications of technology for education and work, such as the need to replace rule-based solutions with expert thinking and complex communication (Levy & Murnane, 2007).

Although there is not a single vision in regards to the substance to be included in these skills, several organizations and partnerships have developed frameworks that provide a fairly consistent set of skills and knowledge. This initiative emphasizes preparation for the digital age and for the workplace in the global economy and has been supported largely by the business community and the government sector. One of the leading organizations, the Partnership for 21st Century Skills (2008), explained its mission: "To successfully face rigorous higher education coursework, career challenges and a globally competitive workforce, U.S. schools must align classroom environments with real world environments by infusing 21st century skills." In this framework, a range of life skills are included that attempt to balance academic, civic, and vocational skills. Nevertheless, the mission statement illustrates that the primary goal for this approach is competitiveness in the global economy by aligning schooling to the needs of the labor market.

One prominent model for 21st century skills outlined four broad categories, each with several specific skills (see Table 6.1) (Burkhardt et al., 2003). This report, entitled "enGauge 21st Century Skills: Literacy in the Digital Age," is based on a synthesis of research, national reports, workforce trends, and input from educators. It outlines four primary categories of skills: digital-age literacy, inventive thinking, effective communication, and high productivity. The specific skills for each category are the following: The aim is to provide a broad, inclusive framework to prepare youth for all aspects of life beyond the classroom, especially work and citizenship. Although broad and detailed, the framework arguably suffers from the same problem of unrealistic goals and a lack of practical methods for reaching them as do some state standards.

The civic dimension, however, which is most evident in the skills "multicultural literacy and global awareness" and "personal, social, and civic re-

---

TABLE 6.1   enGauge 21st Century Skills

Digital-Age Literacy
1. Basic, scientific, economic, and technological literacies
2. Visual and information literacies
3. Multicultural literacy and global awareness

Inventive Thinking
1. Adaptability and managing complexity
2. Self-direction
3. Curiosity, creativity, and risk taking
4. Higher-order thinking and sound reasoning

Effective Communication
1. Teaming, collaboration, and interpersonal skills
2. Personal, social, and civic responsibility
3. Interactive communication

High Productivity
1. Prioritizing, planning, and managing for results
2. Effective use of real-world tools
3. Ability to produce relevant, high-quality products

---

sponsibility," plays a minor role within the broader framework. The framework places clear priority on the role of education in meeting the needs of the labor market. For example, the report refers repeatedly to the idea that schools are the place for "continued renewal of workers' skills" by transforming schools "into high-performance organizations" that resemble businesses (Burkhardt et al., 2003, p. 11). Thus, the emphasis is on cognitive skills rather than deeper understanding of social and political contexts, which disciplines such as history and political science provide, and ignores social inequalities and issues of justice relevant to the acquisition and use of such skills in a world that is growing increasingly unequal. In this respect, multicultural literacy serves businesses competing within a global economy that is multilingual and multicultural, rather than to address civic deficits to build and extend democracy and democratic principles.

Although this framework officially aims to prepare students for different realities of future life, the emphasis is on the rapid alignment of schools with the so-called real world, which typically is a reference to the workplace. The 21st century skills approach is based on the post-industrial notion that the global economy is driven by the production and management of technology and knowledge (i.e., a "knowledge" or "information" economy) rather than by labor and capital. In this context, the purpose of learning 21st century skills is to contribute to the development of human capital and learners are conceived primarily as future workers. For example, the enGauge framework presents a rationale that is based on aligning education with workforce needs in claiming that "Not providing students with opportunities to develop 21st century skills and proficiencies will create a disconnect between the innovative jobs being created and the skills of the workforce" (Burkhardt et al., 2003, p. 9). This framework further aligns with No Child Left Behind legislation and its emphasis on high-stakes testing. The alignment of education to serve the purposes of the labor market has been criticized, as Carlson (1996) described:

> The "basic skills" restructuring of urban schools around standardized testing and a skill-based curriculum has been a response to the changing character of work in post-industrial America, and it has participated in the construction of a new post-industrial working class. (pp. 282–283)

Other scholars have argued that the majority of jobs do not require such broad postindustrial skills and that the testing and skills movements are geared toward basic literacies and familiarity with information technology in preparation for low-wage jobs (Lipman, 2007).

The 21st Century Skills initiative also differs from the Global History and Global Civics approaches in lacking alignment with a specific academic discipline. As a result it may be less coherent with social studies education. Although 21st century skills frameworks generally are designed to complement traditional school subjects, this supposition is questionable, particularly for the skills that are most closely connected with the workplace. As such, it does not contribute to the development of the disciplinary habits of mind in political science, history, and other subject areas that are the foundation of social studies education. Nonetheless, the framework can provide educators with a broad indication of some of the broad communicative and thinking skills that are most relevant for the globalizing world.

CONCLUSION

This chapter has attempted to highlight some of the ways that globalization is affecting learning and to examine some approaches for integrating globalization as a topic in the social studies curriculum. The three approaches that were outlined—global history, global civics and 21st century skills—articulate different understandings of the significance of globalization as a curriculum topic with different implications for students' learning about the world today. In particular, global history and global civics align with the stated, although still largely unfulfilled, NCSS standard for global connections and cross-cultural understanding. The latter approach, 21st century skills, has become a major reform movement that brings important scholarship into the social studies discourse. Each of the three approaches provides important insights into the ways that global and international education can begin to include globalization as a curriculum topic.

One aim of this chapter was to make the case that the study of globalization as a curriculum topic is an imperative for international education in today's schools. Much of what takes place in schools as international education has not changed in terms of curriculum content. My hope is that this chapter will help to expand the conversation about the content of international education within social studies, especially as it pertains to the integration of contemporary social science and humanities scholarship. Ultimately, social studies educators interested in international and global education should take into consideration each of these approaches when considering the role of globalization in the social studies curriculum.

REFERENCES

Appelbaum, R. P., & Robinson, W. I. (Eds.). (2005). *Critical globalization studies.* New York: Routledge.

Archibugi, D., & Held, D. (Eds.). (1995). *Cosmopolitan democracy: An agenda for a new world order.* Cambridge, UK: Polity Press.

Becker, J. (2002). Globalization and global education: Ever the twain shall meet? *International Social Studies Forum, 2*(1), 51–57.

Bender, T. (2006). *Nation among nations: America's place in world history.* New York: Hill & Wang.

Boulding, K. (1995). Expecting the unexpected: The uncertain future of knowledge and technology. In E. Boulding & K. Boulding (Eds.), *The future: Images and processes* (pp. 7–25). Thousand Oaks, CA: Sage.

Burkhardt, G., Monsour, M., Valdez, G., Gunn, C., Dawson, M., Lemke, C., et al. (2003). *enGauge 21st century skills: Literacy in the digital age.* Naperville, IL: NCREL.

Camicia, S. P. (2007). Deliberating immigration policy: Locating instructional materials within global and multicultural perspectives. *Theory and Research in Social Education, 35*(1), 96–111.

Carlson, D. (1996). Education as a political issue: What's missing in the public conversation about education? In J. L. Kincheloe & S. R. Steinberg (Eds.), *Thirteen questions: Reframing education's conversation* (pp. 281–291). New York: Peter Lang.

Castells, M. (1996). *The rise of the network society.* Oxford, UK: Blackwell.

Dower, N. (2002). Global ethics and global citizenship. In N. Dower & J. Williams (Eds.), *Global citizenship: A critical introduction* (pp. 146–157). New York: Routledge.

Dower, N., & Williams, J. (2002). Introduction. In N. Dower & J. Williams (Eds.), *Global citizenship: A critical introduction* (pp. 1–8). New York: Routledge.

Dunn, R. E. (2008). The two world histories. *Social Education, 72*(5), 257–263.

Gardner, H. E. (2007a). *Five minds for the future.* Cambridge, MA: Harvard Business School Press.

Gardner, H. E. (2007b). The synthesizing mind: Making sense of the deluge of information. In M. Sánchez Sorondo, E. Malinvaud & P. Léna (Eds.), *Globalization and education* (pp. 3–18). Berlin: Walter de Gruyter.

Gardner, H. E. (2004). How education changes: Considerations of history, science, and values. In M. M. Suárez-Orozco & D. B. Qin-Hilliard (Eds.), *Globalization: Culture and education in the new millennium* (pp. 235–258). Berkeley: University of California Press.

Geyer, M., & Bright, C. (2000). World history in a global age. In R. E. Dunn (Ed.), *The new world history: A teacher's companion* (pp. 564–575). Boston: Bedford/St Martin's.

Globescan (2004). 19 Nation poll on global issues. Retrieved January 9, 2009, from www.pipa.org/OnlineReports/Other%20Studies/GlobalIss_Jun04/GlobalIss_Jun04_quaire.pdf

Hahn, C. L. (1999). Challenges to civic education in the United States. In J. Torney-Purta, J. Schwille & J.-A. Amadeo (Eds.), *Civic education across countries: Twenty-four national case studies from the IEA civic education project* (pp. 583–607). Amsterdam: IEA.

Held, D., & McGrew, A. G. (Eds.). (2003). *The global transformations reader: An introduction to the globalization debate.* Cambridge, UK: Polity Press.

Held, D. (2002). The transformation of political community: Rethinking democracy in the context of globalization. In N. Dower & J. Williams (Eds.), *Global citizenship: a critical introduction* (pp. 92–100). New York: Routledge.

Held, D., McGrew, A., Goldblatt, D., & Perraton, J. (1999). *Global transformations: Politics, economics and culture.* Cambridge, UK: Polity Press.

Held, D. (1995). *Democracy and the global order: From the modern state to cosmopolitan governance.* Stanford, CA: Stanford University Press.

Hess, D. E. (2005). Moving beyond celebration: Challenging curricular orthodoxy in the teaching of Brown and its legacies. *Teachers College Record, 107*(9), 2046–2067.

Holzner, B., & Holzner, L. (2006). *Transparency in global change: The vanguard of the open society.* Pittsburgh: University of Pittsburgh Press.

Hopkins, A. G. (Ed.). (2002). *Globalization in world history.* New York: Norton.

Junn, J. (2004). Diversity, immigration, and the politics of civic education. *PS: Political Science and Politics, 37*(2), 253–255.

Larson, R. W. (2002). Globalization, societal change, and new technologies: What they mean for the future of adolescence. *Journal of Research on Adolescence, 12*(1), 1–30.

Levy, F., & Murnane, R. J. (2007). How computerized work and globalization shape human skill demand. In M. M. Suárez-Orozco (Ed.), *Learning in the global era: International perspectives on globalization and education* (pp. 158–174). Berkeley: University of California Press.

Lipman, P. (2007). "No Child Left Behind": Globalization, the labor market, and the politics of inequality. In E. W. Ross & R. Gibson (Eds.), *Neoliberalism and educational reform: Marxian perspectives on the impact of globalization on teaching and learning* (pp. 35–58). Cresskill, NJ: Hampton Press.

Manjoo, F. (2008). *True enough: Learning to live in a post-fact society*. Hoboken, NJ: Wiley.

Manning, P. (2003). *Navigating world history: Historians create a global past*. New York: Palgrave Macmillan.

Mansilla, V. B., & Gardner, H. E. (2007). From teaching globalization to nurturing global consciousness. In M. M. Suárez-Orozco & C. Sattin (Eds.), *Learning in the global era: International perspectives on globalization and education*. Berkeley: University of California Press.

Mazlish, B. (2006). *The new global history*. New York: Routledge.

Mead, W. R. (2006). *The state of state world history standards*. Washington, DC: Fordham Institute.

Mittelman, J. H. (2004). *Whither globalization: The vortex of knowledge and ideology*. New York: Routledge.

Myers, J. P., & Zaman, H. A. (2009). Negotiating the global and national: Immigrant and dominant culture Adolescents' vocabularies of citizenship in a transnational world. *Teachers College Record, 111*(11), 2589–2625.

Myers, J. P. (2008). Making sense of a globalizing world: Adolescents' explanatory frameworks for poverty. *Theory and Research in Social Education, 36*(2), 95–123.

Myers, J. P. (2006). Rethinking the social studies curriculum in the context of globalization: Education for global citizenship in the U.S. *Theory and Research in Social Education, 34*(3), 370–394.

National Geographic/Roper. (2002). *2002 global geographic literacy survey*. Washington, DC: Author.

Newlands, D. (2002). Economic globalization and global citizenship. In N. Dower & J. Williams (Eds.), *Global citizenship: A critical introduction* (pp. 213–221). New York: Routledge.

Nussbaum, M. C. (2002). Patriotism or cosmopolitanism. *Boston Review, 19*(5), 3–6.

Partnership for 21st Century Skills (2008). *Mission statement*. Retrieved June 14, 2008, from www.21stcenturyskills.org.

Pew Research Center (2007). *47-nation Pew global attitudes survey*. Washington, DC: Author.

Ravitch, D. (2002). September 11: Seven lessons for the schools. *Educational Leadership, 60*(2), 6–9.

Scheve, K., & Slaughter, M. J. (2006). Public opinion, international economic integration, and the welfare state. In P. Bardhan, S. Bowles & M. Wallerstein (Eds.), *Globalization and egalitarian redistribution* (pp. 217–260). New York: Russell Sage.

Schissler, H., & Soysal, Y. N. (Eds.). (2005). *The nation, Europe, and the world: Textbooks and curricula in transition*. New York: Berghahn Books.

Stearns, P. N. (2006). World history: Curriculum and controversy. *World History Connected, 3*(3).

Steger, M. B. (2004). Introduction: Rethinking the ideological dimensions of globalization. In M. B. Steger (Ed.), *Rethinking globalism* (pp. 1–12). Lanham, MD: Rowman & Littlefield.

Stewart, V. (2007). Becoming citizens of the world. *Educational Leadership, 64*(7), 8–14.

Strand, J. R., Mueller, T. F., & McArthur, J. A. (2005). The essentially contested concept of globalization. *Politics and Ethics Review, 1*(1), 45–59.

Stromquist, N. P. (2002). *Education in a globalized world.* Lanham, MD: Rowman & Littlefield.

Tarrow, S. (2005). *The new transnational activism.* Cambridge, UK: Cambridge University Press.

Tikly, L. (2001). Globalization and education in the postcolonial world: Towards a conceptual framework. *Comparative Education Review, 37*(2), 151–171.

Tomlinson, J. (2003). Globalization and cultural identity. In D. Held & A. McGrew (Eds.), *The global transformations reader: An introduction to the globalization debate* (pp. 269–277). Malden, MA: Polity Press.

VanSledright, B. (2008). Narratives of nation-state, historical knowledge, and school history education. *Review of Research in Education, 32,* 109–146.

Wineburg, S., Mosborg, S., Porat, D., & Duncan, A. (2007). Common belief and the cultural curriculum: An intergenerational study of historical consciousness. *American Educational Research Journal, 44*(1), 40–76.

Yell, M. M., & Box, J. (2008). Embrace the future: NCSS and P21. *Social Education, 72*(7), 347–349.

CHAPTER 7

TEACHER PREPARATION FOR GLOBAL PERSPECTIVES PEDAGOGY

Omiunota N. Ukpokodu
University of Missouri–Kansas City

A child born today will be faced as an adult, almost daily with problems of a global interdependent nature, be it peace, food, the quality of life, inflation, or scarcity of resources. He will be both an actor and a beneficiary or a victim in the total world fabric, and he may rightly ask: "why was I not warned? Why was I not better educated? Why did my teachers not tell me about these problems and indicate my behavior as a member of an interdependent human race? It is, therefore, the duty and the self-enlightened interest of governments to educate their children properly about the type of world in which they are going to live. (Muller, 1985, p. 1)

It was almost two and half decades ago that Robert Muller made this powerful appeal on the need to foster global education and global citizenship skills. In an increasingly diverse and interdependent world, individuals, regardless of their geographic location, must possess the knowledge, skills, and attitudes necessary to negotiate different social, cultural, political, and economic discourses. But more importantly, they need the knowledge about the critical challenges the world faces, and how they can rethink their

Critical Global Perspectives, pages 121–142
Copyright © 2010 by Information Age Publishing
All rights of reproduction in any form reserved.

roles/responsibilities in solving difficulties faced by marginalized people in the world.

We know that people in the world are increasingly becoming interconnected as new technologies are creating electronic networks. New electronic technologies and communication systems now make it more possible to develop communication and cross-cultural exchanges, including making news events more accessible to people around the world. The globalization of the world comes with great benefits as well as unprecedented challenges. The economic aspect of globalization has transformed how labor and capital operates globally, thus reshaping how transnational economy functions. On the other hand, the cultural dimensions of globalization have influenced how people consume popular culture (music, film, etc.) globally. We may ask: What are the implications of the rapid increase of Western fast-food restaurants (McDonald's, Kentucky Fried Chicken, etc.) or products (media, fashion, music, etc.) in Third World societies? These global cultural/economic activities have complexly linked the world together as never before. Yet, it remains to be seen to what extent the poorest of the poor in the Third World are benefiting from the current economic/cultural changes taking place in the world. Without a doubt, today's social, economic, cultural, and demographic realities across national boundaries have made people and cultures more in contact with each other. In fact, nation-states and people in the world have become more interdependent on international economics and are beginning to realize that issues such as environment and wars affect people around the world.

As globalization has reshaped people's lives (for better or worse) and, because of industrialization, it has also threatened habitats and biodiversity in the planet (Annan, 2000). Some of the critical challenges humanity faces today include global warming, which has created unpredictable weather patterns that have devastated many communities nationally and internationally. For instance, the tsunami of 2004 created enormous economic, human, and cultural destruction in several countries in Asia and Africa. Similarly, Hurricane Katrina in 2005 was one of the costliest and deadliest disasters in U.S. history, displacing thousands of people. Issues such as wars, depleting resources, poverty, human rights abuses, and the effects of a burgeoning world population continue to plague societies around the world. Many individuals and groups across the world continue to be dehumanized and marginalized because of the racial, ethnic, gender, religious, and sexual identities they negotiate. However, just as new technologies and communication networks have brought the world closer, they have also further separated the haves from the have-nots. In the United States, economic disparities exist between the rich and the poor neighborhoods and communities are segregated along the lines of race and class. The realities of poverty, economic disparities, and inequities in Third World countries are particularly acute. Even though the world is interconnected, acute economic equalities exist between "developed" and "developing" countries, or what I prefer to call resourced and underresourced nation-states. Ngugi (1993) pointed out that the relationships between developed and developing nations have never been equal. And so begs the question: How do we navigate our way?

In this chapter, I ask: How can we develop a framework that addresses meaningful approaches to global perspective pedagogy—a pedagogy that is attentive to critical issues of our times. I also ask: In what ways do our perspectives shape how we think about the topic of global perspectives and a pedagogy that addresses global perspectives? I do not doubt that many scholars within the field of social studies are committed to global education and have the good intention of preparing teachers for global perspective pedagogy; however, I would argue that there might be differences in how we engage with or interpret the topic of global perspective or global perspective pedagogy. My primary focus in this chapter is to explore and raise questions about preservice and inservice teachers' preparation for global perspective pedagogy in teacher education programs, especially in the social studies. While much has been written about K–12 classroom teachers developing and implementing global education, little is known about what constitutes global perspective pedagogy in teacher education. Also, while much focus is given to preparing teachers for multicultural education in teacher education, little has been done to prepare teachers to teach from a global perspective (Merryfield, 1993, 1998). Thus, my goal in this chapter is to provide a framework that can be used effectively to prepare pre-service and in-service teachers for global perspective pedagogy. First, to contextualize the value of developing global perspective pedagogy, I discuss the findings of a survey that I developed and note its implications to recognizing the different issues multicultural education and global education address. Lastly, the chapter examines suggested practices for global perspective pedagogy in the context of teacher education.

ANALYZING RESULTS OF A SURVEY

While I personally recognize that many scholars and educators have genuine passion for teaching global perspectives, little is known about how teacher educators, especially social studies educators, engage in global perspective pedagogy. If we want our students (pre-service and in-service teachers) to embrace global perspective pedagogy, we need to ask in what ways we are developing pedagogy that values global perspectives. Since the conception of global education, studies have examined its integration into teaching and learning (Gilliom, 1993; Merryfield, 1993; Tye & Tye, 1992), the contextual factors that influence teachers' decisions in teaching from a global perspective (Merryfield, 1998; Tye & Tye, 1992), and the impact of cross-cultural and international experience on teachers' development of a global perspective pedagogy (Merryfield, 1998; Wilson, 1998, 2001). Most of these studies have been researched within the K–12 levels and limited conversation has taken place between the fields of global education and teacher education. Although the importance and imperative for global education are widely acknowledged, research suggests that teacher education programs are doing very little to prepare teachers to develop the knowledge, skills, and dispositions to teach from a global perspective (Gilliom, 1993; Merryfield, 2002; Tye & Tye, 1992; Wilson, 2001). Furthermore, research indicates that the relationship between teacher education and global education has not been adequately examined by scholars as a critical topic of inquiry (Johnson & Ochoa, 1993; Massialas, 1991). For me, this is a serious concern.

In the aftermath of September 11, 2001, global education became a popular discourse in academic circles and, for instance, "globalization" and "global education" became buzzwords and were used quite broadly and without much analysis on what constituted a more critical approach to looking at world events. Needless to say, in academic circles, including in the social studies, there were limited critical conversations about how to theorize or teach about post-9/11 events. Some attention was given to analyzing and debating the effects of the tragedy on students and how teachers should teach about the tragic event. Merryfield (2002) argued that the teaching about 9/11 should not only be linked to pedagogical discourses but that teaching practices needed to open spaces for educators to reassess the value of global education and that teachers needed to incorporate more global content in their teachings. Following the tragic events of 9/11, it was often pointed out how global education should play a critical role in helping students understand the tensions and conflicts around the world, particularly in relation to U.S. wars in Afghanistan and Iraq. Yet, in schools as well as in various academic circles, there was much resistance to teaching and learning about various perspectives surrounding U.S. wars and the violation of civil rights in the post-9/11 climate. For example, those who presented alternative perspectives about the wars, particularly those that were critical of U.S. policies, were criticized and were even constructed as being unpatriotic radicals and as terrorist sympathizers.

In the post-9/11 period, I was troubled by the ways in which educators were narrowly interpreting domestic and international issues surrounding terrorism, civil rights, and war. In the context of social studies, I felt that there was a need to ask whose knowledge, perspective, or story was being privileged when we were speaking about the idea of global perspective. My attempt here is not to delve into the nuances of the rhetoric that surrounded the nature of academic discourse on global issues following the events of 9/11, including among social studies scholars. Rather, my purpose is to explore the value of recognizing different interpretations on what constituted global perspective and global perspective pedagogy. This may help us recognize the multiple ways we come to understand global issues and local–global relationships.

As a teacher educator who is committed to developing transformative pedagogy, I was interested in researching the ways in which professors of social education taught global perspective pedagogy. In particular, in the post-9/11 climate, I was interested in finding out how educators defined the meaning of global perspective and how we could model global perspective pedagogy in our methods courses. Thus, 2 years ago, I initiated a study that investigated teacher educators' approaches to preparing pre-service and in-service teachers for global perspective pedagogy. The study questions were as follows:

1. What is your conception of global education?
2. What is your understanding of global perspectives?
3. What is your conception of global perspective pedagogy?
4. How do you prepare teachers for global perspective pedagogy? Please list/describe specific processes, strategies, and activities.
5. To what extent have you been successful in preparing teachers for global perspective pedagogy?
6. What challenges, constraints, and dilemmas have you faced in your efforts to prepare teachers for global perspective pedagogy?

Unfortunately, the overall response to the survey was very disappointing and troubling. First, the response rate (10%) was very low (the survey was emailed to 300 social studies educators, nationally and internationally). Of those responding, only two educators responded to the entire questionnaire. Some sent in apologies indicating that they could not go beyond the first two questions—conception of global education and understanding of global perspectives. In other words, they could not discuss their conception of global perspective pedagogy and how they prepared teachers toward it. As one participant explained, "I received your questionnaire regarding global perspective pedagogy in teacher education and had paused to think about it. While I personally have a view of global education, the notion/concept is **not** really addressed in our teacher education program here." A few of the participants listed generic responses such as, "I emphasize similarities, not differences about people around the world. All people around the world have common needs, but how needs are fulfilled may be very different." Or "I discuss customs of other countries such as—do arranged marriages make sense?" Or "I have my students develop units on continents/ countries—Asia and Japan."

In addition, I reviewed 15 social studies textbooks used in social studies methods courses. It was also disappointing to find that these books did not have a chapter or threads that explicitly discussed global perspective pedagogy. There was only one textbook, *Teaching Strategies for the Social Studies*, by James Banks (1999), that included a section on human rights issues in the global context. Furthermore, a review of teacher education course syllabi, collected from the Web, also revealed a lack of global perspectives focus. This is not to suggest that a professor may not teach certain discourses even when they are not explicitly indicated in the course syllabus. However, we know that textbooks can dictate course implementation, especially for educators who may have limited content knowledge on a given topic. These disappointing experiences and observations raised my interest about the dearth of conceptual frameworks that addressed global perspectives pedagogy. Upon reflection, I wondered, given the emphasis on diversity/multicultural education in teacher education, are we assuming that preparing teachers for diversity/multicultural education automatically prepares them for global perspective pedagogy? Are we misconceiving multicultural education pedagogy for global education pedagogy? While multicultural education and global education are both needed in helping students develop critical consciousness, there are important distinctions that have not been articulated in the field. In what follows, I discuss the distinction between global education and multicultural education and note its implications to developing a more responsible global perspective pedagogy.

GLOBAL EDUCATION AND MULTICULTURAL EDUCATION

Multicultural education and global education are educational approaches and efforts designed to prepare students for effective citizenship in specific national and global communities. While there are similarities on how both approaches conceptualize differences and citizenship, there are also differences that must be critically recognized. In my article, "Multiculturalism vs. Globalism," I made a distinction between global and multicultural education (see Ukpokodu, 1999; see also Figure 7.1 and Table 7.1). Multicultural education, global education, multiculturalism, and globalism are terms that are often used interchangeably in the literature. Banks (2001) argued that we ought to use caution when using the term "multiculturalism" since the term has often been used to describe dominant approaches to diversity discourses. Similarly, I use the term "globalism" with caution because of the negative connotations that have been associated with the concept, particularly in relation to global approaches that devalues differences across cul-

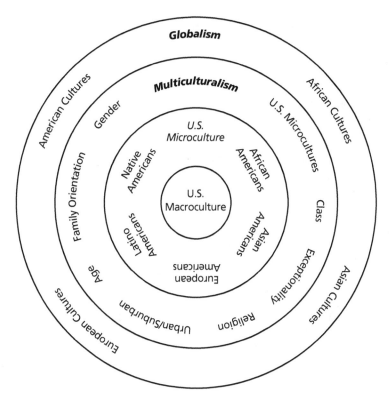

Figure 7.1 Global education versus multicultural education.

tures. For this reason, instead of using multiculturalism and globalism, I use multicultural education and global education, respectively. Figure 7.1 shows a construct representing the relationship between multicultural education and global education. Using the United States as an example, the construct shows the United States as a macro-culture and how its national culture promotes (at least conceptually) democratic ideals to citizens via various political and social institutions. Second, the micro-cultures are subcultures within the United States that have their own unique cultural histories and experiences that stand within and outside of macro-cultures. This may include the cultures of specific ethnic/racial groups: Native Americans, European Americans, African Americans, Latinos and Asian Americans, and sociocultural categories such as class, religion, gender, disability, and sexual orientation. The outer realm of the construct represents the global dimension where ideas, perspectives, and issues from around the globe can be integrated into students' learning experiences. Similarly, Table 7.1 shows the distinctions between multicultural education and global education. On the other hand, global education focuses on issues and events outside of a

TABLE 7.1 Differences between Multicultural Education and Global Education

Multicultural Education	Global Education
• Study of ethnic and cultural diversity within a given society	• Study of cultures and peoples of nations
• A vehicle for understanding and addressing national issues of diversity, equity, and justice	• A vehicle for understanding and addressing global issues of diversity, equity, and social justice
• Aimed at promoting national citizenship	• Aimed at promoting global citizenship
• The transformation of learning environments essential for successfully educating all students and ensuring educational equity	• A focus on human connectedness and interdependency and the challenges that confront humanity as a whole
• Developing multicultural/pluralist perspectives based on diversity within a given society	• Developing a global perspective needed to live wisely in a world that possesses limited resources
• Developing a pluralist perspective needed for understanding differences	• Developing a global perspective for viewing the world and its people with understanding and concern
• Fostering social activism needed to transform a given society	• Fostering social activism needed to transform the world
• Developing a sense of social responsibility for the needs of all microcultural and sociocultural groups and a commitment to finding a harmonious and peaceful coexistence	• Developing a sense of social responsibility for the needs of all people and a commitment to finding just and peaceful solutions to global problems
• Ensuring social justice for all	• Ensuring social justice for all

given nation-state and connects local–global issues.[1] Banks (2009), while noting the linkages between multicultural education and global education on shared goals (social justice, need of diverse curriculum, etc.), cautioned against substituting one for the other. Thus, in terms of developing a pedagogy that addresses global perspectives, it is useful for us to distinguish the different purposes that multicultural education and global education advocate. This may help us not homogenize the different (and shared) goals of both interventions.

THE VALUE OF GLOBAL PERSPECTIVE PEDAGOGY

Giroux and Simon (1989) define pedagogy as a deliberate attempt to influence how and what knowledge and identities are produced within and among a particular learning setting. In particular, pedagogy means "the integration in practice of particular curriculum content and design, classroom strategies and techniques, a time and space for the practice of those strategies and techniques, and evaluation purposes and methods" (p. 239). I define global perspective pedagogy (GPP) as a transformative and critical pedagogy that offers opportunities for teacher–learner engagement in discourses on perspectives, issues, and concerns faced by the global community. Global perspective pedagogy is a pedagogy that (1) aims to challenge and reconstruct given knowledge about the world, (2) argues for the need to further develop perspective consciousness, and (3) aims to engender a sense of social responsibility. Thus, global perspective pedagogy is transformative when it challenges learners to question world realities, their own experiences, beliefs, and values, and helps them rethink the ways that they have come to see the world. And through global perspective pedagogy, students can learn to avoid exotic perspectives of the world. Such an approach allows learners alternative ways of reading the international social context and enables them to be nondiscriminating, change-oriented, and reflective of their beliefs and perspectives (Dewey, 1933; Mezirow & Associates, 2000). Like any other form of transformative pedagogy, global perspective pedagogy is effectively implemented when it creates learning community via dialogue and self-reflection, and that allows learners to question and challenge social issues (Cranton, 1994). It provides not only a self-examination about knowledge and dispositions toward global concerns but also experiential activities that encourage active learning, problem-posing with real-world issues and concerns, and social action–oriented projects.

Rationale for Global Perspective Pedagogy

While most scholars within the field of global education have defined and conceptualized global education and its dimensions, issues related to equity and social justice have been ignored. Today, even as we call for global collaboration and as the world confronts critical socioeconomic challenges, we need to ask broader questions on issues of power and representation, particularly that addresses issues of voice: what counts as legitimized knowledge and the nature of knowledge that is privileged in a given topic of discussion. More than anything else, issues of equity and social justice must become a focus when implementing global education. It is not enough to help students learn and develop knowledge, skills, and attitudes about other cultures without raising their awareness on issues of inequities and injustice that inflict many people across the globe. I ask: How can teacher educators translate theories and conceptions of global education into their practices as they work with pre-service and in-service teachers? That is, how can teacher educators engage with global perspective pedagogy that addresses issues of equity and injustices?

By examining Banks's (1996) analysis on the need to rethink knowledge embedded within social science disciplines, Merryfield (1993) pointed out how U.S. students have much to learn from perspectives shared by people worldwide and that "American-centrism" cannot prepare students for citizenship, let alone educate them for equity and diversity in an increasingly interdependent world. Merryfield argued that if K–12 students are to be educated to understand changes taking place in the global context, they must understand local–global connections and must learn to recognize the voices of people from the margins, both in the national as well as in the international context. In relation to rethinking local–global connections, the discourse of citizenship is similarly important since it helps us rethink traditional conceptions of citizenship that have privileged dominant forms of knowledge (see Banks, 2004). In recent years, teachers have been asked to educate students about *multicultural citizenship* so that they are better able to recognize their rights and responsibilities; and also so that they can critically negotiate their identities as members of their ethnic and national as well as global communities (Kymlicka, 1995). I would argue that each of us possesses a national and global citizenship. Either by our birthright or via the process of immigration and naturalization, individuals can claim, in most cases, national citizenship. On the other hand, global citizenship is a right and responsibility that individuals ought to claim on the basis of their being born in the world and as members of humanity. Global citizenship has no specific geographic identity other than one's sense of belonging (and responsibility) toward the planet and its inhabitants. Thus, as a global citizen, our allegiance should be to the wider world since we negotiate multiple identities—individual, cultural, national, regional, and global. For this reason, educators must help students develop a global consciousness: as world citizens so that they can act to make the world just, equitable, peaceful, and humane.

But how can teachers effectively develop students' global perspectives and consciousness and a sense of social responsibility if they themselves have not developed such perspectives and identifications, let alone the pedagogy to facilitate relevant experiences for their students? Hargreaves (1999) stated that:

> It is plain that if teachers do not acquire and display [the] capacity to redefine their skills for the task of teaching, and if they do not model in their own conduct the very qualities that are key outcomes for students, then the challenge of schooling in the next millennium will not be met. (p. 123)

Clearly, teachers can nurture students' interest and concern over issues such as human rights and environment when teachers themselves are knowledgeable and passionate about such issues (Torney-Purta, Lehmann,

Oswald, & Schultz, 2001). Global education scholars emphasize that prospective and in-service teachers must be adequately prepared so that they can effectively prepare students to develop open-mindedness, respect for diverse worldviews, human dignity, empathy, human rights, and social justice (Hanvey, 1974). Osler and Starkey (1996) clarified more poignantly the rationale for preparing teachers to develop not only a global perspective but the pedagogy for global perspective. They explained that:

> Teachers are responsible for "transmitting" values. They need to be in a position to help their students be supportive of pluralist democracy and human rights, enjoy cultural diversity and be conscious of their responsibilities to the planet and to all those who live on it. This implies that they should themselves share these values. (p. 105)

Taylor (1970) argued that global perspectives ought to be infused throughout the teacher education program and that without the development of global perspectives students will only gain a narrow understanding of the global reality. More importantly, Taylor urged that in an increasingly diverse, interconnected, and interdependent world, teachers and schools must be conscious agents in integrating knowledge about global concerns in curriculum and must advocate the idea of a global community.

GLOBAL PERSPECTIVES PEDAGOGY
IN TEACHER EDUCATION

It is important to understand that, similar to multicultural perspectives, integrating global perspectives into students' curricular and instructional experiences should not be an add-on practice. Global perspectives must be infused within everyday learning experiences that students are provided. Teaching an isolated unit or lesson on a specific country or culture is neither effective nor pedagogically responsible. Second, integrating global perspectives should not be an either–or proposition, such as emphasizing only one country (European, etc.) while avoiding others (African, etc.). Thus, global perspectives must be integrated into the curriculum on a consistent and explicit basis. Third, integrating global perspectives is not about a one-week activity or endeavor. Thus, global perspective pedagogy should be deliberate, systematic, critical, and ought to permeate the teacher education conceptual framework within a given institution. In other words, the importance of global perspective should be explicit in the following areas: (1) course descriptions and objectives, (2) content integration, (3) instructional resources and materials, (4) delivery strategies, and (5) assessment of self-transformation.

Course Description and Objectives

Clearly, the syllabus is an important pedagogical component that reflects an educator's values, knowledge, expectations, passion, and commitment. The following fundamental questions can be helpful in developing course descriptions and objectives that reflect the need to value global perspectives: (a) How does this course raise and heighten teachers' awareness of global issues and cultures? (b) How does the course prepare teachers to live and teach in today's inequitable and culturally diverse world? (c) How does my course prepare teachers for global perspective pedagogy? (d) How does my course help teachers understand the goal of preparing their students for an interdependent world?

One strategy that I have used in my methods courses is to administer a pre–post survey about global concerns (Ukpokodu, 2006). The survey requires students to rank in order of importance (1 = low to 5 = high) their level of awareness, the importance, the extent to which they feel affected by global concerns, and their disposition toward teaching about global concerns. The survey consists of 13 items related to critical global concerns and challenges that the world faces (environmental degradation, poverty, overpopulation, AIDS, terrorism, hunger, human rights abuse, threats of nuclear weapons, depleting resources, trade and economy, drug trafficking, slave labor, and gap between developed and developing countries). The items were developed by adapting and modifying concepts from the 2000 UN Executive Summit Report that was delivered by the Secretary-General of the United States at the dawn of the third millennium (Annan, 2000). The survey asks participants to identify their "before" and "after" level of perception of the 13 items in light of the September 11 terrorist attacks. Students find the survey thought provoking since it helps them rethink the critical issues the world faces and how they have a responsibility in teaching critical global issues.

Content Integration

Banks (2006) explained content integration as a method of incorporating content from multiple perspectives. In the context of promoting global perspectives, the goal of content integration is to expand the curriculum by infusing perspectives, issues, and events from various parts of the world. For example, common themes or concepts taught in the social studies reflect experiences and histories of people, places, and cultures across time and space. At the elementary level, educators can explore social studies themes such as self, family, community, immigration, human and civil rights, governance, and so on. For instance, a unit on immigration would include perspectives about immigration realities in various parts of the world—Australia, Great Britain, Canada, Japan, and South Africa. The American Revolution is a popular theme taught in the upper elementary grades and throughout high school. A global perspective approach would involve globalizing the understanding of revolution since many countries around the world have experienced various forms of revolutions. In Figure 7.2, students have the opportunity to learn about the places in the world where revolutions have taken place. A theme such as revolution provides a critical opportunity for students to learn, question, and understand how people across time and space resisted oppression, exploitation, and injustice. This global perspective approach gives students a broad understanding of the commonalities and differences across cultural experiences. For example, in studying about revolution, students can examine events of pre- or post-colonial aspects of revolution and discern the similarities and differences across geographic contexts. For instance, students can explore the following essential questions: What has precipitated revolutions across time and space? How have revolutions taken place in various geographical locations? How do revolutions change the course of events in people's lives? Global perspective pedagogy ensures that global perspectives are infused throughout the entire course rather than being limited, as a token approach, to a week or two for a particular topic. Integrating global perspectives is about advocat-

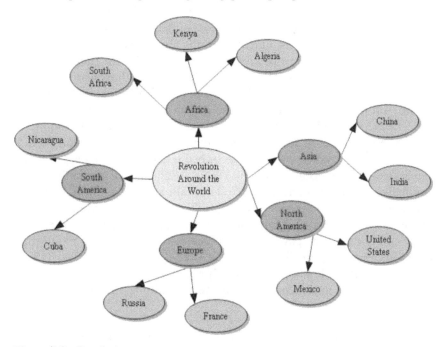

Figure 7.2   Revolutions across space.

ing balanced and multiple perspectives. Merryfield (2002) described how it is important for teachers to examine colonial and racist assumptions about the Other and how the center and periphery binaries have sustained the image of the United States or the West as being superior and benevolent. Clearly, planning and organizing the social studies curriculum is one of the most critical aspects of a social studies methods course and it is critical to ask: How am I modeling a unit construction for pre-service and in-service teachers? And we also need to ask: What perspectives and issues are included and excluded in my course readings? From what regions of the world have I drawn examples from and what regions are yet to be included?

Knowledge Construction and Reconstruction

In examining the topic of content integration, global perspective pedagogy also examines the nature of global knowledge included in a given curriculum. For example, a number of scholars have noted the need to recognize how people in the Western, industrialized world tend to view people and cultures of Third World societies in biased ways (see Said, 1993). Viewing Others through stereotypes creates dichotomous perspectives, which leads to the talk about "us" and "them," First world versus Third world countries, and how one is civilized and the Other is uncivilized. Over the years, textbooks in many U.S. schools and media outlets have presented negative images, myths, stereotypes, and distortions about peoples, cultures, and histories of the Third World, and Africa in particular. In thinking about knowledge, we need to ask: How has knowledge about those who are on the outside been represented? How has Europe's domination and exploitation of the continent of Africa been represented and justified within curriculum knowledge? Banks (1996) argued how hegemonic knowledge promotes the interest and agenda of the powerful, elite groups. Banks maintained that educators must become aware of not only the knowledge that is produced but also about the producers who use their social, cultural, and political positionality to construct and produce dominant knowledge. Even facts and theories that we believe have been scientifically generated are influenced by the knower's social and cultural interests. This is particularly true when we examine the perspectives that have been written regarding topics such as colonization, imperialism, and culture. The scholarship of Said (1993) and Mazrui (1986) has been particularly enlightening on how Western representations have misrepresented non-Western history and culture. For example, Said argued that

> The tendency in anthropology, history, and cultural studies in Europe and the United States is to treat the whole of world history as viewable by a kind of

Western super-subject, whose historicizing and disciplinary rigor either takes away or, in the post-colonial period, restore history to people and cultures "without" history. (p. 35)

Like Said, Mazrui critiqued Western accounts of African history and culture through the provocative documentary series *The Africans: A Triple Heritage.* Over the years various scholars have debated the effects of colonialism on Africa and European scholars have argued that colonialism was beneficial since the colonial legacy "civilized" Africans. Mazrui challenged this dominant view and described how Western imperialism and colonialism was destructive to African cultural makeup and that the current problems in African societies can be connected to the legacy of European colonialism. Similarly, Ngugi (1993) challenged the Western hegemonic knowledge base in regards to how Western historians claimed universal nature of human history, yet which treated Third World histories as being marginal and inferior. He challenged the view of the world that claimed Western superiority in the field of language, literature, and culture, and spoke of the need to move "the centre from the assumed location in the West to a multiplicity of spheres" (p. xvi). I would argue that the concept of knowledge construction, as defined by Banks (1996), is important in how we can rethink how we have imagined the continent of Africa. Banks noted how, because of implicit cultural assumptions and frames of references, curriculum knowledge has remained biased and that educators need to learn to integrate new knowledge into the curriculum. Speaking about issues of knowledge, Merton (1972) spoke about the importance of considering events and accounts from both the *insider* and *outsider* viewpoints. As he argued, a subject may claim the status of an *insider* because he or she is a member of a specific community and brings perspectives of the group's history and culture to the discourse. On the other hand, the *outsider* subject can also claim legitimacy because of his or her nonmembership to a cultural community, thus offering new insights on particular issues.

In terms of considering knowledge construction and reconstruction, we need to ask: How can teacher educators, especially social educators, help pre-service and in-service teachers become aware of the marginalization of Others' histories, cultures, and lived experiences? When we rethink issues of knowledge construction, we can go deeper into the analysis on how we have imagined curriculum and the decisions we have made about the nature of knowledge we have included or excluded within curriculum. How would the events/issues we tell be different if they were told from a different perspective? Whose story is silenced? Whose action is represented as being "uncivilized" and undemocratic even when such actions are practiced or seen as "normal" in the so-called "developed" and "civilized" societies? Too often, U.S. students have learned to see the Other through European and American perspectives and that oppression of European colonialism and imperialism are frequently glossed over and rarely connected to contemporary problems that non-Western societies face (Merryfield, 1998). And, quite often, pre-service and in-service teachers have been socialized into viewing the world in narrow ways and it is important that students learn to deconstruct biased worldviews. I have found the book *Rethinking Globalization: Teaching for Social Justice in an Unjust World* by Bigelow and Peterson (2002) useful in helping students gain diverse perspectives about the realities and events in diverse parts of the world.

Instructional Resources and Materials

Pedagogy also involves the careful selection of and the appropriate use of instructional resources and materials for teaching and learning. Resources may include textbooks, film, videos, photos, various Internet resources, and newspapers. Over the years, textbooks have been criticized for presenting biased perspectives, distorting history and misleading students by omitting viewpoints. For example, Commeyers and Alvermann (1994) conducted a content analysis of three high school world history textbooks and their findings revealed that (1) Third World countries were underrepresented in textbooks, (2) there was no mention of major Third World historical events, (3) emphasis was placed on (the benefits of) European imperialism, and (4) reports on current conditions of Third World countries depicted only bleak conditions. For example, the instructional materials on Africa have, in most cases, focused on the exotic aspects—the safari, the wildlife, the Massai people, and so on. African people have been stereotyped and depicted in instructional materials as primitive, barbaric, undeveloped, and uncivilized. Irrespective of the developments that have taken place over the years, these stereotypes persist and continue to be perpetuated in the curriculum as teachers continue to use outdated materials. Similar to many Third World cultures, the continent of Africa and African people have been misrepresented in a systematic way in the curriculum and instructional materials. Bennett (1995) argued that:

> The truth about Africa has been so distorted among non-Africans that with the emergence of Africa on the world scene in 1980—most Westerners were ignorant about the earth's second largest continent. For centuries perceptions of the "Dark Continent" had been clouded over with myths and stereotypes, and Africa was greeted then as now with all the myths and stereotypes. (p. 7)

A global perspective pedagogy advocates that educators critically select and use appropriate resources, including textbooks. The social studies texts selected for the methods course should be carefully reviewed for unbiased and multiple perspectives on a given issue. When selecting a particular resource, educators need to ask pertinent questions such as: Why am I using the texts/materials for the course? Have I critiqued the resources for its invisibility, linguistic bias, and stereotypes (Sadker & Zittleman, 2007)? More importantly, course professors should heighten students' awareness about global issues by critiquing mainstream resources and supplementing them with resources that provide multiple perspectives on a given topic. Although instructional materials have improved greatly in the last few years in terms of providing balanced viewpoints, many resources still contain stereotypes and biases.

Delivery Strategies and Activities

Course delivery is at the heart of teaching and learning. Oftentimes social studies methods courses focus too much on unit/lesson constructions. First, all methods instructors should recognize that all societies around the world are shaped by their respective histories and culture that influence people's beliefs, values, and worldviews. It is also important for teachers to be engaged in exploring their own cultural values as they begin to recognize the similarities and differences between what they know and what they need to know. This self-awareness can help students recognize how their socialization and worldviews have impacted their perceptions, interactions, and relationships with others. In methods courses, I have used the Alpha-Bafa (Ukpokodu, 2002) simulation activity to help students gain insights about cultural dynamics across cultures. The Alpha-Bafa simulation is a short exercise that simulates cross-cultural interactions between two cultural groups with different worldviews, experiences, and language backgrounds. It places participants in contexts where they have to negotiate cultures they are not familiar with. As the participants interact, they experience conflict and discomfort because each participant has to negotiate situations that are unfamiliar, including cultural norms that have been historically constructed as being abnormal, deficient, and uncivilized. The interactions help students recognize how misunderstandings, conflicts, and tensions develop when different cultures/people come into contact with each other. But more importantly, it raises students' awareness on how various societies in the world negotiate heterogeneous cultures. The simulation also helps students better understand their own location and cultural identities.

Another strategy for promoting global perspective pedagogy that I have used in methods courses is the *problem-posing* approach (Shor, 1992). This approach contextualizes a particular issue (war, poverty, etc.) within the global context and asks students to critically respond to questions such as:

Why are the people in the world unable to coexist peacefully and harmoniously? How do global events and issues affect us differently? What does it mean to be a global citizen? What is my role in educating for global citizenship and how should teachers educate K–12 students for global citizenship? For example, as a way to promote the idea of global citizenship, I ask students to consider how they may have connected with the world in their everyday interactions. For the past 16 years teaching social studies methods courses, I have come to realize that most of my students do not read newspapers or pay attention to the news on a daily or on a consistent basis. Students attribute the nonengagement with international news to a "lack of time." To help students develop global perspectives, I require students to examine news events at local, state, national, and global levels, and I have asked students to pose a problem about a news event that they have recently read about. The exercise often creates a forum for discussing diverse viewpoints on global perspectives in the methods courses.

Assessing Self-Transformation

Because of the way we see the world, we are selective about the nature of knowledge we include and do not include in the curriculum. When global perspectives are emphasized in our courses, we help teachers realize that global perspectives are important and that they should not be marginalized when developing curriculum. Clearly, this is a question about self-assessment: how to evaluate the ways we have mobilized intellectual passion and commitment toward global aspects of social change. When individuals transform themselves, they can effect change for a better world. A genuine transformation can take place when we re/examine our knowledge base, recognize and clarify our multiple identities, and value the notion of global citizenship and global social responsibility. A critical self-reflection can enable us to recognize our positionalities and can help us teach global issues in transformative ways. Such self-examinations may begin by asking how we are committed to global education and how we have integrated global perspectives within our courses. Or we may begin by asking how we have connected local and global issues in our teaching so that we can critique stereotypes and racism that divides people in the world.

CONCLUSION

Global challenges defy unilateral national solutions: they call for collaborative and collective responsibility and solutions. I would argue that there is a need to recognize and work toward social justice, particularly that is attentive to the needs of economically and culturally marginalized people in the world. Therefore, the role of education, particularly global education, cannot be underestimated in fostering a critical consciousness about important global issues. Thus, global education is not only essential today but should be an integral component of school curriculum on every grade level. Present and future students must cultivate a pluralist and global perspective and possess the essential knowledge, skills, and dispositions for individual and collective responsibility (Merryfield, 2002; National Council for the Social Studies, 1994; Ukpokodu, 2006). Although projects such as international research collaborations, cross-cultural learning exchanges, and World Wide Web learning creates spaces to learn about new knowledge, it also raises questions about issues of access and equity, which further dis-empowers those who do not have access to power and those who are attempting to preserve indigenous knowledge from being exploited. Classrooms must become spaces that offer opportunities for students to develop global perspectives, social consciousness, and local–global responsibility.

Research on global perspective pedagogy in teacher education has historically been marginalized. In this chapter, I have argued for the need to raise awareness about global perspective pedagogy in social studies methods courses and the need to make global education a legitimate field of inquiry within social studies methods courses. Given the complex realities and challenges that our world is confronting, global education has a strong ethical dimension that all teacher educators must take responsibility for. As our world becomes more interconnected, preparing students to develop the knowledge, skills, and dispositions for collaboration and social responsibility becomes even more important. Furthermore, educators must teach students to approach the problem in the world as a member of a global society. This includes being willing to change one's lifestyle and consumption habits to protect the environment, and being willing to critique human rights violations in the global context (Kubow, Grossman, & Ninomiya, 2000, p. 132). Without systematically integrating global perspectives into students' curricular experiences, we limit their ability to understand the world beyond their immediate confines. We know that discourses on power, human rights, civil rights, social justice, equality, ethnicity, and gender are marginalized when teaching about global perspectives. Integrating these issues into students' everyday learning broadens their knowledge about themselves and the world. Although the notion of multiple perspectives is often emphasized as a useful pedagogical tool, rarely does the approach include a deliberate, explicit, and systematic integration of global perspectives into the curriculum. Sadly, pre-service and in-service teachers are often encouraged to create instructional units/lesson plans on peoples and cultures of nation-states that often reinforce stereotypes and trivialize global cultures. A relevant and transformative approach to global education is not celebratory, tokenistic, superficial, or a once-a-year activity. A transformative approach is critical, problem/issue-based, and is a practice that questions mainstream perspectives on global issues. A transformative practice also engenders a commitment to produce change in local–global contexts. If teacher educators do not model transformative global perspective pedagogy in their teachings, how would pre-service and in-service teachers value the need to infuse global perspectives in their classrooms?

NOTE

1. For the purpose of this chapter, I define global education as an approach that develops students' knowledge, skills, and dispositions to promote individual and collective responsibility for a sustainable, equitable, just, humane, and peaceful world. In specific terms, first I view global education as a way to prepare students to develop a critical perspective that would allow students to view the world with critical understanding and concern. Second, I see global education as a method of helping students develop a sense of social responsibility and commitment to finding just and peaceful solutions to global problems. Third, global education is about critically studying cultures, peoples, and systems of various nation-states yet which must avoid exotic understandings of cultural practices. Fourth, global education should promote global issues such as diversity, equity, and social justice, especially issues of power, privilege, oppression, racism, sexism, classism, xenophobia, exploitation, etc.

REFERENCES

Annan, K. (2000). Issues in global education. *Newsletter of the American Forum for Global Education, 156,* 1.

Banks, J. A. (1996). The canon debate, knowledge construction, and multicultural education. In J. A. Banks (Ed.), *Multicultural education transformative knowledge and action: Historical and contemporary perspectives* (pp. 3–29). New York: Teachers College Press.

Banks, J. A. (1999). *Teaching strategies for the social studies: Decision making and citizen action.* New York: Longman.

Banks, J. A. (2001). *Cultural diversity and education: Foundations, curriculum and teaching.* Boston: Allyn & Bacon.

Banks, J. A. (2004). Introduction: Democratic citizenship education in multicultural societies. In J. A. Banks (Ed.), *Diversity and citizenship education* (pp. 3–15). San Francisco: Jossey-Bass.

Banks, J. A. (2009). *Teaching strategies for ethnic studies.* Boston: Pearson.

Bennett, C. (1995). *Comprehensive multicultural education: Theory into practice.* Boston: Allyn & Bacon.

Bigelow, B., & Peterson, B. (2002). *Rethinking globalization: Teaching for justice in an unjust world.* Wisconsin: Rethinking Schools Publications.

Commeyers, M., & Alvermann, D. E. (1994). Messages that high school world history textbooks convey: Challenges for multicultural literacy. *The Social Studies, 85*(6), 268–274.

Cranton, P. (2006). *Understanding and promoting transformative learning: A guide for educators of adults* (2nd ed.). San Francisco: Jossey-Bass.

Csikszentmihalyi, M. (1993). *The evolving self.* New York: HarperCollins.

Dewey, J. (1933). *How we think: A restatement of the relation of reflective thinking to the education process.* New York: D.C. Heath.

Gilliom, M. (1993). Mobilizing teacher educators to support global education in preservice programs. *Theory into Practice, 32*(1), 40–46.

Giroux, H., & Simon, R. (1989). Popular culture and critical pedagogy. In H. Giroux & P. McLaren (Eds.), *Critical pedagogy, the state, and cultural struggle* (pp. 236–252). New York: State University of New York Press.

Hanvey, R. (1974). *An attainable global perspective.* New York: Center for Global Perspectives in Education.

Hargreaves, D. (1999). The knowledge-creating school. *British Journal of Educational Studies, 47*(2), 122–144.

Johnson, M., & Ochoa, A. (1993). Teacher education for global perspectives: A research agenda. *Theory into Practice, 32*, 64–68.

Kubow, P., Grossman, D., & Ninomiya, A. (2000). Multidimensional citizenship: Educational policy for the 21st century. In J. J. Cogan & R. Derricott (Eds.), *Citizenship for the 21st century* (pp. 131–150). London: Kogan Page.

Kymlicka, W. (1995). *Multicultural citizenship: A liberal theory of minority rights.* New York: Oxford University Press.

Massialas, B. G. (1991). Education for international understanding. In J. P. Shaver (Ed.), *Handbook of research on social studies teaching and learning* (pp. 448–458). New York: Macmillan.

Mazrui, A. (1986). *The Africans: A triple heritage.* Boston: Little, Brown.

Merryfield, M. M. (1993). Reflective practice in teacher education in global perspectives: Strategies for teacher educators. *Theory into Practice, 32*(1), 27–32.

Merryfield, M. M. (1998). Pedagogy for global perspectives in education: Studies of teachers' thinking and practice. *Theory and Research in Social Education, 26*(3), 342–379.

Merryfield, M. M. (2002). Rethinking our framework for understanding the world. *Theory and Research in Social Education, 30*(1), 148–151.

Merton, R. K. (1972). Insiders and outsiders: A chapter in the sociology of knowledge. *The American Journal of Sociology, 78*(1), 9–47.

Mezirow, J., & Associates. (2000). *Learning as transformation: Critical perspective on a theory in progress.* San Francisco: Jossey-Bass.

Muller, R. (1985). *The need for global education.* Paper presented at the annual meeting of the World Federalists of Canada, Sally Curry.

National Council for the Social Studies (NCSS). (1994). *Expectations of excellence: Curriculum standards for social studies* (Bulletin 89). Washington, DC: Author.

Ngugi Wa Thiong'o. (1993). *Moving the centre: The struggle for cultural freedoms.* New York: Heinemann.

Osler, A., & Starkey, H. (1996). *Teacher education and human rights.* London: David Fulton.

Sadker, D., & Zittleman, K. (2007). Gender bias: From colonial America to today's classrooms. In J. A. Banks & C. A. Banks (Eds.), *Multicultural education: Issues and perspectives* (pp. 135–169). Hoboken, NJ: Wiley.

Said, E. W. (1993). *Culture and imperialism.* New York: Vintage Books.

Shor, I. (1992). *Empowering education: Critical teaching for social change.* Chicago: University of Chicago Press.

Taylor, H. (1970). *The world as teacher.* New York. Doubleday.

Torney-Purta, J., Lehmann, R., Oswald, H., & Schultz, W. (2001). *Citizenship and education in twenty-eight countries: Civic knowledge and engagement at age fourteen.* Amsterdam: International Education Association.

Tye, B. B., & Tye, K. A. (1992). *Global education: A study of school change.* Albany: State University of New York Press.

Ukpokodu, N. O (1999). Multiculturalism vs. globalism. *Social Education, 63*(5), 298–300.

Ukpokodu, O. N. (2002). Breaking through preservice teachers' defensive dispositions in a multicultural education course: A reflective practice. *Multicultural Education, 9*(3), 25–33.

Ukpokodu, O. N. (2006). The effects of 9/11 tragedy on preservice teachers' perspectives and disposition toward global concerns. *Social Studies Research and Practice, 1*(2), 178–200.

Wilson, A. (2001). Growing toward teaching from a global perspective: An analysis of secondary social studies preservice teachers. *The International Social Studies Forum, 1,* 127–143.

Wilson, A. (1998).Oburoni outside the whale: Reflections on an experience in Ghana. *Theory and Research in Social Education, 26*(3), 410–429.

CHAPTER 8

SEEKING A CURRICULAR SOUL

Moving Global Education into Space/ Place, with Intimacy, and Toward Aesthetic Experience

William Gaudelli
Teachers College, Columbia University

One would be hard pressed to find an educational institution that does not invoke *global* in their mission statement. And one would be equally challenged to find such calls enacted in the realities of daily life in those same institutions. *Going global* in education may suffer from the misfortune of having too much interest that is too widely spread, such that rationales for global education are shallow, diverse, and often contradictory. Some raise alarms about the lack of academic competitiveness among U.S. students as the central point of a rationale, a claim that resonates in other countries (Clough, 2008). Others seek the maintenance of U.S. power internationally, economically, and otherwise (Burack, 2003; Smith, 2006). Still others want global education for humanitarian reasons, such as promoting cross-

Critical Global Perspectives, pages 143–160

cultural understanding (Merryfield, 2002; Merryfield & Kesai, 2004), global citizenship (Gaudelli, 2003; Gaudelli & Heilman, 2009; Myers, 2006; Osler & Vincent, 2002), and economic and social justice (Bigelow & Peterson, 2002; McLaren & Farahmandpur, 2005). While such diverse and discordant calls enrich curricular discourse by inviting a varied conversation of possibility, the complexity of rationales may also thwart the development of global curriculum projects in the places that need them the most: schools.

Despite increasing discourse about just how global curriculum ought to be and from which perspectives, U.S. schools remain remarkably unmoved by exhortations to *go global.* No Child Left Behind (2001), for example, includes nary a reference to learning about the world. The International Baccalaureate school program in the United States is often resisted by many communities as being anti-American and for endorsing one-world curriculum (Smith, 2006). In general, the U.S. public, despite the massive U.S. involvement in world affairs through commerce, war, militarization, and energy consumption, remains widely uninformed about the world. Unfortunately, schools have fallen short in educating students about critical global issues. A 2006 National Geographic–Roper Public Affairs study, for example, found that 37% of U.S. students could not find Iraq on a map while 88% could not identify Afghanistan, despite the presence of U.S. military forces in both countries (*www.nationalgeographic.com/roper2006*). Why does this pattern persist? Perhaps U.S. schools avoid teaching about the world because a critical study of the world can compel serious conversations about significant changes needed in our society. Or, global problems may be viewed as too severe such that moving beyond the comfort of the nation-bound curriculum is viewed as not being practical and thus untenable.

The need for learning about the world, however, has seemingly never been more pressing. In just the first decade of the 21st century, great social catastrophes have occurred, including Hurricane Katrina and its woeful social response in North America and a massive tsunami in the Asia/Pacific region. We have witnessed migrant labor riots in European cities coupled with the rise of white-identity nativist politics, the nuclearization of Pacific Rim countries, and the potential rise of nuclear states in southwest Asia. Add to these the rekindling of deforestation in Latin America, rapid desertification, an HIV/AIDS epidemic in Africa, genocide in Darfur, and massive ecological devastation globally, including China. Furthermore, there is continued resource exploitation in the United States and beyond and food shortages in many parts of the world. In the summer of 2007, scientists indicated that there was melting of Arctic sea ice equivalent to the area of six California(s). Indeed, we have reasons to be concerned about the state of the planet (Revkin, 2007). Globally, mass species extinctions, burgeoning human population growth, resource exploitation, wars, genocide, and nuclear proliferation continue to threaten the sustainability of many life forms on the planet, including people.

So how can it be that while global events unfold with devastating and manifold results, global education remains at the margins of U.S. curriculum? Some may point to the lack of international experiences of people in the United States for the lack of critical engagement with global issues. Zakaria (2008) calls this the cosmopolitan gap, or the difference between those who travel internationally and are therefore conversant with the world and those who generally do not. This might also be called the Palin–Obama gap, as the once governor of Alaska only got a passport in 2007 while President Obama lived for years outside the United States, the only president in U.S. history that can reasonably be called a global citizen. A *go-it-alone, you're either with us or against us* attitude has pervaded the United States after 9/11 as a direct result of the Bush Administration's policies, fomenting the public's hostility and apathy toward critical global issues.

An examination of internal problems within global education as a curriculum field is warranted. In this chapter, I turn attention to the field itself to examine how it has missed the opportunity, at least for now, to strike when the global is hot. Global education, and schools in general, have erred on the side of technical and rationalist aims at the expense of space/place, relationships, and aesthetic experiences, or what I am broadly referring to as the soulful dimensions of curriculum. Instead of focusing solely on learning about the world as if it were a massive entity to be known for potential future benefits, developing a curricular soul is about a journey that is open ended and that strives to connect why global consciousness should matter in the lives of young people. This reorientation is in line with scholars who have argued that education has become too focused on rationalistic ends that belie the aesthetic possibilities inherent in something as wonderfully life-giving and spiritual as learning and teaching (Palmer, 1998).

SPACE/PLACE

Space is a set of relations and forms shot through with layers of meaning and power (Lefebvre, 1974/1991, p. 116). While space has typically been viewed as an actual location, or place, that is characterized by the objects within it, a rethinking of the concept of space helps us understand how it is more than a container to be filled with contents but is itself a content instantiated through processes, information, and flows. People, thus, are viewed as mediators of space, who create "the action of groups, factors within knowledge, within ideology, or within the domain or representations. Social space contains a great diversity of objects, they possess discernible peculiarities, contour, and form" (p. 77). Soja's (1989) work helps situate

Lefebvre's notion of space by examining how urban landscapes are structured in particular ways for determined ends. Soja seeks "to create a more flexible and balanced critical theory that re-entwines the making of history with the social production of space" (p. 11). Soja employs the backdrop of Los Angeles to identify the cyclical nature of capital's use of *space/place* to serve its ends by fragmenting communities in times of economic crises, redistributing populations and means of production to suit capital, and thereby remaking the urban landscape in the service of capital rather than social needs. Such an analysis is critical in understanding how and why resources have been spatialized as *belonging* to a certain group, region, or nation and how such stratification has contributed to the gap between global haves and have-nots: the ways in which resource extraction and development have deteriorated ecology, and what can be done in local communities and elsewhere to address differential access to resources.

Castells (2000) argues that the *network society* is one wherein flow, rather than place, has a more central role in how networks operate. "The space of flows refers to the technological and organizational possibility of organizing the simultaneity of social practices without geographical contiguity" (p. 14). Use of the Internet may serve as an illustration of Castells's argument since the technical hardware of the PC, fiber optic line, and servers are associated with its operation. Yet, the space of flow that Castells refers to suggests that the social practices occurring within this media space, which are neither geographically proximate nor linear, are constitutive of the meanings of the space. Information flows simultaneously within and beyond the system as it creates new, permeable, and ephemeral social locations that are sites of meaning-making. Using this notion of space/place and flows to consider the global is to recognize that social practices continually reconstitute space such that fixity is impossible, and unending contingency is typical, with abundant global ramifications.

Issues of space/place resonate differently since I have recently traveled to India a number of times. I am currently working on a curriculum and professional development project with a nongovernmental organization in India and travel there for 1–2 weeks at a time. As a middle-class, white professor from an elite research university, I realize my social location affords me many privileges. While in India, I am never stopped and asked what I am doing when entering a hotel, restaurant, or shop, which typically happens to locals, as my skin color and dress provide me with access bequeathed by a legacy of imperialism. I am treated with an embarrassing level of respect and deference that I do not typically receive (and prefer not to get), but here again, the status of being a white male in India from the United States matters in these social relations. Most striking is my experience of the separateness of social life in India, as I often travel by private car from hotels that sit behind high, guarded walls to meeting places that are typically located on large campuses, also walled off from the larger community. While the social relations are abundant in the work I develop there, they are clearly shot through with power, ever fluid and flowing, and contingent on my identity as it reconstitutes over time and space.

As I write this, I am sitting in a hotel in New Delhi. I look out my window and see a hyperdeveloped urban landscape that is filled with vehicles of all types, from horse-drawn carts to SUVs, all beneath a sun-drenched and hazy atmosphere. One cannot help but be reminded of the making of space in this post- (or neo-) colonial city. Just beneath my window is a woman washing white linens, probably from the hotel where I am staying. She dips them in water and repeatedly spins them in the air and smacks them against a wood plank, later placing them in the sun to dry with the help of two assistants. What set of social relations is evident in this vignette of the spatialized world? How is power evident here? From the window of his Western hotel, an observer from the United States sees women laboring in intense heat. Meanwhile, the observer sits in the comfort of an air-conditioned room to write and then later rests on the linens that are these working women's toil. The scene is replete with power, to be sure, as one gets to view and the other is viewed while they act and I am served. The problem captured in this episode, of which there are many, is that the power differences are taken to be *normal*: as space has assigned these social relations their normality. This small vignette is reenacted daily in countless ways while it is part of a long chain of historical events and movements that has construed this space in a particular way, events bound up with colonial hegemony, dispossession, and violence of which we cannot help but be implicated.

Focusing on space/place in curriculum means helping students to ask specific questions about their lived situation and local community: this helps them (re)consider how social space has been produced in their communities. My global teaching occurs at Teachers College, in the Morningside Heights community of New York City that sits adjacent to Harlem. As to issues of space, I ask students to examine the ways that these communities are constructed differently and how the differentiation that is classed, raced, and gendered is resonant in communities around the world. The lesson for global education is clear: Do we examine Harlem in light of Hanoi, Harare, and Helsinki? Do we examine the space/place of class and the class of space/place when we engage students in learning geography? If we teach about the world in a manner that ignores problems in our own neighborhood while fetishizing other places as wondrously exotic then we may generate some interest in the world, but we may do so in such a way that abstracts students from seeing their places *as in* the world, *as if* the global were somewhere out there, beyond the complicated terrain of here.

Focusing on space/place is an attempt, albeit insufficient, to address the break of people from their experiences. Lefebvre (1974/1991) points to the development of language as both indispensable and dangerous as it allows "meaning to escape the embrace of lived experience, to detach itself from the fleshy body" (p. 203). Lefebvre is seemingly pointing to the same condition that Dewey lamented, or the schism between academic learning and experiential knowing. Dewey related a telling anecdote offered by the superintendent of Moline, Illinois, schools wherein some students were learning the geography of the Mississippi River but did not connect the body of water that flowed through their town as the same one studied in their textbook (Dewey, 1990, p. 75). Viewed in this light, the fact that U.S. students cannot identify Afghanistan on a map is really not surprising considering information is typically presented in a way that does not give students access to substantive issues surrounding U.S. military engagement in Afghanistan. Rather, information is often presented in an abstract way so that the critical knowledge about the topic often becomes fundamentally unknowable and lacking in substantive meaning.

Global education can address some of this distancing by making more explicit the way that power permeates the social relations in the local communities of students. Global educators have generally bought into the belief that in order to be globally educated, one must move beyond the boundaries of the U.S. While international travel is helpful in creating dissonance about one's assumptions and confronting the alterneity of life, it alone cannot guarantee that one develops a global perspective. Perhaps the best illustration of this limitation of othered space/place learning is the ubiquitous phenomenon of international student trips. Most universities and secondary schools use these as curricular enhancements to demonstrate their *global hipness.* Too often these excursions are viewed as individualized enrichments for the traveler as visitor and voyeur in a quest to slake their thirst to know the other, to find their own *personal native.*

After taking summer graduate courses in Kenya, I went on a safari, traveling in the company of two young Dutch couples. As we traversed the highways of Kenya, my Dutch friends were quite alarmed that the young children would not wave back to them enthusiastically, concerned that they were not getting a "real experience with the natives," as they put it, since they were not being received as exotic white people. They were, in a sense, yearning for the Africa of their grandparents' generation, where whiteness was currency and undisturbed *people of the bush* a curiosity. Not much has changed. Kenya was for these visitors a place like an interactive diorama in a living museum, all there for the taking-in, all available to be witnessed and carried out in digital video memories of the *other.*

If global education is to be soulful, if it is to be more than learning to satisfy one's curiosity and fill one's memory box with souvenirs of others, then space/place needs to take a more prominent role, particularly how all communities, local and more distant ones, consist of myriad social relations filled with power. One means of doing so is to have students engage with locals about matters of space/place. While I was in Kenya and during my trips to India, the tourist attractions were and still remain some of the least interesting aspects of travel. Rather, I am interested in the meaning-making opportunities that occur in conversations with people about their lives and mine. I have often found these to be profound learning experiences as I am offered a semblance of how, or if, the unique patterns I see are meaningful to locals and consonant with my life. But perhaps most importantly, I have the opportunity to return home with these insights and apply them to my community and engage them in my work. Conversations like these, either through direct contact, letter/email exchange, or video teleconference, provide students with needed insights about the conditions of others. What's more, such interactions become a new space, one where the flow of interpretations about social being are shared in ways that the global is not an exotic location of the other but a present reality of shared being.

INTIMACY

The second revision I want to propose to global education curriculum is to make it more intimate. I am not referring to the neo/colonial aspect of intimacy that attempts to fully know or to master the other. Intimacy is the vulnerability that we invite when we come into close contact with another person, our sense of empathy for their well-being, our vicarious pain when they are hurt, our listening to the stories of others as a way of better understanding them and ourselves, and our caring for others beyond ourselves (Prager, 1995). While this constellation of ideas is not exhaustive, of course, it provides a sense about what is intended. A more challenging question beyond the definitional one relates to appropriateness: Is it appropriate to speak about *global intimacy*, a term that sounds oxymoronic? Or, put another way, can we truly care about the world or be intimate with global others? My response is both no and yes: no meaning that caring is an abstract moral idea, or simply willing yourself to care as if it were just a mental state, but also yes, meaning caring in the sense that it embodies action by the one-caring toward a completion of the caring act. Noddings (1984) writes,

> I am not obliged to care for starving children in Africa, because there is no way for this caring to be completed in the other unless I abandon the caring

to which I am obligated. We cannot refuse obligation in human affairs by merely refusing to enter relation; we are, by virtue of our mutual humanity, already and perpetually in potential relation. Instead, we limit our obligation by examining the possibility of completion. (p. 86)

So if caring is enacted through active relations that seek completion, then what can we say for caring about the world? Helping children to live truly in relation to one another, rather than as a means to other ends, is to have them live intimately. And if they live intimately they are likely to carry a disposition of relational caring. Giddens's (1992) work provides rich commentary on how the break of modernity created a split in intimacy from which educators have much to learn. He argues that as societies increasingly *detraditionalize* in an era of globalization, the tally of benefits and costs has shifted. While some people are given a great deal more autonomy through this economic order, most people have an increased sense of destabilization. Giddens argues that plastic sexuality, or the individualization and ownership of sexuality, has created a new terrain on which love and sex are less dictates of social norms and more choices of free and egalitarian people. Intimacy is no longer a contractual domain that joins and solidifies families, estates, and territories but has generally become a choice of people with free will. While most view this as a benefit to social life, the cost according to Giddens is a loss of security. Given our egalitarian ethos, we accept as a condition of modern life the anxiety that our intimate ties may be severed at any time due to circumstances completely beyond our control. Recognizing the ephemeral nature of our intimate relations contributes to uncertainty and anxiety. This change explains in part the rise of addictions in post-traditional societies, as people search for a form—be it work, alcohol, sex, drugs, pornography, fast-food, texting/email, shopping, or exercise—as a means of providing stasis, however unreal its promises, in a world of pervasive uncertainty. These *stand-ins* for intimacy though only serve to further exacerbate widely diffused anxiety. And to no one's surprise, these are some of the commodities with which our young people are often transfixed.

What healthy experiences most interest young people? Relationships are what most of my students in high school cared about, though they often employed substitutions (obsession with pop culture icons, etc.) in place of real intimacy. Indeed, at some level relationships are what we all care most about. So, when we exhort students to care about the world, think globally, be a global citizen, these calls ring hollow unless we have engaged them in a full exploration of what it means to care, to love, to befriend, to be intimate. If global education is to be soulful, it must seek new ground that situates relations as crucial to knowing and being ourselves in the world. Put another way, how are we to love the world if we cannot fully love ourselves and those closest to us?

What would it mean to be intimate in global education? First, it requires a fuller sense of relationship among young people. Schools too often promote a self-serving ethos that situates students as customers, teachers as providers, and knowledge as commodity. This linear, contractual connection does not seek a healthy and rich context to develop mutual understanding as students are viewed as being *in line* for the commodities that will give them access to the next level. Detailed by Meier (2002), schools such as Central Park East demonstrate how students living in relation to one another, their teachers, and curriculum benefit from the wholeness of such experience. There is a sense of togetherness that allows people to flourish individually while remaining integrated with others in their school community. Global education requires that such relationships, fostered in the school community, reach out toward others in the world community and develop relationships with them. This may be accomplished through a host of activities, including study abroad, digital communication projects, joint community action work, and interacting with nearby students of different backgrounds. At the core of these activities, though, needs to be explicit attention to the development of relationships such that caring and intimacy are integral to the aims of the project.

AESTHETIC EXPERIENCE

Global education rarely suggests conversations about aesthetic experience, as it conjures rational thinking about massive problems such as global warming, famine, epidemics, human rights, and war rather than the aesthetic experience possible from viewing a piece of art, listening to a song, watching a film, being audience to a theatrical performance, or hearing a poem. To refer to aesthetic experience emanating from the study of the world seems, at some levels, absurd. While fine art points to aesthetic experience, common happenings outside the museum, the theater, and the art gallery can also be viewed as artful. Teaching can be aesthetic, and indeed, it is in these moments that the possibility of transcendence becomes fleetingly visible in pedagogy. Aesthetic experience can appear in the "harmonious proportion of parts" that move toward a completed whole, regardless of the medium involved (Dewey, 1934, p. 130). Dewey argued that experiences that have (1) a flow of consecutive elements that build on each other, (2) a move toward completion, and (3) an eye toward the whole process as a harmonious event constitute for Dewey aesthetic experiences that take on dimensions of lived beauty.

Dewey (1922/1983) defined an aesthetic form in terms of completeness of relations within a shared activity.

> But "relation" is an ambiguous word...in its idiomatic usage denotes something direct and active, something dynamic and energetic. It fixes attention upon the way things bear upon one another, their clashes and uniting, the way they fulfill and frustrate, promote and retard, excite and inhibit one another. (p. 139)

Integral to this clash is Dewey's notion of rhythm, which he defines as an ordered variation of energy, rather than a mechanical recurrence of sameness. Applying this notion to speech acts, those often associated with democratic processes, the cacophony of voices moving through an issue toward a new synthesis of energies previously opposite manifests as a new ordering of rhythmic exchanges. Those engaged in speech acts that recognize their potentially democratic ends, and the aesthetics therewith, can syncopate speech-acts toward a rhythmic filling-in that at once challenges and builds the energy of the opposition into a newly energized whole.

How does a social organism, a person, interpret such experiences? Dewey's notion of habit, or social practices, is integral to the development of capacity and fluidity in thinking. Take, for example, a young child learning to swim. At base, this is rightly viewed as a psychomotor response to a given environment, such as water. As she develops the ability to move in the water, she is led to broadened experiences. She can access the deep end of the pool, objects on its surface, sensations of being submerged, and eventually, other waterscapes. The psychomotor skill is originally an interest that becomes the avenue for future, diverse experiences. Perhaps she takes up surfing, which enhances and complicates the swimming skill, enriches her knowledge of water and its environment, and develops an appreciation for nonhuman animal life associated with oceans.

These directed experiences, or what others might call chance encounters, may lead her to develop associations with similarly interested people, such as ocean biologists, who have a scientific background that deepen and extend her experience, or a lifeguard, who appreciates the water's landscape. The activity of experience has become an organ of intelligence through engaging with people within a given social situation. Swimming, as articulated, is not an end unto itself, but an activity that leads to further ends and thoughtful engagement in the social world beyond itself. As such, this is a habit, or social practice, that broadens, deepens, and enriches the lives of both the swimmer and to a lesser degree the people with whom she interacts.[1]

But in this conception of aesthetic experiences, harmony only occurs through discord and tension. Imagine a rubber band being pulled apart, its sinewy energy building as you stretch it. Or consider a disagreement with a colleague about the quality of a dissertation. These are situations filled with energy and when that energy is expressed, the rubber band loosened and the colleague confronted, the point of friction and disagreement loses its tautness as masses collide, creating a situation of instability. The situation with a colleague takes a turn, a compromise sought, and a tenuous harmony arises for a period, only to be upset by a new energy of discord that leads to a new collision of energy that once again seeks harmonious stasis. Such energies in conflict can and should manifest in classrooms as persistent and deep questioning and careful inquiry about how to live together as a society. Students' experience of ideas and working through their expressions of what is and *ought* to be, or the tension of values massed against one another, can synthesize into a common energy through engagement of global social issues. This is the ultimate expression of living democratically, and potentially, living for transcendence.

I offer two vignettes from my work as a teacher educator and researcher that illuminates what I mean, or how I interpret Dewey's notion of aesthetic experience in teaching. I do not offer these as *best practices*, but moments of being fully *wide awake* as a teacher (Greene, 1978).

VIGNETTE 1: READING THE HOLOCAUST

The sun streamed into our classroom, torrents of energy that glared so brightly even the tinted windows could not dull it. Students were sitting in a horseshoe of desks, chatting about their student teaching placements and the ups and downs of life in classrooms. I interrupted, "Let's get started. Today, I have a series of documents for you to examine related to the Holocaust. As you read these, I'd like you to use Hilberg's (1992) analysis of the Holocaust and think about which category best fits the people in the document: perpetrator, victim, bystander, and rescuer." The students sauntered off to their collaborative groups and began reading a variety of primary source documents, from a Jewish man's suicide note just prior to the German attack on the Warsaw Ghetto, to an officer of the *Einsatzgruppen* (or, mobile killing unit) writing a letter home to his wife and children, to documents related to the Norwegian resistance of German deportation orders. These are documents that I have used in the past so I knew the emotional effect they would likely have on students and the opportunity they provided for a rich discussion of these events, both in the specifics of each case and the general contours of the period.

Small talk completely ceased after a brief period of reading as their now laser-like attention on the documents was palpable. As they began to process the ideas raised and use the Hilberg typology, I heard a variety of questions, including those related to the particulars of the events described (e.g., Where is the place he is referring to? What is the *Einsatzgruppen?*) as well as the questions of disbelief (e.g., How could you write a letter detailing the attempts to kill people more efficiently and then ask your wife how the children are doing?).

I asked each group to report out to the larger group about one of the documents. As they began, the resulting conversation was intense. Students grappled with the horror of these narratives, the unspeakable acts committed against the individuals, and the banality of evil at the hands of the perpetrators. Perhaps the best indication that students were truly engaged by this activity was their earnest questions. They would preface what they said with obligatory "I know I've studied this before, but..." and launch into passionate inquiries about why people were so willing to perpetrate mass murder. As the last group reported about the suicide note of the Jewish man living in the Warsaw Ghetto, the woman doing most of the talking had difficulty completing her thoughts as her eyes became teary and her lip trembled. She was quickly aided by her group who finished giving the report but all were visibly shaken by her courageous expression of what was being felt by everyone. When the last group finished, the room was filled with stunned silence such that I can vividly recall thinking that I had done this activity many times before but this was the first time it ever took on a life of its own in this way. Rather than fully debriefing the pedagogical implications of this work, which I often do in such classes, I simply closed with a rhetorical question: "So, isn't this the type of learning experience that you want to create with your students?" to which the group paused for a long time and then left.

This was a moment of wide awakeness for me and my students, to be sure, such that the energy of the exchange was felt by all. There was a great deal of genuine discord in the group as they truly struggled to understand how this and other grotesque episodes of human depravity occur. And the discord that was felt, while thoughtfully considered in an attempt to provide rational explanation, lingered even after unanswerable questions were seemingly answered. The activity had an internal rhythm as students spoke, listened, and empathized as well as filling in the gaps for each other as they spoke about the conditions that those described in the documents faced.

VIGNETTE 2: READING GLOBAL MEDIA

The second vignette is taken from a focus group study of students reading global media that I completed in Spring 2007. Two separate groups of high school students consisting of 12 participants each viewed a variety of media forms, such as a feature film, documentary film, online video game, blog, and music video in six sessions. After participants viewed the media for 30–

60 minutes, they engaged in an open-ended dialogue about their interpretations of the texts, what questions or issues were raised, and their views about the contents and processes of media development and viewing. In this illustrative extract from the data, students are struggling with the contrast of two media texts, Al Gore's *Inconvenient Truth* and Canadian Broadcasting Corporation's special series *Doomsday Called Off* (available widely on YouTube). In this excerpt, students are weighing the significance of global warming:

Chad: So, seeing these two movies, you see this issue from two different sides. You're just kinda left with, "Which one do I believe." You know, you have Al Gore who's obviously a prominent, well-known person and you have the Canadian Broadcasting Corporation, which we assume is a reputable source and they're not out there to ruin anyone's idea or anything. I think that they're both presenting the same issue, but from different sides. So, how do you feel that there are other people out there viewing this media, seeing these two videos, how it affects their perception of the future?

Aaron: Well, personally, I don't know if anyone has ever heard of the CBC one, which says global warming doesn't exist or doesn't exist to an extent. Most of the media has been pushing this *Inconvenient Truth*, it has been showing in schools. Has anyone ever been shown anything from the other side? *An Inconvenient Truth* is in school and any media on TV and stuff like that. I personally had the ideas that the CBC, the Canadian Broadcasting Company, had before *Inconvenient Truth* began. I usually get ripped apart when I bring that up, because all people know is the bias, the opinion given by *Inconvenient Truth* has become general fact. Even CBC was saying that it's just the opinions of a small group of scientists. And now if you look on, if you read a newspaper, look on CNN.com, Drudge Report, the articles are actually saying most scientists don't believe in the extent of global warming, it's the opinion of these small groups of people and these lobbyists. I just think that when you have so much media coverage on a certain side, a lot of people aren't educated about the other side. I'm saying it's really good to see both sides.

Alice: What they're trying to argue is that you can't completely know whether it's natural or unnatural until either more information is observed or it becomes more of a problem. It might sound like a bad way to think of it, but we're very far from it being a true problem, I mean, you're not having lakes dry up yet. [Group interrupts each other.] I feel that's a less positive message. I don't think it would kill us to work on cars that don't rely on as much gas, as much oil. I don't think that environmental activism would ever hurt anybody.

Aaron: But, the argument is do you put billions if not trillions of dollars required to make a shift like that based on the entire industry of this planet run on CO_2 emissions.

[*Group responds loudly to each other.*]

Patty: I wish we could watch the whole movie because he [Gore] goes into other countries. The United States has not done anything whereas hundreds of other countries are trying.

Janice: The fact that our school doesn't recycle...what are we doing!? We can be doing more, but the movies I think are trying to show, especially *Doomsday*, is not that we shouldn't do that by any means, they're not putting down environmental activism, I just think that they're kind of like *don't panic*. There's no need to go into this crazed panic. Yet there's ways to make our environment better, making it healthier into driving a better car, a bike, let's not be wasteful. Those could always help in any situation. But I think they're saying that this is not something that has just been caused, just now by us, but it's something our world has gone through before.

Tony: I don't think it was like that, I thought you guys were trying to say that with the whole billions of dollars—

[*Group responds loudly to each other.*]

Aaron: We shouldn't shift our entire economy, industrial base—

Tony: Right.

Alice: We should create better industry, a better quality of life.

Albert: Like, France runs completely on nuclear power and it saves them a lot of money. It's more efficient. There's more energy. Like, it is cleaner. Like—it's cheaper in the long run.

Aaron: Oh, don't get me wrong. I just think the problem will fix itself instead of putting in billions and billions of dollars.

Albert: How's it going to fix itself?

Aaron: We're already getting the hydrogen energy. I just think we're going to lower our CO_2 emissions and we're always going to find technological advances.

Chad: I think what's, what I found is most compelling in *An Inconvenient Truth* is that they actually have the photographs of glaciers melting. They have photographs of lakes drying up. And like the entire Antarctic is shrinking and like huge ice-shelves are breaking off. And it doesn't seem like that, to me, doesn't seem like that's sort of a natural thing. We need the ice caps because they reflect the sun off from our planet,

> so the fact that they're melting is a bad thing—The ozone
> hole thing—CFCs in the atmosphere is that they found the
> problem, they eliminated the problem, and now the hole
> is clearing up. We have done something about it and it's
> better. So, I think that's the same way, why now today we can
> say, you know, implement new technologies to reduce our
> CO_2 emissions. Then, the problem would get better.

A few insights are evident from this excerpt. First, the students are highly engaged in the conversation, as they lead themselves through the discussion without any prompting by the teacher or researcher. Second, they are contributing to the flow of the talk and truly listening to one another, such that the conversation meanders and develops through rising conflicts and points of harmony. And third, the students often break into spontaneous talk that draws from their engagement with the visual text and the implication of comparing them. This excerpt represents an aesthetic experience for these students about a potentially catastrophic phenomenon, though rendering it in writing makes translating this sense of cohesion, discord, and syncopated harmony impossible. To witness the exchange, however, gave one a full sense of the energy within the conversation and the flow that permeated its development. Reflecting on these excerpts taken together, both are related to issues and historical events that are very disturbing such as global warming and the Holocaust. Despite the potentially dire nature of the conversations themselves, there is a sense of wholeness, syncopated discord, and group cohesion about the experience that drives it toward more fully illustrating what they think, feel, and know about the social world through the lenses of these social texts that are themselves discordant and powerful.

CONCLUSION

Those who read the current global context as one that suggests the need for increased learning about the world have a strong foundation on which to build. There is ample evidence in the current world situation to demonstrate a clear and abundant need for more global learning. But we also need to be more circumspect about the type of curriculum that we promote and how it is too often tethered to rationalistic ways of thinking that are necessary but insufficient for a satisfying, and perhaps transcendent, expression of one's life. When I speak to parents about their children's education or when my wife and I think about the education of our son, rarely do parents express a concern that their child is not learning and thinking enough. More often than not, they are concerned about their child's sense of satisfaction with their lives, the feelings of contentedness and happiness that come with learning and feeling connected to others and their community.

It is easy to lose sight of this truism about what really matters most in the lives of young people, particularly within a social milieu that has become obsessed with test scores as indicators of achievement. My sense is that global education's marginality has caused some who are concerned about the state of the field to readily forge its identity as yet another academic curriculum among many, a new set of contents to achieve long-standing goals. And yet, just as I believe the world is being radically changed in this most recent era of globalization, I also contend that we need to carefully rethink the nature of learning, especially in light of its aims and materials, tools and methods. I have proposed three revisions for global education—ones that attend to issues of space/place, intimacy, and aesthetic experience—that may do a great deal to rebalance our efforts in a way that is more soulful. Without a sense of the transcendent that can accompany aesthetic experience, and of real intimacy and richly textured understandings of space/place, global education may be mired in its own rationalist premises and fail to develop a meaningful soul, a path we can ill afford at this critical juncture.

ACKNOWLEDGMENTS

Special thanks to those who participated in presentations at Michigan State University and Seton Hall University where these ideas initially took shape, to Binaya Subedi for inviting me to write for this project, and to my outstanding editor and writing guru, Janelle Gendrano.

NOTE

1. This paragraph and the previous two are drawn from W. Gaudelli and R. Hewitt (in press), The aesthetic potential of global issues curriculum. *Journal of Aesthetic Education.*

REFERENCES

Bigelow, B., & Peterson, B. (2002). *Rethinking globalization: Teaching for justice in an unjust world.* Milwaukee, WI: Rethinking Schools Press.
Burack, J. (2003). The student, the world, and the global education ideology. In J. Leming, L. Ellington, & K. Porter-Magee (Eds.), *Where did social studies go wrong?* New York: Fordham Foundation. Retrieved January 9, 2008, from http://www.edexcellence.net/foundation/publication/publication.cfm?id=317&pus ub d=907

Castells, M. (2000). *The rise of the network society* (2nd ed.). Oxford, UK: Blackwell Publishing.

Clough, G. W. (2008). Wanted: Well rounded students who can think. *School Administrator, 65*(2), 28–32.

Dewey, J. (1990). *The school and society and the child and the curriculum.* Chicago, IL: University of Chicago Press.

Dewey, J. (1934/1980). *Art as experience.* New York: Perigee.

Dewey, J. (1922/1983). *Human nature and conduct.* In J. A. Boydston (Ed.), *John Dewey: The middle works, 1899–1924* (Vol. 14). Carbondale: Southern Illinois University Press. (Original work published 1922)

Gaudelli, B., & Hewitt, R. (in press). The aesthetic potential of global issues curriculum. *Journal of Aesthetic Education.*

Gaudelli, W. (2003). *World class: Teaching and learning in global times.* Mahwah, NJ: Erlbaum.

Gaudelli, W., & Heilman, E. (2009). Reconceptualizing geography as democratic global citizenship education. *Teachers College Record, 111*(11), 2647–2677.

Giddens, A. (1992). *The transformation of intimacy.* Stanford, CA: Stanford University Press.

Greene, M. (1978). Wide-awakeness and the moral life. In M. Greene (Ed.), *Landscapes of Learning* (pp. 42–52). New York: Teachers College Press.

Hilberg, R. (1992). *Perpetrators, victims, bystanders: The Jewish catastrophe, 1933–1945.* New York: Aaron Asher Books.

Lefebvre, H. (1991). *The production of space* (D. Nicholson-Smith, Trans.) Malden, MA: Blackwell. (Original work published 1974)

McLaren, P., & Farahmandpur, R. (2005). *Teaching about global capitalism and the new imperialism: A critical pedagogy.* Lanham, MD: Rowman & Littlefield.

Meier, D. (2002). *The power of their ideas.* Boston: Beacon Press.

Merryfield, M. M. (2002). The difference a global educator can make. *Educational Leadership, 60*(2), 18.

Merryfield, M. M., & Kesai, M. (2004). How are teachers responding to globalization? *Social Education, 68*(5), 354–359.

Myers, J. P. (2006). Rethinking the social studies curriculum in the context of globalization: Education for global citizenship in the U.S. *Theory and Research in Social Education, 34*(3), 370–394.

No Child Left Behind Act (2001). Retrieved March 25, 2009, from http://en.wikipedia.org/wiki/No_Child_Left_Behind_Act

Noddings, N. (1984). *Caring: A feminine approach to ethics and moral education.* Berkeley: University of California Press.

Osler, A., & Vincent, K. (2002). *Citizenship and the challenge of global education.* London: Trentham.

Palmer, P. J. (1998). *The courage to teach: Exploring the inner landscape of a teacher's life.* San Francisco: Jossey-Bass.

Prager, K. J. (1995). *The psychology of intimacy.* New York: Guilford Press.

Revkin, A. C. (2007, October 2). Arctic melt unnerves the expert. *New York Times.* Retrieved April 27, 2008, from http://www.nytimes.com/2007/10/02/science/earth/02arct.html.

Smith, F. (2006). Global superpower: The unique International Baccalaureate program sparks both admiration and controversy. Retrieved February 18, 2008, from http://www.edutopia.org/global-superpower on.

Soja, E. (1989). *Postmodern geographies*. New York: Norton.

Zakaria, F. (2008). *The post-American world*. New York: Norton.

CHAPTER 9

EDUCATION FOR A GLOBAL ERA

Reflections of an Asian Teacher Education Faculty

Guichun Zong
Kennesaw State University

As American culture, demography, economics, and politics become increasingly globalized, teacher educators today are faced with an urgent responsibility. This responsibility includes the need to transform curriculum and pedagogy so that teachers can help students obtain a more broad understanding about diversity issues in the global contexts. Social studies educators have long called for a critical inclusion of global education in both K–12 classrooms and pre-service teacher education programs. The terrorist attacks of September 11, 2001, and its aftermath have again challenged the American public in general and educators in particular to rethink what Americans know and should know about the world (Dunn, 2002; Kagan & Stewart, 2004; Kirkwood-Tucker, 2004; Merryfield & Wilson, 2005; Shapiro & Purpel, 2005). The leading professional organization in social studies

Critical Global Perspectives, pages 161–179
Copyright © 2010 by Information Age Publishing
All rights of reproduction in any form reserved.

education, the National Council for the Social Studies (NCSS), suggests that an effective social studies program must include global education to respond to the reality that people are constantly being influenced by transnational, cross-cultural, multicultural, and multiethnic interactions.

Colleges and universities have attempted to respond to these calls by increasingly adding a global curricular dimension to teacher education programs through a variety of policies and practices, including encouraging the study of foreign languages, creating internationally focused courses, and organizing cross-cultural fieldwork experiences. Universities have also offered extracurricular activities that are internationally oriented, and professional development programs to help prospective and practicing teachers gain knowledge, skills, and dispositions to teach from a global perspective. Research studies have been conducted to examine the impact of various initiatives on prospective and practicing teachers' global knowledge and global mindedness (Cushner & Brennan 2007; Quezada & Cordeiro, 2007; Zong, 2009b). However, very little is known about international faculties' experiences and perspectives on teaching about the world from a global perspective. This chapter aims to contribute to the existing literature by examining one Asian/Chinese teacher education faculty's efforts to introduce the relevance and centrality of global perspectives into social studies education.

INFLUENTIAL THEORIES AND RESEARCH

I have drawn upon theory and research in both teacher education and global education to frame and guide this writing, including research on the power of teachers' stories and narratives (Connelly & Clandinin, 1999), self-study in teacher education (Cochran-Smith, 2000; Hamilton & Pinnegar, 2000; Ladson-Billings, 1996), and the impact of lived experiences on the development of multicultural and global educators (Gay, 2003; Merryfield, 2000; Paccione, 2000; Wilson, 1982, 1998). Guided by the tenets of interpretive autobiography and reflective inquiry to investigate social interaction and lived experiences (Angrosino, 1989; Denzin, 1997; Ellis & Bochner, 2003), I use my personal experience and autobiographic voice (Creswell, 1998; Davies, 1999) to craft this chapter. The account is based on my own recollections of and reflections on classroom events, and a close reading of documents such as student evaluations, syllabi, discussion notes, and samples of students' work. I also locate this inquiry within the growing field of self-study in teacher education, a type of research undertaken by teacher-educators that emphasizes personal professional development and that also provides a deep understanding of teacher-education practices (Asher, 2005; Kubota, 2002; Milner, 2007; Obidah, 2000). Part of the motivation to write from a self-study perspective is to acknowledge the teacher-educator's role in shaping prospective and practicing teachers' experiences in their educational programs. Narrative and self-study in teacher education have the most important implications for this research.

Narrative Inquiry in Teacher Education

As research methodology, content, and pedagogy, narrative inquiry is becoming increasingly recognized as a valid and viable way to explore the complex nature of teaching and learning examined by educational researchers, theorists, and practitioners. Narrative inquiry has been used extensively to explore cultural diversity in teacher education as well as professional development in in-service teacher education (Gay, 2003; He, 2002). According to McEwan and Egan (1995), narrative is "essential to the purpose of communicating who we are, what we do, how we feel, and why we ought to follow some course of action rather than another" (p. xiii). Because the "function of narrative is to make our actions intelligible to ourselves as well as others, narrative discourse is essential to our efforts to understand teaching and learning" (p. xiii). hooks (1994) explained that autobiographical narratives enable us to look at aspects of our past experiences from different perspectives and that we can critically utilize the knowledge we have gained for the purpose of self-growth and social change.

Similarly, Gay (2003) suggested that multicultural teaching is both a personal and professional process that requires deep personal engagement, commitment, advocacy, and agency and that by "engaging in dialogue with ourselves and sharing our stories with other travelers, we can find confirmation, companionship, and community" (p. 5). Gay argued that traditional styles of academic writing have not been productive to capturing some of the subtle nuances of becoming and being multicultural educators. Instead, personal narratives serve the dual function of helping us to look inward and outward in becoming multicultural educators.

As an immigrant faculty member of Chinese origin, my experiences and understandings about people, places, and perspectives deeply shape my teaching decisions with my students in the teacher education programs. In this discussion, I attempt to capture the multiple stories around border crossing I experienced as a way to better understand my own practices (my curriculum decision and my pedagogy choice) as well as the multiple tensions inherent in enacting global pedagogy in teacher education contexts. I also agree with Gay's (2003) analysis that within the context of multicultural and global education it is important to emphasize process over products, which means that we should value our own emerging knowledge, thoughts, beliefs, and skills about the field. Through purposeful articulation of the dilemmas, experiences, and tensions, reflective processes will help us re/construct knowledge on teaching about the world, a practice that has implications for understanding and refining global learning theory and practice.

Self-Study and Reflection in Teacher Education

This chapter is a teacher essay, a type of conceptual teacher research wherein "teachers recollect and reflect on their experiences to construct an argument about teaching, learning, and schooling" (Conchran-Smith & Lytle, 1993, p. 35). In recent years, there has been growing recognition for self-study among teacher educators to engage in systematic examination of their own practice to improve their work (Cochran-Smith, 2000; Hamilton & Pinnegar, 2000; Ladson-Billings, 1996). Hamilton and Pinnegar (2000) expressed concern that much of the teacher education discourse is absent of teacher educators' voices and perspectives: "We do not hear the voices of those who create living educational theories" (p. 235) in teacher education. Bullough and Pinnegar (2000) suggested that the aim of self-study research is to "provoke, challenge, and illuminate rather than confirm or settle" (p.20). Zeichner (2007) believed that self-study research can maintain this important role in opening up new ways of understanding teacher education and of highlighting the significance of contexts of inquiry while joining the discussions and debates about issues of importance to teacher educators, policymakers, and those who conduct research about teacher education. He further argued that self-study research in teacher education should contribute to the improvement of teacher education practice and to broader knowledge about particular questions of significance to teacher educators and policymakers. Zeichner suggested that teacher educators who engage in self-studies should make an effort to better situate self-study research within existing and newly emerging research programs and need to expand public knowledge about critical questions and problems in the field.

This study responds to this call by situating my inquiry in the emerging research that addresses the complexities of theorizing lived experiences in relation to multicultural and global pedagogy. I also locate this inquiry within the growing field of self-study in teacher education. This line of research emphasizes the importance of looking at the self as the critical element for change in teacher education research and practice (Torres-Guzman & Carter, 2000a, 2000b).

Research on Lived Experiences

What aspects of lived experiences have more direct impact on teachers' and teacher educators' pedagogy? I found research studies conducted by Merryfield (2000) and Paccione (2000) to be helpful in situating my inquiry. Merryfield examined the lived experiences of successful teacher educators in both multicultural and global education and found childhood and family experiences, educational background, teaching experiences or interactions with students, and cross-cultural experiences to be influential in teacher educators' decisions to commit to multicultural and global education. Similarly, Paccione's survey study revealed that the most salient life experiences associated with the development of a commitment to multiculturalism were influence of family/childhood experiences, discriminations due to minority status, interactive/extended cultural immersion experiences, initiative from job situations, influence of mentor, and the context of education and training.

In this chapter, by recounting my own journey—a girl who grew up during the Mao Era of China to a faculty member in universities in the American South—I try to analyze how my past experiences, specifically my roots, have shaped my work and commitment to cross-cultural dialogue and global learning. By writing about my own trajectory and by reflecting on my adjustments, challenges, struggles, and interventions, I hope this analysis of my own journey sheds light on questions of much wider scope, such as: How do you address complex global issues in social studies curriculum? What are the core concepts and critical debates that should be examined? What pedagogical strategies are more aligned with teaching that promotes global learning?

REEXAMINING PERSONAL HISTORY/EXPERIENCE

Family and Global Learning Experiences

I was born in a small city located in the northeastern region of China in the mid-1960s, the year when the Chinese Cultural Revolution began. The province that I grew up in is part of the historically known Manchuria area, which was occupied by Japan in the 1930s. It also borders North Korea. My childhood education and my initial understanding of the world were significantly influenced by how the area was represented as a historical significant region because of its unique geographical location, a region that had witnessed many conflicts. Growing up, internationalism was emphasized in schools to teach children about the need for oppressed people around the world to unite in fighting against imperialism and foreign invasions.

At home, I grew up listening to my father's stories about how he and his college peers were treated badly in this native land by Japanese imperialists and how they were stripped of their cultural identity. This included only being permitted to learn and speak Japanese and being forced to change their Chinese names into Japanese names. My father's generation's struggle to resist the Japanese colonialism and to maintain cultural identity and dignity took place during one of China's most difficult and turbulent times, an experience very similar to the one encountered by the Koreans (a topic that was recently chronicled in a young adult book, written by Linda Sue Park, titled *When My Name Was Keiko*).

Another part of my early global awareness was in relation to North Korea and very vaguely about the United States, which was mostly constructed by watching movies. I remember singing songs and watching movies that featured Chinese heroes in North Korea who were fighting against the U.S. invasion during the Korean War. Because of this early exposure to this topic, I have always been curious about the U.S. involvement in the Korean War. Recently, I developed a related research project in the social studies context that examines how the Korean War (often dubbed as the "Forgotten War" in the United States due to lack of attention by the media) is being portrayed in both Chinese and American middle school and high school history textbooks and curriculum standards.

Upon graduating from high school in 1984, I passed the national college entrance exam and was admitted to Beijing Normal University (BNU). As one of the leading national universities in China, BNU's prestige lies not only in its rigorous academic standard, but also in its long history of students' active participation in the nation's social and political movements, including the famous May Fourth movement in the 1920s (BNU, 2008). The students at the university were selected from each province, autonomous region, and municipality in China, and represented many of the 56 official ethnic groups or nationalities. During my 7 years of academic training at BNU, I studied and worked together with students from many ethnic groups across China, such as Mongolians, Tibetans, Uighurs from the northwest, Koreans from the northeast, and Miao, Yi, and Zhaung people from the southwest part of China. This experience provided me with valuable cross-cultural learning experiences on how China was not a homogenous entity but an ethnically, linguistically, and religiously heterogeneous space.

During the 1980s when I was studying at BNU, China was going through many profound and rapid changes, economically, ideologically, and socially. One of the major changes was that China gradually opened up to the international community after decades of isolation during the Mao Era. Fascinated by the dynamic changes taking place in the society and by the social sciences courses that I was taking at the university, I decided to switch my major from math and science education to social science education. There were many different student organizations on the BNU campus, such as Education Forum (Jiao Yu Xue She), History Society (Chun Qiu Xue She), and May Fourth Literature Club (Wu Si Wen Xue She). These student organizations often brought guest speakers with competing views to dialogue on the dynamic changes taking place in China, which always drew huge crowds of young and enthusiastic students.

My experiences in China have impacted me on how I currently negotiate my identity and how I position myself in U.S. academia, including the ways I teach global issues. Because I am a Han Chinese, the largest ethnic group in China (both culturally and numerically)—which makes up over 92% of the nation's population (Zou, 2000)—and also because I was from a region in which standard Chinese is spoken, I had always been part of the majority culture as well as the majority linguistic group. For a long time, I didn't realize that I was part of a majority group. Because I did not grow up as a member of a marginalized group in China, the development of my self-identity was not significantly influenced by discourses on oppression, racism, or minority/majority relationships.

In the summer of 1995, I left Beijing, China, and moved to the United States to pursue my doctoral degree in social studies and global education. More than a decade of living in the United States has reshaped how I think about China and has provided me with new perspectives on reading events in China in a way that I probably couldn't have realized while living in China. When I began my academic work in the United States, I came to the realization that there were multiple mainstream media stereotypes of Asians, including about China and Chinese people. In fact, it took me a very long time to recognize that my accent, my skin color, my national origin, and my ethnicity situated me as a marginal scholar/subject in U.S. academia. Along with my awareness of my minority identity and marginalized subjectivity in the United States, which developed much later after I had lived here, and because my experiences and knowledge gained in China, I developed a sense of self-confidence to be self-critical of my identity. Through such experiences, I also learned the language to be critical of dominant discourses that represented Asian (women) subjects as "feminine passiveness and permissiveness." In this process, I also learned the language to resist the imposition of Chinese/Asian identity as "invisible and outsider." Such experiences, along with a later experiential understanding of discrimination and outsider status encountered in the United States, have significantly shaped my consciousness on nationality, class, culture, race, gender, and ethnicity.

It is this critical consciousness that has influenced me on how I perceive myself, my identity, and how I teach and conduct research; and these experiences have prompted me to make global and multicultural awareness and action the centerpiece of my teaching and scholarship. Research studies conducted by both Merryfield (2000) and Paccione (2000) indicated that travel and cross-cultural experiences often provide people with increased understanding of human diversity and allow subjects a more sustained interaction with a wider and complex world. Cross-cultural learning has the potential to enable the development of transformative perspectives about human differences and also has the potential to trouble stereotypes and generalizations about groups of people. My own journey and travel have offered spaces of learning experiences in helping me become an educator committed to global education.

PROFESSIONAL AGENCY: TEACHING GLOBALLY

My commitment to global education has grown out of the interaction between my own personal background and professional responsibility at the university working with pre-service and practicing social studies teachers who are mostly from the southeastern part of the United States. My philosophy of teaching has been informed by the tenets of global pedagogy, which posits that teaching social studies from a global perspective differs from traditional approaches to studying communities, cultures, geography, and history (Case, 1993; Hanvey, 1976; Kniep, 1989; Merryfield, 2001; Wilson, 1997). My earlier work was influenced by Hanvey's (1976) five dimensions of global perspectives: perspective consciousness, state-of-the-planet awareness, cross-cultural awareness, knowledge of global dynamics, and awareness of human choices. More recently, I have found Hicks's (2003) synthesis particularly helpful in framing global teaching. Hicks identified four core elements that all global education programs should address:

1. Issues dimension—including issues such as inequality/equality, injustice/justice, conflict/peace, environmental damage/care, alienation/participation;
2. Spatial dimension—referring to exploring local–global connections that exist in relation to these issues, including the nature of both interdependency and dependency;
3. Temporal dimension—exploring the interconnections that exist between past, present, and future in relation to such issues and in particular scenarios of preferred future: a process of helping young people think more critically and creatively about the future, especially in relating to creating a more just and a sustainable future;
4. Process dimension—a participatory and experiential pedagogy that explores differing value perspectives and leads to developing politically aware local–global citizenship (p. 271).

Merryfield and Wilson's (2005) work has also shaped my conceptual understanding and practical implementation of global education. Both scholars have long argued that in order for education to be truly global or world-centered, it is critical to examine how the educational legacy of imperialism has shaped mainstream academic knowledge. A critical argument the two scholars make is that there is a need to incorporate the experiences, ideas, and knowledge of people who are usually omitted, marginalized or misrepresented in mainstream academic knowledge.

In contemporary contexts, these principles guide my curricular and instructional decisions, which are student centered and world oriented. The central aim of my teaching is to translate these theoretical principles into instructional practices to help prospective and practicing teachers understand various global connections and to tap into their sense of themselves as global citizens and as intercultural beings. My work has also been guided by Noddings's (2005) vision that global education should prepare students to become citizens who are concerned about social and economic injustice, protection of the Earth, preservation of cultural diversity, and cultivating peace. In keeping with this theoretical vision, I work to build a curriculum that is world oriented and I attempt to craft a pedagogy that employs experiential, student-centered strategies that are based on a constructivist approach to teaching and learning.

I have created a range of teaching–learning experiences to engage my students in pursuit of these goals. These include asking students to write an autobiography so that they begin to reflect on personal experiences; conducting community inquiries to explore real-life connections between local communities and people and places around the world; participating in computer-mediated global discussion forums to practice cross-cultural experiential learning; integrating literature and other narratives in learning about people, places, and perspectives; and engaging in critical analysis of discourses on globalization to deepen students' understanding on global connections and interdependence (Zong, 2005, 2009a). In what follows, I focus on two areas: teaching through the use of autobiography and the value of critically examining the concept and processes of globalization in social studies teacher education program.

BEGINNING WITH AUTOBIOGRAPHY: ANALYZING STUDENTS' EXPERIENCES

Muchmore (2004) argued that teaching is an autobiographical endeavor. "It is autobiographic in the sense that the values and beliefs that guide teachers' actions are inevitably shaped by their personal histories. All of their past experiences—as children, as students, as preservice teachers, and as adults—play a significant role in determining the kinds of teachers that they become" (p. 6). He further argued that teacher educators have the responsibility to help prospective and practicing teachers to "discover the interplay between their personal histories and formal theories of teaching and learning" (p. 6). The way that I have tried to foster this connection between global education theory and personal histories is through creating a series of reflection activities for both pre-service and practicing social studies teachers. In the past, I had adopted Merryfield's (1993) "Tree of Life" activity and Wilson's (1997) "Hierarchy of Intercultural Experiences" model to guide students in thinking about the impact of their life experiences on their worldviews in general and social studies learning experiences in particular. More recently, I have used the assignment of writing global learning autobiographies. It is an assignment in which one uses an autobiography format to identify and reflect upon what values, beliefs, experiences, and knowledge have shaped one's views of themselves, diverse peoples, and the workings of the world in general. These initial understandings shape to some extent what my students will learn from my courses. My goal is also to create opportunities that allow students to see themselves in my curriculum, instructional practices, and classroom climate. Fostering student development on global understanding also demands that I challenge their perspectives, their beliefs, their views of self and others.

In their completed autobiography assignments, students share stories about how their parents, teachers, colleagues and friends, churches and communities, and trips to foreign countries have shaped their knowledge on what constitutes global. A majority of the students' reflection indicates how they have come to learn about differences through cross-cultural contact and experiences. Over the years I have found that the autobiography assignment, which requires emotional and intellectual effort of working through one's story of crossing cultural borders, has been a powerful activity for students to connect their personal experiences with theoretical discussions on differences. When read as a whole, these narratives tell the legacy of unique racial history rooted in the American South. As a starting point, I often find it useful to dialogue with students on local experiences on differences so that they can ultimately make global connections. Students' writings not only focus on the process of developing worldviews, but they also have the effect of stimulating considerable interest and excitement about the process of reflection and learning from one's own and others' beliefs and experiences.

For example, one African American teacher candidate wrote about the cultural shock he had experienced when he first entered a predominantly white college and how that experience had made an impact on his view of social studies education in general and encountering difference in particular:

> I grew up as a southern Baptist in a small town right outside of Macon, Georgia, and was raised in the church. The way I grew up the whole community was responsible for educating and raising the children of community. After completing high school with a 3.89 GPA, I chose to play basketball in a state college located in a predominantly white county. For a young African American male I was up for a rude awakening going to this city. The people here

loved their local college but hated people that were somewhat different from them. There were not too many African Americans, Latin Americans, or Asian Americans at the time. If you were one of the ethnic minority groups at this college you were either an athlete, an exchange student, or you were on academic scholarship. Most African American students were indeed athletes or aspiring athletes. This puzzled me because I was so used to everyone being totally equal. Going to this college made me question my own blackness, and where I stood as an African American male and what I actually knew about my own history as well as the history of others. This gave me the desire and dedication to want to teach young people about who they are as well as how to better understand others.

A female graduate student reflected upon her limited cross-cultural learning experiences before going to college:

As a child growing up in the South, I was taught to be skeptical of people from different ethnic groups other than my own. My grandparents and parents were openly prejudiced against any race other than their own. Even in my church, I remember the pastor teaching that it is in the Bible that we should not be "unequally yoked" with others.... I spent the majority of my childhood years in a community where the population was very homogenous. My school system at the time was probably 98% white. The only time that I encountered members of another race or culture was when our football team played a neighboring school that was majority black. We attended the football game on the other campus, but we did not interact with the other students. My first encounters with other races came when I attended a state university. To me, global education should bridge differences among people.

For many of my students, the sharing of stories and experiences became a space to analyze their emerging conceptualization of teaching and learning from a global perspective. Indeed, the act of being reflective helps develop a theory of experience (hooks, 1994). Through the autobiography assignment, students gained important insights into perspective consciousness and cross-cultural understanding, two of the major concepts in global education (Hanvey, 1976). As a teacher educator, I also learned that it is important to connect global content to students' backgrounds, interests, and communities and to explore the intersection between multicultural education and global education. Understanding students' diverse backgrounds and how they read differences helps me intervene critically in the classroom, particularly on what or how I need to teach to make students learn about the global aspect of differences. As people continue to have access to global knowledge, it is critical for educators to teach how learning about local cultures/histories is an important starting point of becoming a global citizen. I encourage students to blend their life experiences in the discussions of the required readings on global perspectives.

One white female student discussed her learning about friendship through cross-cultural contact:

> I grew up in a typical suburban town, which is mostly populated with middle- to upper-class European Americans. It was not until I began working as a pharmacy technician that I was able to fully experience other cultures. I was surrounded by coworkers from all parts of the world including China, Egypt, Mexico, Nigeria, Philippines, and Uganda. My coworkers took me under their wings as they explained some of the intricacies of their culture, as well as some of their past experiences. The friendships that I formed with them prepared me greatly in alleviating the feelings of culture shock that one feels when thrust into a new environment with different surroundings. Additionally, being surrounded by various cultures piqued my quest for a deeper understanding of my own German heritage.... My experiences with other cultures will enable me to better present a centered worldview of various issues. Ultimately, I am motivated by the ability to have a positive effect on society and the world by helping to create mindful and compassionate individuals.

TEACHING ABOUT GLOBALIZATION

Globalization, as an explicit concept, commonly referred in relation to the acceleration of interregional contacts, has become one of the most contested topics in the last two decades. It has been linked to almost every purported social change in recent years, from an emergent knowledge economy, the declining authority of the state, and the demise of traditional cultural practices, to the spread of neoliberal economic regimes and the advent of a postmodern consumer culture. Observers and theorists of globalization have argued that the rapid increase in cross-border economic, social, technological, and cultural exchange is a new source for optimism in a world that has witnessed much economic, cultural exploitation and human suffering. Proponents of globalization argue that the movement of people, money, and information across national and cultural boundaries allows people the access to markets, cultural practices, and products as never before and this access clearly has the potential for enriching people's lives. Critics of globalization tend to draw attention to the links between past and present global economic policies and social realities such as widespread hunger and poverty, the massive displacement of small farmers, sweatshop working conditions, the breakdown of community, the rise of ethnic and religious fundamentalism, increased social conflict, and an array of severe ecological crises.

Globalization has been seen as one of the most important social science theories in recent years. Theoretical and empirical research on globalization has generated a vast and growing literature in social sciences during the last two decades. The *International Bibliography of Social Sciences* (IBSS) records articles published in the most prestigious academic journals and it appears that the first article with the term globalization in either the title or the keywords appeared in 1983. In 1990, only 15 articles included the term. By 1998, this figure had risen to over 1,000 and, in 2003, stood at 2,909. During the 20-year span, from 1983 to 2003, there were 12,859 articles dealing substantively with issues related to globalization. This proliferation only provides a feel for the increasing importance of the topic, as many articles deal with issues surrounding globalization less explicitly (Murray, 2006, p. 17).

Despite the growing attention by the scholars in social sciences, research and scholarship in teacher education on globalization is rather minimal. In the latest edition of the *Handbook of Research on Teacher Education: Enduring Questions in Changing Contexts*, edited by Cochran-Smith, Feiman-Nemser, McIntyre, and Demers (2008), there is no mention of global education or globalization as a topic of discussion. Sadly, the word *global* is not mentioned nor is the word *international* noted in the book. Similarly, in the much-publicized AACTE award-winning book on teacher education research, *Studying Teacher Education: Report of the AERA Panel on Research and Teacher Education* (Cochran-Smith & Zeichner, 2005), global education or globalization is not included as a topic of inquiry. Because of such omissions, very little is known about the policy, research, and practice that connect the global domain to teacher education. It is no wonder that teachers lack critical knowledge about issues of globalization and global perspectives (Mansilla & Gardner, 2007). The teachers that I have worked with over the years also report that globalization is one of the concepts they feel least prepared to teach in either high school or middle school social studies curriculums.

To address this gap, I decided to explicitly teach globalization in the social studies teacher education program and have developed the following essential questions to guide the selection of course readings, organizing activities, assignments, and course assessment: How can globalization be defined? What has driven historical and contemporary aspects of globalization? Is globalization homogenizing global society? How has the regional economic integration and evolution of global economy affected spatial division of labor? What are the existing discourses and measurement of development? What are the impacts of globalization on the power of the nation-states and on the world environment? What causes the anti-globalization movement? Ultimately, how should social studies educators rethink teaching about the world in the era of globalization?

I have drawn scholarly work on globalization from fields such as economics, geography, anthropology, sociology, history, philosophy, religion, and feminist theories to engage students in exploring the various concepts, theories, processes, and impacts of globalization on various societies (Cooper, 2001; Guillén, 2001; Heald, 2004; Sachsenmaier, 2006; Sniegocki, 2008; Stromquist, 2002). In organizing the scope and sequence of the course, I found Mansilla and Gardner's (2007) conceptual map helpful in framing the core concepts and critical debates associated with globalization. This model highlights four areas that are central to understanding the complexities and contingencies of globalization:

1. *Economic integration*, emphasizing the opportunities and costs for economies, societies, cultures, and individuals associated with the flux of capital and production around the globe;
2. *Environmental stewardship*, raising awareness of the state of the global environment (including global health) and what we can and should do to ensure its long-term sustainability and well-being;
3. *Cultural encounters*, examining the forces of homogenization, hybridity, and localization that shape how nations, cultures, and small groups exchange ideas, people, and cultural products;
4. *Governance and citizenship*, comprehending emerging tensions between national and supranational forms of government, as well as the extent to which individuals enjoy global rights and responsibilities as a function of their humanity (p. 52).

I begin the course by asking students to read *The World Is Flat: A Brief History of the Twenty-First Century* (Friedman, 2007) and *Plan B 3.0: Mobilizing to Save Civilization* (Brown, 2008) to illustrate the concepts of economic integration and environmental stewardship. Both books have used China extensively in their arguments for impacts of globalization. Friedman's book emphasizes how globalization has provided people the tools and ability to connect, compete, and collaborate, and how China's transition to free markets has helped to create more jobs, increased income level, and reduce poverty. Brown's writing stresses the environmental costs of recent economic growth. Citing the example of the 1998 flood in China's Yangtze River valley, Brown argues that the Western economic model—the fossil fuel–based, automobile-centered, throwaway economy—may not be productive for China. By utilizing the two texts, I share my own experiences and observations in China to critique the ideas presented in the books and add that what is missing in the books are issues of social justice, including environmental justice.

In addition to academic readings and discussions, pre-service and practicing teachers are also expected to explore the impact of globalization within local communities. In the community inquiry project, students research one issue within areas of economy, arts, government, and so on, and how globalization has shifted people's values and beliefs or how a particular issue (economy, etc.) has changed over time within the community. Students are encouraged to use various historical inquiries such as analyzing primary sources and conducting interviews to reconstruct the globalizing forces on the development of the local community. This assignment has served as a powerful teaching tool to help students discuss and debate the global economic and social changes on educational policies and practices within local levels. For example, in the region where I teach, during the last 3 years, announcements were made on closing one local General Motors plant and one Ford plant. Moreover, a Korean automaker, Kia, is building its first plant in North America in the state and is expected to generate 2,500 new jobs. I have also addressed current issues on the controversies and challenges about teaching immigrant children, including refugee children (St. John, 2009). The examination of the local issues can be linked with theories in global education, particularly those that addresses issues of cross-cultural learning and addressing stereotypes.

To draw the connections between globalization and social studies teaching and learning, the culminating activity for the course is a critical curriculum review assignment. In this assignment, students apply knowledge, understanding, and perspectives from the course to examine the representations of one region or one country in the current state curriculum standards or textbooks. We use Wilson's (1995) article and Ukpokodu's (1996) writing on examining Africa in the social studies curriculum as examples. As a class, we also read more recent writings, such as Davis's (2005) "Teaching African History in an Era of Globalization," Dunn's (2008) "Two World Histories," and Morgan's (2008) paper, "Contesting Europe: Representation of Space on English School Geography" to encourage broad conversations on how social studies educators should rethink teaching about the world in the era of globalization.

Collectively, we have examined how current state standards and commonly used textbooks have written knowledge about Africa, Central Asia, East Asia, the Caribbean, and Latin America. Students often find the review an engaging assignment as it reveals whether the curriculum depiction of the region or country is accurate and adequate, or whether it addresses issues of agency on the part of the people being portrayed. Based on the review results, we discuss how teachers, as the curriculum "gatekeepers," should incorporate current events and other resources to enrich teaching and learning about the world.

In recent years, the world financial markets and economy continue to face serious challenges and severe uncertainties. The Group of Twenty (G-20) finance ministers and central bank governors from both industrial and emerging-market countries often meet to tackle the international financial and economic crisis, restore worldwide financial stability, and lead international economic recovery. It is worth noting that major U.S. and

Chinese newspapers such as the *New York Times*, the *Wall Street Journal, China Daily*, and *People's Daily* offer different perspectives on economic issues. For instance, various newspapers often publish articles on comments made by the Chinese Premier Wen Jiabao about China being worried about its huge stock of U.S. Treasury securities. According to the news report, in September 2008, China had surpassed Japan as the largest foreign holder of U.S. Treasury debt. As of December 2008, it owned $727.4 billion in such securities. The current U.S. administration is implicitly asking China, along with other nations, to buy more government debt to finance its $787 billion stimulus package and other crisis-related spending. One can find hundreds of readers from both countries expressing their views through the online discussion of the report. Because of technological changes, readers from all over the world can add their views to the report and their views will be instantly displayed on the websites. Reading through the articles and the readers' comments help us recognize the deep interconnections between the two large world economies as well as alarming gaps in peoples' understanding of the other country. The pre-service and practicing teachers in my social studies education classes have been intrigued about the fact that the U.S economy is heavily dependent upon borrowing money from China. Such information may not be included in the state official curriculum or textbooks, but can certainly serve as teachable moments to help social studies educators understand how global economy functions. Such a move has the potential to transform curriculum and pedagogy so that students will have the ability to make informed decisions.

REFERENCES

Angrosino, M.V. (1989). *Documents of interaction: Biography, autobiography, and life history in social sciences perspective.* Gainesville: University of Florida Press.

Asher, N. (2005). At the interstices: Engaging post-colonial and feminist perspectives for a multicultural education pedagogy in the South. *Teachers College Record, 17*(5), 1079–1106.

Beijing Normal University. (2008). Brief history of Beijing Normal University. Retrieved on June 10, 2008, from http://www.bnu.edu.cn/focus/survey/history.htm.

Bullough, R., & Pinnegar, S. (2001). Guidelines for quality in autobiographical forms of self-study research. *Educational Researcher, 30*(3), 13–21.

Case, R. (1993). Key elements of a global perspective. *Social Education, 57*(6), 318–325.

Cochran-Smith, M., Feiman-Nemser, S., McIntyre, D., & Demers, K. (Eds.). (2008). *Handbook of research on teacher education: Enduring questions in changing contexts.* New York, NY: Routledge.

Cochran-Smith, M., & Lytle, S. (1993). *Inside/Outside: Teacher research and knowledge.* New York: Teachers College Press.

Cochran-Smith, M., & Zeichner, K. (Eds.). (2005). *Studying teacher education: Report of the AERA panel on research and teacher education.* Mahwah, NJ: Lawrence Earlbaum.

Cochran-Smith, M. (2000).Blind vision: Unlearning racism in teacher education. *Harvard Educational Review, 70*(2), 157–191.

Connelly, F. M., & Clandinin, D. J. (1999). *Shaping professional identity: Stories of educational practice.* New York: Teachers College Press.

Cooper, F. (2001). What is the concept of globalization good for?: An African historian's perspective. *African Affairs, 100,* 189–213.

Cushner, K., & Brennan, S. (2007). *Intercultural student teaching: A bridge to global competence.* Lanham, MD: Rowman & Littlefield.

Creswell, J. W. (1998). *Qualitative inquiry and research design.* Thousand Oaks, CA: Sage.

Davies, C. (1999). *Reflective ethnography.* London: Association of Social Anthropologists.

Davis, R. (2005). Teaching African history in an era of globalization. *History Compass, 3*(1), 1–5.

Denzin, N. K. (1997). *Interpretive biography.* Newbury Park, CA: Sage.

Dunn, R. (2002). Growing good citizens with a world-centered curriculum. *Educational Leadership, 60*(2), 10–13.

Dunn, R. (2008). Two world histories. *Social Education, 72*(3), 257–263

Ellis, C., & Bochner, A. P. (2003). Autoethnography, personal narrative, reflexivity. In N. K. Denzin & Y. S. Lincoln (Eds.), *Collecting and interpreting qualitative materials* (pp. 199–258).Thousand Oaks, CA: Sage.

Gay, G. (2003). *Becoming multicultural educators: Personal journey toward professional agency.* San Francisco: Jossey-Bass.

Guillén, M. (2001). Is globalization civilizing, destructive or feeble?: A critique of five key debates in the social science literature. *Annual Review of Sociology, 27*(1), 235–260

Hamilton, N., & Pinnegar, S. (2000). On the threshold of a new century: Trustworthiness, integrity, and self-study in teacher education. *Journal of Teacher Education, 51*(3), 234–240.

Hanvey, R. G. (1976). *An attainable global perspective.* New York: Center for Global Perspectives in Education.

He, M. (2002). A narrative inquiry of cross-cultural lives: Lives in the North American academy. *Journal of Curriculum Studies, 34*(5), 513–533.

Heald, S. (2004). Feminism and teaching about globalization: Contradictions and insights. *Globalisation, Societies and Education, 2*(1), 117–125.

Hicks, D. (2003). Thirty years of global education: A reminder of key principles and precedents. *Educational Review, 55* (3), 265–275.

hooks, b. (1994). Eros, eroticism, and pedagogical process. In H. Giroux & P. McLaren (Eds.), *Between borders: Pedagogy and the politics of cultural studies* (pp. 113–118). New York: Routledge.

Kagan, S., & Stewart, V. (2004, November). International education in the schools: The state of the field. *Phi Delta Kappan,* pp. 229–235.

Kirkwood-Tucker, T. F. (2004). Empowering teachers to create a more peaceful world through global education: Simulating the United Nations. *Theory and Research in Social Education, 32*(1), 56–74.

Kniep, W. M. (1989). Social studies within global education. *Social Education, 53*(6), 399–403.

Kubota, R. (2002). Marginality as an asset: Toward a counter-hegemonic pedagogy for diversity. In L. Vargas (Ed.), *Women faculty of color in the white classroom* (pp. 293–307). New York: Peter Lang.

Ladson-Billings, G. (1996). Silences as weapons: Challenges of a black professor teaching white students. *Theory into Practice, 35*(2), 79–85.

Mansilla, V., & Gardner, H. (2007). From teaching globalization to nurturing global consciousness. In M. Suarez-Orozco (Ed.), *Learning in the global era: International perspectives on globalization and education* (pp. 47–66). Berkeley: University of California Press.

McEwan, H., & Egan, K. (1995). *Narrative in teaching, learning, and research.* New York: Teacher College Press.

Merryfield, M. M. (1993). Reflective practice in global education: Strategies for teacher educators. *Theory into Practice, 32*(1), 27–32.

Merryfield, M. M. (2000). Why aren't teachers being prepared to teach for diversity, equity, and global interconnectedness?: A study of lived experiences in the making of multicultural and global educators. *Teaching and Teaching Education, 16*, 429–443.

Merryfield, M. M. (2001). Moving the center of global education: From imperial worldviews that divide the world to double consciousness, contrapuntal pedagogy, hybridity, and cross-cultural competence. In W. Stanley (Ed.), *Critical issues in social studies research for the 21st century* (pp. 179–208). Greenwich, CT: Information Age.

Merryfield, M. M., & Wilson, A. (2005). *Social studies and the world: Teaching global perspectives.* Washington, DC: NCSS.

Milner, H. R. (2007). Race, narrative inquiry, and self-study in curriculum and teacher education. *Education and Urban Society, 39*(4), 584–609.

Muchmore, J. (2004). *A teacher's life.* San Francisco: Daddo Gap Press.

Murray, W. (2006). *Geographies of globalization.* London: Routledge.

Noddings, N. (2005). *Educating citizens for global awareness.* New York: Teachers College Press.

Obidah, J. (2000). Mediating boundaries of race, class and professorial authority as a critical multiculturalist. *Teachers College Record, 102*(6), 1035–1061.

Paccione, A. (2000). Developing a commitment to multicultural education. *Teachers College Record, 102*(6), 980–1005.

Quezada, R., & Cordeiro, P. (2007). Guest editors' introduction: Internationalizing schools and college of education educating teachers for global awareness. *Teacher Education Quarterly, 34*(1), 3–7.

Sachsenmaier, D. (2006). Global history and critiques of western perspectives. *Comparative Education, 42*(3), 451–470.

Shapiro, H., & Purpel, D. (Eds.). (2005). *Critical issues in American education: Democracy and meaning in a globalizing world.* Mahwah, NJ: Erlbaum.

Sniegocki, J. (2008). Neoliberal globalization: Critiques and alternatives. *Theological Studies, 69*(2), 321–340.

St. John, W. (2009). *Outcasts United: A refugee team, an American town.* New York: Spiegel & Grau.

Stromquist, N. (2002). *Education in a globalized world.* Lanham, MD: Rowman & Littlefield.

Torres-Guzman, M., & Carter, R. (2000a). Looking at self as the critical element for change in multicultural education: Pushing at the seams of theory, research, and practice—Part I. *Teachers College Record, 102*(5), 861–863.

Torres-Guzman, M., & Carter, R. (2000b). Looking at self as the critical element for change in multicultural education: Pushing at the seams of theory, research, and practice—Part II. *Teachers College Record, 102*(6), 949–952.

Ukpokodu, N. (1996). Africa in today's social studies curriculum. *Social Studies, 87*(3), 125–133.

Wilson, A. (1982). Cross-cultural experiential learning for teachers. *Theory into Practice, 21,* 184–192.

Wilson, A. (1995). Teaching about Africa: A review of middle/secondary textbooks and supplemental materials. *Social Studies, 86*(6), 253–230.

Wilson, A. (1997). Infusing global perspectives throughout a secondary social studies program. In M. M. Merryfield, E. Jarchow, & S. Pickert (Eds.), *Preparing teachers to teach global perspectives: A handbook for teacher education* (pp. 1–24). Thousand Oaks, CA: Corwin Press.

Wilson, A. (1998). Oburoni outside the whale: Reflections on an experience in Ghana. *Theory and Research in Social Education, 26*(3), 410–429.

Zeichner, K. (2007). Accumulating knowledge across self-studies in teacher education. *Journal of Teacher Education, 58,* 36–46.

Zong, G. (2009a). Developing preservice teachers' global understanding via communication technology. *Teaching and Teacher Education, 25*(5), 617–625.

Zong, G. (2009b). Research and practice in teacher education for global perspectives. In T. Kirkwood-Tucker (Ed.), *Visions of global education* (pp. 71–89). New York: Peter Lang.

Zong, G. (2005). Road less traveled: An Asian woman immigrant faculty's experience practicing global pedagogy in American teacher education. In G. Li & G. Beckett (Eds.), *"Strangers" of the academy: Asian women scholars in higher education* (pp. 251–265). Sterling, VA: Stylus Publishing.

Zou, Y. (2000). The voice of a Chinese immigrant in America: Reflections on research and self-identity. In E. T. Trueba & L. I. Bartolomé (Eds.), *Immigrant voices: In search of educational equity* (pp. 187–202). Lanham, MD: Rowman & Littlefield.

CHAPTER 10

UNLEARNING THE SILENCE IN THE CURRICULUM

Sikh Histories and Post-9/11 Experiences

Rita Verma
Adelphi University

The earliest South Asian immigrant groups to settle in the United States were Sikh communities who had migrated from the northern areas of India. Sikhs landed on the American shores in the early 1900s and worked as agricultural laborers in California. Their contribution (and presence) has been all but absent from school curriculum despite their growing visibility over the last century. Given the current global and national political climate, especially after 9/11, it is important that educators give due consideration to the impact of this silence, particularly the misrepresentation of Sikh communities in the media and how local and global discourses have impacted Sikh experiences in the United States. Undeniably, because of 9/11, youth of South Asian (specifically those of Indian, Pakistani, Bangladeshi, and Sri Lankan descent) and Muslim heritage have come under unwarranted scrutiny in multiple ways. Since many Sikh youth wear turbans, they have especially faced scrutiny and have become the victims of racist acts, both

Critical Global Perspectives, pages 181–197
Copyright © 2010 by Information Age Publishing
All rights of reproduction in any form reserved.

subtle and overt. For example, a 2006 study of Sikh youth in Queens, New York, indicated that 77% of Sikh youth were victims of hate and prejudice (The Sikh Coalition, 2007).

What politics are in place that racialize Sikh communities in the United States? How do local/global events impact how we have come to know about Sikh histories and experiences? This topic is important in social studies research, particularly in relation to how we can teach about the local/global Other (see Crocco, 2005; Merryfield, 2001). I argue that decolonizing mainstream knowledge about local/global issues requires a careful understanding of current Islamophobic and xenophobic attitudes. This requires that we critically interrogate hegemonic discourses and their oppressive structures.

Historically, Eurocentric knowledge has influenced how people have come to know people who are considered different and who are seen as "uncivilized." Helping students learn through a global perspective is critical to unlearning racist ideologies that divide people (Willinsky, 1999). Contemporary political rhetoric over national security, which is often situated within discourses of terror and terrorism, often blames the foreign brownskinned "Other" as the one to be feared. In this discussion, I explore two interrelated topics that are very much related to how we can rethink local–global relationships in social studies classrooms. First, I explore the usefulness of studying the historical context of Sikh migration to the United States, particularly the events that led Sikhs to migrate in the post-1984 period. This topic, I believe, will help social studies educators understand cultural dimensions of global history and contemporary immigrant experiences. Second, I explore how Sikh students have been racialized in schools in the post-9/11 period—a topic that is connected to the mission of social studies in teaching about global citizenship and diversity. Overall, I argue that by being knowledgeable about cultural histories and experiences, we can be critical of prejudicial acts that have incited hatred in our school hallways, particularly in the post-9/11 context. As we continue to discuss what counts as "legitimate knowledge" to be learned in school curriculum, there has been little discussion on the need to educate students about the experiences of marginalized groups such as Sikhs and their experiences.

SIKHS WITHIN THE CONTEMPORARY POLITICAL CLIMATE

As many as 83 percent of Sikh respondents say they or someone they knew personally had experienced a hate crime or incident and 35 percent of Pakistani Muslims say they considered leaving the United States because of the hostile atmosphere created in the aftermath of the terrorist attacks. Eighty-six percent of Pakistani Muslim respondents also said they became more interested in domestic and international politics and generally they felt more of a desire to participate politically. The study was done by the Discrimination and National Security Initiative (DNSI), an affiliate of the Pluralism Project at Harvard University. The report released on the fifth anniversary of the terrorist attacks in New York and Washington was based on interviews conducted over the last two years. June Han, who authored the report, said, "We now live in an era in which individuals who are or are perceived to be Arab or Muslim, including South Asians, are viewed with suspicion because of their religious background and/or the colour of their skin. (*Hindustan Times,* September 11, 2006)

The BBC (British Broadcasting Corporation) characterized September 11th as the "day that shook the world." Reactions to the 9/11 events in the United States were unpredictable and Sikhs often became the victims of racist acts, including hate crimes, discrimination, harassment, and murder. The policing of bodies and organized surveillance of the dangerous "Other" contributed to immigrants and "foreigners" being seen as the undesirable Other who was to be hated and feared. On September 13, 2001, the *Washington Post* conducted a poll that revealed that 43% of U.S. residents that were polled thought that the attacks would make them more suspicious of people who "appear to be of Arab descent."[1] Following 9/11, President George W. Bush vowed to "rally the world" in the "fight against evil" and to "rally the armies of compassion" to fight against evil, and Bush reassured people that the "civilized" world would win. Utilizing the discourse of fear, President Bush called the "civilized" world to wage war against the "uncivilized" world. Various political and religious leaders made derogatory statements about Islam and glorified the greatness of Christianity. Sikhs, Muslims, and various immigrant communities found themselves being constantly scrutinized and being treated as the enemy of the United States.

In the aftermath of 9/11, Osama Bin Laden was viewed as the representation of the irrationality of the Third World. And mainstream media culture was often successful in painting Muslim and Arab societies as being deviant. The creation of the "evil Arab" who is dark-skinned, bearded, and turbaned became synonymous with the terrorist figure or villainous identity—a symbol of national security threat. "Oppressed women" were depicted as those wearing a *hijab.* The fact that there was a sharp rise in hate crimes against Arabs, Muslims, Sikhs, and South Asians indicated how many Americans viewed the Other as being undesirable. In many countries, including the United States and France, efforts were made to ban the wearing of turbans or *hijab* in public spaces.

Dichotomous representations limit the ways we can read the world. Kellner (1993) argued that through binary conceptions of worldviews the arbitrary line of demarcation is stabilized by the constant production and reproduction of attributions, differences, desires, and capacities that separate the West from the non-West. The West is rational, the third world is not. The West is democratic, the third world is not. The West is virtuous, moral and the side of the good and right; the third world is vicious, immoral and on the side of evil. Indeed the electronic media images generated around United States' ongoing conflict with Iraq exploits precisely these dichotomies in order to help the American viewer separate the cause of the U.S. and the West from that of the bad guys of the Middle East—Saddam Hussein and the Iraqis. (cited in McCarthy, 1998, p. 124)

Taken together, in the post-9/11 context, the media fueled and revived anti-Arabism and Islamophobia, which led to the rise in hate crimes and racist attacks against anyone who looked like a "terrorist." The post-9/11 representations were not new in the sense that, as McCarthy (1998) pointed out, the dichotomous representation of the Third World cultures has historically treated non-Western people as being deviant subjects who have had no claims to "civilized" culture or religion.

VIOLENCE, MIGRATION, AND UNCERTAINTY

Since the 9/11 attacks, numerous *gurudwaras* (Sikh temples) across the United States and the world have been vandalized, looted, and burned down. Mosques also have suffered similar attacks. Such acts were often violent and were designed to send the message to Sikh immigrants that they were not welcome or that they did not belong in the United States. In order to understand the psychological trauma faced by Sikh immigrants after 9/11, it is important to understand the historical context of Sikh migration into the United States. For many Sikhs, the post-9/11 targeting, misrepresentation, and violence invoked painful memories of life in India during 1984 and beyond, particularly after the Indian Government's campaign, Operation Blue Star. In 1984, the Indian Army entered the Golden Temple (located in the city of Amritsar, in the state of Punjab), which is considered to be an important spiritual site for Sikhs. The entry of the army is a controversial topic and there are many interpretations of the events to this day. The entry was an attempt to eradicate the Khalistan movement that sought to create an independent Sikh state. Regardless of the political motivations of the violent raid, it is important to recognize that everyday citizens became victims of the attack. During the Operation Blue Star attack, hundreds of innocent temple goers were fired upon by the army. Sikh communities in India and globally reconsidered their patriotic or national affiliation in the aftermath of the invasion since the event marked a sense of loss of a homeland. Many felt that India was no longer a community or home for them. Many Sikhs in India who were members of the Khalistan movement felt betrayed by India and felt that they were alienated from a country toward which they had made extensive contributions (Helweg, 1999). Following the entry of the Indian military, the state of Punjab was placed under martial law and Sikhs were represented as the enemy of the state of India. Groups such as Amnesty International reported random arrests, secret detentions and disappearances, extrajudicial killings and systematic practices of torture conducted by the Indian security forces. Following the raid, Sikhs were seen as being subversive agents and Hindus were constructed as "real" Indians who symbolized the "goodness" of the Indian nation-state.

After Operation Blue Star, Sikh notions of imagined community began to pick up momentum worldwide. Such visions of community have been called the diasporic imaginary since: "The diasporic imaginary indicates a precise and powerful kind of identification that is very 'real' and specifies processes by which formations of temporality and corporeality have become integral to the relations of recognition and alienation forming the Sikh subject and the Sikh homeland" (Axel, 2001, p. 154). Sikhs who lived through the tragedy felt a sense of displacement and felt that the Indian state had betrayed them. During the assault by the India army and its aftermath, many families feared for their lives and thousands of Sikhs left Punjab during the 1980s. In order to escape discrimination and violence in India, many sought political asylum in Canada, the United Kingdom, and the United States. The growth of the independence movement in Punjab, however, forced many people to rethink the meaning of what it meant to be an Indian, a Punjabi, and a Sikh (Axel, 2001). The diasporic Sikh conception of what constituted a "home" helps us understand how immigrants negotiate their identities in their "new" home, which can be shaped by political events in "old" countries (see Rumbaut,1996). The politicization of religion in Punjab created tensions within Sikh communities and raised questions over what it meant to be a Sikh and an Indian. Families and communities, hence, encountered difficulties in deciding where they stood on issues on negotiating Sikh and/or Indian identities.

For many Sikh people, seeking political asylum in the United States became an option to avoid state-sanctioned violence in India. Although Sikhs have often been targets of discriminations in the United States, many Sikhs viewed the United States as a safe place where they could strengthen their Sikh identity and could freely practice their religion. One may ask: What happens when families escape oppressive regimes in their countries of birth yet face a different type of oppression in the adopted homelands? Although Sikhs had not being targeted by the American government in a systematic way in recent years, the discriminations they faced after 9/11 often reminded them of the events following Operation Blue Star. For many families, 9/11 served as a stark reminder on how ideas such as freedom and citizenship were conditional. Sadly, although in a different context, for many Sikh communities, the kinds of oppression that they had escaped/encountered in India had once again resurfaced in the United States. Thus, even prior to 9/11 events, Sikh communities in the diaspora had been accustomed to the feeling of being displaced and had felt the sense of distrust of institutional politics.

SEPTEMBER 11TH AND SCHOOLS

An alarming number of the post-9/11 incidents against Asian Americans occurred in the workplace and in schools. In a number of cases, students were the targets of racial slurs by their classmates, and some were even physically attacked while in school (*India Abroad*, March 22, 2002):

> In a bid to raise cultural awareness about the Sikh community, all public elementary students in California will receive a new coloring and activity book which explains why Sikh boys and men wear turbans and refrain from cutting hair. (*Indian Express*, May 2, 2003)

> In October 2001, the Bush administration launched a series of initiatives aimed at prescribing patriotism among the nation's 52 million schoolchildren. Government officials urged students to take part in a mass recitation of the Pledge of Allegiance, and called upon veterans to teach "Lessons for liberty." (O'Leary & Platt, cited in Scraton, 2002)

In the post-9/11 period, schools became the prime vehicle for (re)educating youth about patriotism and loyalty to America. There were more recitations of the Pledge of Allegiance, including increased displays of American flags and increased discussion about 9/11, yet rarely were there attempts made to distinguish or educate children about who specifically was responsible for the tragic day. Similarly, rarely were efforts made to understand the event in its historical and contemporary political contexts. The aftermath of September 11th was punctuated by a renewed sense and eagerness to assert national belonging, and perhaps to eliminate (or to deport) those that were "unpatriotic." School policies of "zero tolerance for intolerance" and efforts to address the safety concerns of Sikh students (perceived by mainstream students as being like hijackers) were largely silenced, as evidenced by the unending acts of violence and harassment encountered by Muslim or students of Middle Eastern and South Asian backgrounds.

Mainstream students were quick to name Arabs, Muslims, or people from certain nation-states (Pakistan, Iraq, etc.) as being dangerous and as potential terrorists. My ethnographic study took place from October 2001–June 2003 in an urban Midwestern setting. I interviewed 12 young Sikh males and females that were high schoolers and, in this chapter, I have included the narratives of five male students. Interviews were conducted in students' communities, *gurudwaras* (Sikh temples), and schools. During my interviews with Sikh youths, they pointed out how they were subliminally as well as in overt ways discriminated in schools. The youth also indicated how school officials did little to address the racism that they had encountered. Prior to 9/11, the youth had felt prejudice yet they shared how the level of racism increased after 9/11. Three young males, who wore turbans, shared the following experiences. Harmeet, a male high school student, described how his peers interacted with him prior to 9/11 events in the following way:

> I was feeling good. I was feeling like I was allowed to be myself, with my turban. Students would ask about it and then sometimes we would joke around in a nice way. I was doing work with the student government and I felt good and like I belonged to the school.

Then Harmeet pointed out how the 9/11 political context changed how he was viewed in the school.

> I thought I had found my freedom. I was fooled. America can be just like India. We don't want you, get out you Sikh!! I feel so angry sometimes, but look.... I will not cut my hair!

Harmeet's experience reveals the sense of isolation and racial experiences students face because of national and international events. Thus, we can see how global–local events are intimately connected in what Harmeet encountered in his schooling experiences. Although he felt that he belonged (in some ways) within the school prior to 9/11, his response after the 9/11 event reveals the marked changed in his view and his experiences. He questions his sense of freedom and belonging in the school and the pressure he felt to look mainstream. His reference to "I will not cut my hair!" is a critique of dominant discourse that equates the wearing of turban by Sikh boys to the image of a terrorist, particularly in relation to the image of Osama Bin Laden and his followers. By cutting their hair and hoping to fit in, some of the young males felt that they would be less of a target of discrimination. Cutting their hair, however, meant erasing a part of their identity in order to be accepted by their peers. Jasgit, another male youth, similarly shared how he was viewed in the post-9/11 context:

> I tried to speak with other girls about who I was, but they refused to listen, they were like "Well... you are an oppressed woman from Saudi Arabia—that is why you don't cut your hair." The girls that used to say my long hair was pretty were now treating me in a bad way.

The above statement indicates how Jasgit's male identity is feminized in an exotic way and is perceived as an antithesis of "normal" male identity. The reference to an oppressed woman in Saudi Arabia is not framed within any sort of historical or cultural context. The experience that Jasgit shares is a reflection of the contemporary political discourse that assumes European American cultural/gender as being modern, civilized, or superior. Using Eurocentric norms, it assumes that men or women are oppressed because of their appearances; and, similarly, Sikh religious and cultural identity is conflated with assumed cultural practices in Saudi Arabia. In other words, it assumed that the Other is the same (different, oppressed, etc.) no matter where he or she may live. In a similar context, Maninder, another male student, explained how his world had changed in the following way:

> Everything changed. I was not reelected to the student council. People did not talk to me the same way anymore. I am so angry. My friends here also cut their hair and no longer wear their turbans! Why did they let all of this change them? I don't want to cut my hair. I will not.

> In school, I sit down when the other kids pledge allegiance to the American flag. The students then threw rotten eggs at me when I was walking home from school.

A number of Sikh youth that I spoke with indicated how they were willing to make drastic decisions to avoid unwanted attention and hostility. As noted above, some of the Sikh students who wore turbans cut their hair and no longer wore their turbans to school. They described how the increase in prejudice had triggered these decisions. Because of the lack of institutional support, the youth often spoke about how their attempts to educate others in schools about Sikhism had been unsuccessful. And the racial slurs, harassment, and unwelcome attitudes they had encountered impacted how they socialized with non-Sikh students. Because of the hostile climate in schools, students often shared how a once familiar school setting had become unfamiliar to them since they were often viewed as unwanted strangers.

SCHOOLS AS A SPACE OF CONFLICT, TENSION, AND SILENCE

Overall, in the 9/11 aftermath, Sikh youth described schools as being a place of conflict, tension, and silence. As noted earlier, many spoke about how they had begun to question their prior beliefs about their sense of being somewhat comfortable at school despite being seen as different. Many described how they were continually harassed and singled out as being objects of ridicule. Because of racial incidents, for instance, Balvinder, a high school student, indicated how he had "never felt comfortable at...and 9/11 just made my life worse and like hell!" The reference to the changing climate in the school reflected how the post-9/11 period was a difficult time for Sikh youth who were often perceived as being the Other. Sadly, many noted how they had encountered teacher apathy and how reports of harassment had been largely silenced. It seemed to the students that their voices were continually ignored, and the students felt that the discriminations they encountered were part of the retribution for what had taken place during 9/11.

Maninder pointed out how he had "tried my best to explain about Sikhism and how we were not terrorists or to be feared." Many Sikh youth made attempts to educate other students and their teachers on the distinction between Sikhism from other cultures and religions. As a way to counter stereotypes, students developed PowerPoint presentations, invited guest speakers to the schools, and even spoke with local news organizations. These efforts, however, did not lessen the racism and were often not well received by their school peers. Thus, they often silenced themselves in order to not bring unwanted attention. For instance, Mankaran, a male student, noted:

> I did not want to be noticed and not wearing the turban helped me out. I wanted to pass for...something. But it seems the harder I tried to go unnoticed, I was noticed.

Because of the marginalization they had felt, the youth spoke about how they had become reluctant to participate in school leadership positions and, in general, school activities. Yet, they also felt that they needed to participate or be visible in order to claim their Americaness or to claim their citizenship that was denied to them. In addition to trying to reclaim their citizenship identities, they faced additional pressures in school to behave or perform as "model minorities." The dominant discourse of model minority codes various Asian or Asian American groups as being obedient and academically intelligent students because of their Asian racial identity. In the post-9/11 period, the model minority perception quickly faded in school settings since the youth began to be seen as violent and dangerous. Thus, the youth were viewed not only as exotic subjects but were also constructed as subjects to be feared and to be avoided. For instance, Harmeet indicated how he was once asked in school: "Oh, are you learning to bomb us?" Thus, the once "intelligent" mind of the immigrant subjects was now being considered as being corrupt and deviant. Many youth indicated how their grades had suffered as a result of the increased isolation they had felt. Many spoke about how they had considered dropping out of school and not attending college. A number of students made comments such as "School is stupid" or "Why do I need an education? I don't have a chance." For many Sikh students, dislike of school significantly grew in the period after 9/11.

AMBIVALENCE TOWARD CITIZENSHIP IDEALS

Most of the students that I spoke with indicated how they felt a sense of being defeated and were ambivalent about the possibility of ever being accepted in the United States. A number of students shared how their parents must have felt in India in the aftermath of the 1984 events when Sikhs were viewed as the national problem. The youth pointed out how the United States may have seemed like an attractive place for their parents to emigrate to in order to escape the political persecution, oppression, and violence of India. The freedom to openly worship Sikhism, build *gurudwaras,* and to not fear detainment, torture, and humiliation had all been incentives for the families to remain in the United States. In the post-9/11 period, the youth and their families questioned the possibility of having the freedom to practice their Sikh culture and religion, and to be fully accepted as citizens. Virtually all of the Sikh students shared how their chances of being recognized as a legitimate citizen had decreased because of 9/11 events. Because of the prejudice they had faced, the youth pointed out how their parents had begun to question the seemingly value-free conceptions such as citizenship, justice, and democracy in the United States. Similarly, the question of what constituted home and a sense of not belonging in India or in the United States was an issue that the youth felt they were now able to understand from their parents' experiences.

The Sikh students' experiences help us understand how diverse students encounter more explicit forms of racism because of national and international events. Rizvi (1993) pointed out that racism ought to be viewed as a dynamic ideological construct that is continuously changing, being challenged, interrupted, and reconstructed, and that it often operates in contradictory ways. Indeed, racial forms of prejudice are complex, multi-faceted, and historically specific. The youth experiences also critique the racist model minority discourse that exoticizes Asian identities and that assumes that all Asian immigrant or Asian Americans undergo the same experiences in school. As the youth remind us, because of 9/11 experiences, the students were not perceived as high academic achievers but as threats to school or to the imagined national community.

Social studies educators have rightly pointed out how diverse immigrant students' racial experiences and cultural identities (racial, ethnic, religious, etc.) are often marginalized in schools (see Subedi, 2008; Urietta, 2004). Bhabha (1994) introduced the idea of "in-between-ness" to capture the essence of the immigrants' paradoxical existence. The immigrant is viewed as living on the borderline, thus negotiating national and international, local and global identities. DasGupta (1997) stated that the "in-between space that the Asian Indian immigrant occupies represents a transnational hybridity where the world of linkages and connections comes alive and throws all those concerned into the paroxysms of confusion and conflict" (p. 45).

The youth experiences demonstrate how religious forms of prejudice function in schools, a topic that has received limited attention within social studies research. As noted by Joshi (2006), "religious affiliation, like race, has been the basis for exclusion and discrimination throughout American history" (p. 118). Joshi argued that:

> Religious oppression manifests the majority's belief in the superiority of Christianity and the inferiority of Hinduism, Islam and Sikhism and the oppressor's desire for a homogenous nation.... Religious oppression in the United States exists and is perpetuated by and through a specific combination of facts and acts, each building upon its precedent: first one particular group, Christians, has the power to define normalcy; second, the histories and belief systems of Hinduism, Islam and Sikhism are misrepresented and/or discounted; third, harassment, discrimination and other forms of differential treatment towards non-Christians are institutionalized; and fourth: religious oppression is manifested through violence or the threat of violence. (p. 123)

The racial/religious forms of discriminations faced by Sikh students help us understand how we cannot assume that all immigrants or students of color undergo similar struggles in schools (Gibson 1988; Gibson & Ogbu, 1991). Forms of racism encountered by various school subjects are historically situated and are shaped by specific cultural discourses. Sikh and Muslim students are often racialized in schools because such students are believed to negotiate different and dangerous religious and ethnic identities in school and society.

EXPANDING GLOBAL AND MULTICULTURAL CURRICULUM

The experiences of Sikh youth help us understand the interconnected themes of culture, racism, and the politics of knowledge that are very relevant in teaching about global perspectives. Although Sikhism may be superficially covered in world history courses, the struggles Sikh people have faced in India and in the United States are often silenced in social studies curriculum. This absence has much to do with how the teaching about Asia has filtered through Orientalist frameworks. As Said (1979) argued, Orientalism is a discourse through which dominant Western representation exoticizes and renders the Other different and inferior, a topic that is intimately connected to issues of knowledge and power. In the historical context, Orientalism was embedded within discourses of literature, art, philosophy, and culture and from which Westerners learned to construct the Orient or non-Western societies as inferior and different. Thus, within Western discourses, the: "Theses of Oriental backwardness, degeneracy, and inequality with the West most easily associated themselves early in the nineteenth century with ideas about the biological bases of racial inequality" (Said, 1979, p. 206). For instance, as reflected in Rudyard Kipling's fictitious stories of colonial India, too often Western authors made clear distinctions between East and West, with the West being constructed as being civilized and modern. And, too often, non-Western societies were represented as being homogenous and incapable of transforming their societies. Said argued that new forms of Orientalism shaped how Third World societies continued to be mis/represented in mainstream media and popular culture discourses.

As I have argued, the ways in which Sikhs are being represented as exotic and dangerous suggests how Orientalist thinking is prevalent in the United States. Clearly, educational systems are complicit in further perpetuating Orientalist perspectives that construct the world into civilized and uncivilized entities (Merryfield, 2001). Considering that countries such as India, Pakistan, and Bangladesh are represented as being culturally impoverished, immigrant students from such countries feel the burden and the responsibility to clarify the misrepresentations or the misconceptions that are not addressed by teachers.

The learning of Sikh histories and experiences also has implications to understanding the interconnected nature of multicultural and global discourses. The resurgence of neoliberal and neoconservative alliances in England and in the United States are responsible for the creation of Sikhs, and immigrants in general, as the Other in school settings. I would argue that the Sikh youths' experiences help us develop a more open-minded curriculum vis-à-vis diasporic ethnic experiences and citizenship in the global context. For example, in relation to critiquing American imperial discourses, Maira and Shihade (2006) explained how "the current form of empire and a discussion of how ethnicization, racialization, and citizenship within the multicultural nation are constructed in relation to imperial power that extends globally and that co-opts the very notion of cultural difference" (p. 8). The hegemonic/imperial alliance of conservative groups in the United States and England encompasses a wide array of political or cultural entities. Hegemonic discourse is not characterized by a total control, but rather a partial exercise of control by dominant groups, or by an alliance of dominant groups in various spheres of society (Apple, 1996). Such discourses offer a "commonsense" approach to education that adheres to romanticized notions of Eurocentric values, cultural norms, and traditional knowledge. Clearly, these measures serve to enhance or protect neoliberal agendas. Similarly, the hegemonic neoliberal discourse plays an influential role in shaping the curriculum content, academic standards, and in general how teachers are being prepared to teach about world history and cultures.

Despite contributions that have been made by Asian and Asian American immigrants in the United States, they are often excluded from what is considered "core" knowledge, including in the social studies curriculum (Halagao, 2004). Whenever elements of Asian immigrant and Asian American histories and experiences are incorporated within social studies curriculum, they are incorporated in relation to the experiences of dominant groups. And, too often, Asian subjectivities are written as being the silent and the obedient Other. Thus, it is critical to consider the diverse experiences of immigrant groups when teaching about Asian or Asian American experiences in the United States. In relation to the need to address the distinct South Asian histories and cultures, Shankar and Srikanth (1998) noted how

> South Asians want their unique attributes to be recognized and their particular issues discussed; and some of them want this to occur, initially at least, within the Asian American paradigm, for they think that they must surely belong there. Yet, they find themselves so unnoticed as an entity that they feel as if they are merely a crypto group, often included but easily marginalized within the house of Asian America. (p. 3)

Similar to the term Asian American, the term South Asian American is broad and encompasses the experiences, history, and cultures of various ethnic groups, including Sikh experiences. Clearly, because of religious, cultural, and linguistic differences, South Asians (for instance, from India) do not interpret histories and experiences in the same way. In order to fight for their specific struggles, a large part of the struggle for the Sikh diaspora has been about mobilizing a distinct political project that is part yet distinct from the larger South Asian constituencies.

Apple (1996) argued that educators need to constantly interrogate what constitutes "core knowledge" and who is defining the very meaning of core knowledge to be learned in schools. Clearly, Sikh histories, whether in the context of North America or in the global context, is yet to be included in American or the global history curriculum. Sadly, what constitutes global or multicultural knowledge to be learned in school continues to be defined via mainstream lenses that celebrate narrow conceptions of democracy and citizenship. Conservative interpretation of curriculum continues to construct the binary of "we" (the dominant group) versus "they" (the Other), which attempts to reproduce dominant values and power. The right-wing resurgence in both England and the United States is aimed at creating a "new majority" that calls for the need to return to traditional values and morality.

UNLEARNING THE SILENCES

Discussions in regard to 9/11 in schools have tended to center around the attacks on American soil by certain "enemies." The images of the enemies are reduced to men in turbans who have beards and dark skin. Although the figure of Osama bin Laden may not be present in the American television screen every evening as it was a few years ago, the image has become part of the American "commonsense" and popular culture. The image of Osama bin Laden wearing a turban is ingrained in the memories of the general public, and people who wear turbans or who look like Muslims continue to be victims of racial violence. The term "Taliban" has now become a racial slur and is used commonly against minority groups. I would argue that the challenges faced by Muslim and Sikh groups parallel the violent racial experiences faced by various racial and ethnic groups in the United States. This popular racism, as described by Rizvi (1993), claims itself as the "truth" and appeals to those who are not critically engaging with dominant discourses.

When educators are resistant to unlearn or to dissect racist language and assumptions about marginalized groups, oppressive structures will continue to remain intact. When racism permeates in schools, students of color will find it difficult to negotiate their identities and feel marginalized, which impacts their self-confidence and self-esteem. All students desire to belong in schools and the lack of inclusion of students' cultural knowledge further devalues their ways of knowing. As Nieto (2002) argued, "curriculums in many United States schools today are perceived by students as being irrelevant to their lives and experiences. As a result, these students become disengaged from school" (p. 54). Nieto suggested that educators examine the "hidden curriculum" of schools and how monocultural education disempowers all students. As noted earlier, critical aspects of Sikh histories and experiences have been largely left out of school curricula, and writings on South Asian experiences have often been written from Eurocentric perspectives. How Sikh, and in general South Asian history and cultures, are represented in school curriculum can leave all parents with greater challenges as they attempt to engage with what is taught in schools.

In schools, the interpretation on what counts as "multicultural" practices have, for the most part, been superficial attempts to include token holidays and heroes and have yet to critically deconstruct mainstream curriculum. What I call for in my work is a transformative paradigm that accounts for multiple perspectives on critical histories and experiences of marginalized people. I agree with Nieto (2000) that educational reform cannot be envisioned without taking into account both micro- and macro-level issues that may affect student learning. Micro-level issues include the cultures, languages, and experiences of students and their families, and how these are taken into account in determining school policies and practices. Macro-level issues include the racial, social class, and gender stratification that helps maintain inequality and how resources and access to learning are provided or denied by schools. Freire (1970) pointed out that a critical task for educators is to create space through which teachers can engage in productive dialogue with students so that all participants can become transformative subjects who are capable of changing society. I find it useful to teach students the importance of searching for multiple sources, the value of challenging their own assumptions, and the need to envision a critical world. Addressing students' fears and encouraging them to think about ways to engage in critical global understanding needs to be an important component of social studies curriculum. Teachers' initiatives can clearly promote discussions on issues of prejudice and stereotyping, including dialogue on how the media continues to shape people's understanding about cultural experiences.

In recent years, various social groups have developed resources to critique dominant perceptions of Muslim and Sikh communities. For instance, websites such as *tolerance.org, ADC.org*, and *Sikheducation.com* provide alternative resources on Sikh and Arab-American experiences. The Sikh Coalition has developed a comprehensive website for Sikh youth and educators called Khalsa Kids. This was developed in conjunction with a New York City–wide report that was titled *Hatred in Our Hallways*. The report addressed racism felt by Sikh youth in Queens, New York, and provided curriculum to unlearn the racist discourse that had arisen since 9/11. "The Sikh Next Door" project similarly distributed resources that provide transformative knowledge about Sikh experiences in the Unites States. Unfortunately, as the pressure for high-stakes testing increases, social justice education is increasingly being placed on the periphery. Children in schools need to learn to be critical readers and:

> Those committed to a more participatory curriculum understand that knowledge is socially constructed, that it is produced and disseminated by people who have particular values, interests and biases. This is simply a fact of life, since all of us are formed by our cultures, genders, geographies and so on. In a democratic curriculum, however, young people learn to be "critical readers" of their society. When confronted with some knowledge or viewpoint, they are encouraged to ask questions like: Who said this? Why did they say it? Why should we believe this? Who benefits if we believe this and act upon it? (Apple & Beane, 2007, p. 151)

There is a broader need to decolonize knowledge about global histories and cultures, including the need to see how local discourses are connected to global issues (see JanMohamed, 1987). The prejudice Muslim and Sikh students face in schools is historically situated and is connected to, as I have argued, national and international events. When educators address controversial issues and provide multiple perspectives about global issues, all students will have the opportunity to learn transformative knowledge.

When there is little attempt to unlearn or dissect racist language and assumptions about groups, cycles of oppression are left unbroken. When hegemonic ideas permeate school settings, the groups that are negatively affected face similar tensions within school walls that they experience outside of the school community. Racist messages directly impact students' self-confidence and self-esteem. Issues of self-esteem and "fitting in" are critical in the formation of cultural identity and a sense of belonging in school for students. Nieto (2002) suggested that educators need to examine the "hidden curriculum" reflected in bulletin boards, extracurricular activities, and other messages given to students about their abilities and experiences. For this reason, it is important to encourage students to search for facts, challenge their own assumptions, and envision what an anti-oppressive and a peaceful world may look like. Addressing students' fears and encouraging them to think about the ways to engage in global understanding should be important elements within social studies education.

NOTE

1. Retrieved June 27, 2002 (ABC News/*Washington Post* Terrorist Attack Poll #2, September 13, 2001) from http://www.icpst.umich.edu:8080/ABSTRACTS/03290.xml.

REFERENCES

Apple, M. (1996). *Cultural politics and education.* New York: Teachers College Press.
Apple, M. W., & Beane, J. A. (2007). *Democratic schools: Lessons in powerful education.* Portsmouth, NH: Heinemann.
Apple, M. W. (1995). *Education and power.* New York: Routledge.
Axel, B. K. (2001). *The nation's tortured body: Violence, representation, and the formation of the Sikh "diaspora."* Durham, NC: Duke University Press.
Bhabha, H. (1994). *The location of culture.* New York: Routledge.
Crocco, M. S. (2005). Teaching *Shabanu:* The challenges of using world literature in the US social studies classrooms. *Journal of Curriculum Studies, 37*(5), 561–582.
DasGupta, K. (1997). Raising bicultural children. In B. B. Khare (Ed.), *Asian Indian immigrants: Motifs on ethnicity and gender* (pp. 57–69). Dubuque, IA: Kendall Hunt.
Freire, P. (1970). *Pedagogy of the oppressed.* New York: Continuum Press.
Gibson, M., & Ogbu, J. (Eds.). (1991). *Minority Status and schooling: A Comparative study of immigrant and involuntary minorities.* New York: Garland Publishing.
Gibson, M. (1988). *Accommodation without assimilation: Sikh immigrants in an American high school.* Ithaca, NY: Cornell University Press.

Halagao, P. E. (2004). Holding up the mirror: The complexity of seeing your ethnic self in history. *Theory and Research in Social Education, 32*(4), 459–483.

Helweg, A. (1999). *Punjabi identity: A structural/symbolic analysis.* New Delhi: Oxford University Press.

Hinustan Times, September 11, 2006, p. 1.

India Abroad, March 22, 2002, p. 1.

JanMohamed, A. (1987). Toward a theory of minority discourse. *Cultural Critique, 6,* 5–11.

Joshi, K. (2006). *New roots in America's sacred ground: Religion, race and ethnicity in Indian America.* New Brunswick, NJ: Rutgers University Press.

Kellner, D. (1993). *Media culture: Cultural Studies, identity and politics between the modern and postmodern.* New York: Routledge.

Maira, S., & Shihade, M. (2006). Meeting Asian/Arab American Studies: Thinking race, empire and Zionism in the U.S. *Journal of Asian American Studies, 9*(2), 177–140.

McCarthy, C. (1998). *The uses of culture: Education and the limits of ethnic affiliation.* New York: Routledge.

Merryfield, M. M. (2001). Moving the center of global education: From imperial worldviews that divide the world to double consciousness, contrapuntal pedagogy, hybridity, and cross-cultural competence. In W. B. Stanley (Ed.), *Critical issues in social studies research for the 21st century* (pp. 179–208). Greenwich, CT: Information Age.

Nieto, S. (2000). *Affirming diversity: The socio-political context of multicultural education* (3rd ed.). New York: Longman.

Nieto, S. (2002). *Language, culture, and teaching: Critical perspectives for a new century.* Mahwah, NJ: Erlbaum.

Rizvi, F. (1993). Children and the grammar of racism. In C. McCarthy & W. Crichlow (Eds.), *Race, identity and representation* (pp. 126–139). New York: Routledge.

Rumbaut, R. (1996). The crucible within: Ethnic identity, self-esteem, and segmented assimilation among children of immigrants. In A. Portes (Ed.), *The new second generation* (pp. 119–170). New York: Russell Sage Foundation.

Said, E. (1979). *Orientalism.* New York: Random House.

Scraton, P. (2002). *Beyond September 11: An anthology of dissent.* London: Pluto Press.

Shankar, L. D., & Srikanth, R. (Ed.). (1998). *A part, yet apart: South Asians in Asian America.* Philadelphia: Temple University Press.

Sikh Coalition. (2007). *Hatred in the hallways: Preliminary report on bias against Sikh students in New York City's public schools.* Retrieved March 20, 2008 from www.sikhcoalition.org/advisories/documents/HatredintheHallwaysFinal_000.pdf hallways

Subedi, B. (2008). Fostering critical dialogue across cultural differences: A study of immigrant teachers' interventions in diverse school. *Theory and Research in Social Education, 36*(4), 413–440.

Urietta, L., Jr. (2004). Dis-connections in "American" citizenship and the post/neo-colonial: People of Mexican descent and whitestream pedagogy and curriculum. *Theory and Research in Social Education, 32*(4), 433–458.

Willinsky, J. (1999). *Learning to divide the world.* Minneapolis: University of Minnesota Press.

CHAPTER 11

TRAVEL DIALOGUES OF/TO THE OTHER

Complicating Identities and Global Pedagogy

Sharon Subreenduth
Bowling Green State University

How do we make sense of the global Other—as educators and students? And how does our sense of the Other impact the ways in which we teach content knowledge about the Other? These are fundamental questions that guide this chapter. As an international subject in U.S. classrooms and as a director of an educator exchange program between U.S. and South African educators, I write about the ways in which we—*me as a foreign Other in the United States as well as U.S. educators*—made sense of our travels, engagements, and cross-cultural collaborative practices. In this chapter, I utilize my personal narrative of being confronted or confronting the ways in which I am imagined, consumed, and interpreted in the United States. I also include teacher reflections to demonstrate how U.S. teachers critically participated in an international educator exchange. I present the narratives

Critical Global Perspectives, pages 199–222
Copyright © 2010 by Information Age Publishing
All rights of reproduction in any form reserved.

as a means to contextualize the complexities of U.S.–global diversity and connectedness that challenges the ways in which we teach about local-global diversity in our classrooms. Furthermore, I utilize personal narratives to highlight my ideological and lived commitments to engendering social justice opportunities, particularly in relation to providing meaningful, critical, and challenging opportunities for U.S. educators to engage with the Other in South Africa. Seldom do educator exchanges or study abroad opportunities offer sustained and critical engagement with Othered geographies and people (Dolby, 2004). Often these exchanges serve to offer cross-cultural awareness and understanding, but do little to connect individuals and institutions in mutually productive collaborations and partnerships. Our sharing of these experiences, whether in our teaching, social interactions, academic or research endeavors, seldom interrogate the ways in which we and others consume, translate, or replicate these experiences.

Clearly, the starting point for what and how we teach begins with our personal beliefs, investments, and professional commitments. Thus teachers do not discard their personal beliefs before entering their classrooms. These beliefs, their constructed knowledge and perspectives, influence their interactions with others and shape their interpretations of the curriculum content and pedagogy. In an attempt to locate the personal and particularly travel as a pedagogical construct within which self-reflection, complex interpretations of global societies, and cross-cultural differences are exchanged, I examine the ways in which U.S. educators consumed knowledge and experiences within South Africa. I also trace how the focused educational exchanges offered meaningful complex interactions and dialogue. Insights into the ways in which U.S. teachers translate these experiences to produce a more complex self-understanding as well as curricula to teach about South Africa and the United States offer alternative global discourse about non-Western, often marginalized countries like South Africa. In this chapter, I examine the creative possibilities of teaching global perspectives from more authentic perspectives. I do so by analyzing discourses on lived experience, traveling narratives, and ethical collaborative practices across differences, particularly between U.S. and South African educators.

CALLS FOR MORE COMPLEX READING(S) AND PEDAGOGY OF OTHERS

As a result of the prolonged war in Iraq, a historic election, and an economy spinning out of control, U.S. citizens, for the first time in decades, have been most keenly and consciously aware of the world around them. This current dynamic in conjunction with the recent growth of critical approaches to teaching international issues have expanded discussions on race, gender, ethnicity, social class, religion, politics, history, and culture. The recent publication of Merryfield and Wilson's (2005) *Social Studies and the World: Teaching Global Perspectives* highlights the need for students to be informed by the ways in which their lives and the lives of others are impacted by the same (global) issues. Important in Merryfield and Wilson's NCSS bulletin is their attempt to ensure that teachers "deal with the concept of globalization both historically and currently as they prepare students to participate in the world (p. 5). Banks's (2004) *Diversity and Citizenship Education: Global Perspectives* is positioned to provide crucial dialogue on the core social studies concept of democratic citizenship (Parker, 2003). Within the larger spectrum of educational theorizing, educational theorists such as Smith (1999) and Rizvi (2004) have discussed the need to make connections among indigenous, multicultural, as well as global discourses to help us better understand contemporary issues such as poverty, oppression, and religion. Social studies is a contested and controversial terrain partly because the discipline plays a critical role in shaping students' national/cultural identities and the ways in which they come to understand local-global issues, and in general, citizenship discourses. Since the teaching of controversial topics is often viewed with skepticism or disapproval, in recent years a number of social studies teachers have lost their teaching positions or have been reprimanded for utilizing critical global perspectives in teaching about the 9/11 attacks, the war on terrorism, or the war in Iraq. These incidents testify to the fact that infusing global perspectives in social studies curricula is a controversial practice (see, e.g., Faulconer & Freeman, 2005; Patterson & Chandler, 2008).

As our local environments become increasingly implicated in global operations via our material, technological, or cultural consumptions, we need to give considerable attention to how we rethink and rearticulate the global-local implications of citizenship, identity, history, culture, and politics. Changing global demographic mobility and interaction insists on critical engagement with colonized educational histories and identities. This positions social studies teaching as a critical subject to engender this engagement. Thus Merryfield's (2002) study on how/why teachers are not being prepared to teach about diversity, equity, and global connectedness underscores the gaps in teacher preparation and professional development programs across the United States. While this gap has continued to remain, the recent strong and fervent calls by critical global educators have highlighted the shortfalls of teacher preparation, teacher comfort level, and authentic knowledge about global societies, politics, histories, and peoples. Thus, it is necessary to highlight the urgent need to develop and implement more critical global perspectives in teacher preparation and professional development programs. What I attempt to demonstrate in this chapter is how purposeful interaction and collaboration among U.S. and South African educators can lead to U.S. educators developing a more critical and in-depth sense of the power of their curricular choices in teaching about societies such as South Africa. Although it is not discussed in this chapter, this is true for South African educators, too.

The recent productive growth of critical approaches to theorizing international issues (Banks, 2004; Merryfield & Wilson, 2005), as well as the number of contested academic freedom cases of K–12 educators (see Faulconer & Freeman, 2005; Patterson & Chandler 2008) testify to the increased attention given to discussions about global perspectives. In U.S. classrooms, the teaching of global perspectives is viewed as a controversial arena and remains a marginalized field of knowledge. Thus, critical dialogue about global issues is often marginalized in schools. Thus projects that work toward critically internationalizing curricular studies is urgent for our current historical moment as it offers much-needed alternative spaces to conceptualize local–global relationships of curriculum theory and practice. Alternative conceptualizations call for an interrogation of Eurocentric forms of knowledge that continue to sanction monolithic ideas of truth and reality (McLaren, 1997). Additionally, alternative conceptualizations of knowledge interrogate the political context of knowledge production and how knowledge shapes the inclusion or exclusion of perspectives in schools (Giroux, 1992). What constitutes really useful knowledge? Whose interests does it serve? What kinds of social relations does it structure and at what price? How does school knowledge enable those who have been generally excluded from schools to speak and act with dignity? (Giroux, 1992, p. 16).

TEACHING ABOUT AFRICA[1]

Despite its increased economic, global, cultural, and political impact, Africa continues to remain a marginalized, misrepresented, and misread continent in the United States. It is therefore not surprising that even today students, educators, and people in general in the United States are misinformed about the vast continent of Africa. Too often, students will ask, among other queries, about the wild animals as pets, whether there are cars, airplanes, music, hamburgers, the hunger and poverty of "stateless" nations, HIV/AIDS, killings and corruption. Their impressions are no doubt circulated by media images that reinforce negatives and perpetuate stereotypes about poverty and exotica. Such images often remain intact and are rarely critiqued in social studies classrooms. It is therefore unfortunate that the majority of U.S. students will never glimpse the positive aspects of Africa—whether it is its lush beauty; magnificent physical features; complex, diverse, and rich cultures; hardworking populace; technological advancements; resources; and Africa's sincere attempts at engaging with their democracy and democratic institutions, rights and responsibilities. In addition to the above, recent demographic surveys have shown that African peoples are rapidly becoming one of the nation's (U.S.) larger immigrant populations. Undoubtedly this global mobility and changing demographics impact curriculum knowledge production and consumption in U.S. classrooms. Educators need to engage themselves and their students in a critique of the dominant Eurocentric and canonical forms of knowledge found in textbooks, easily accessible resources, popular culture, and mainstream media. Willinsky (1998), for example, highlights how the legacies of colonialism and imperialism continue to inform contemporary discussions on science, history, geography, and race in education and thus the colonial context of knowledge production has implications for the ways in which issues such as history and culture are taught in K–12 classrooms.

Educators, and more particularly social studies educators, will soon be forced to address the implications of this new immigration trend and be challenged to find ways in which to disrupt dominant conceptualizations of the Third World and Third World peoples in the United States. Not only will they be challenged to rethink the ways they teach such students, but more importantly *what* and *how* they teach about Africa. Subedi (2008) has highlighted the ways in which immigrant teachers in the U.S. opened up more critical dialogue among their students by offering curricular interventions that enabled such critical inquiry. The politics of being immigrant and Othered in U.S. society enabled the immigrant educators in Subedi's study to offer their immigrant and nonimmigrant students more complex curriculum knowledge about cultural differences across racial/ethnic groups.

There is a growing research within social studies that examines the power of teaching global perspective, including the need to understand multiple perspectives, the need to challenge stereotypes, and the value of addressing histories, experiences, and cultures of non-Western society. Global education has historically emphasized how international histories, cultures, and current events ought to be infused within the social studies curriculum (Hanvey, 1975). In the past and in contemporary contexts, curriculum knowledge within social studies has served the interest of people in power (Apple, 1996; Banks, 1996; Willinsky, 1998). Scholars have argued that the teaching and learning of social studies ought to consider the cultural context of classroom settings (Banks, 1996; Ladson-Billings, 1993; Ross, 2001), particularly via providing global perspectives on curriculum knowledge. Scholars in the field have called for the need to further research how people negotiate global perspectives differently and that influences how they negotiate their identity and politics (Asher & Crocco, 2001; Merryfield, 2000).

My pedagogical interactions with mainly mainstream Caucasian pre-service and practicing teachers indicate that their inability to effectively integrate global perspectives in their social studies teaching is often connected to their lack of focused meaningful contact with the Other. In addition, the absence of opportunities for deliberation and dialogue with the Other creates a vacuum in critical pedagogy, particularly about marginalized geographical location such as South Africa—still commonly referenced as Africa! Rarely are there opportunities for U.S. educators to engage with social education practitioners in Africa so that focused meaningful interactions can take place.

While I acknowledge that resistance to including authentic multiple perspectives to teaching about the histories of especially Third World regions exists, my experiences with both pre-service and practicing teachers is not always that they prefer not to teach about Africa, or intentionally misinform their students. Rather, their lack of confidence and discomfort with teaching about Africa is often derived from their lack of knowledge about Africa, which can be attributed to their use of the easily accessed teaching strategies, resources, and content. In addition, those educators who do teach about Africa and utilize a curricular and pedagogical approach that promotes trivialization and reinforcement of existing stereotypes and misconceptions seldom have had mutually productive opportunities to interact with people from Third World regions. The educator exchanges, collaborations, and partnerships offered through the project I direct offers U.S. educators with multiple (South) African perspectives that convey the depth and complexity of a continent that is often misunderstood, misrepresented, or dismissed as unimportant. In a shrinking global environment, alternative and multiple perspectives are needed to critically engage our youth, for example, on issues such as global–local democratic citizenship and histories that encompass not simply an understanding of other cultures, peoples, and politics but also possibilities for them to actively participate in crucial issues that affect them inter/nationally and locally. With the U.S. currently implicated in a number of global conflicts like the war in Iraq and the war on terrorism, Mahalingam and McCarthy (2000) call for curriculum studies to be situated within transnational frameworks is urgent for the field of global studies in order to offer alternative spaces to conceptualize and impart curriculum knowledge about the rest of the world

Such a transnational engagement with Third World content and pedagogy can engender a more complex and critical thinking, including the possibilities of making the self an informed and critical decision maker (e.g., as citizens, consumers) who engages with difference beyond the tolerance discourse. The educators' experiences and reflections included in this chapter allows them (and us) to interrogate the taken-for-granted construction, interpretation, and practice of marginalized histories, events, and experiences—all of which has implications for the ways in which they/ we teach about Third World regions in U.S. classrooms.

RESEARCH CONTEXT

As an attempt to understand the complex tensions of being the Other in the United States and trying to work through this complexity in the classroom and U.S. society, I utilize personal narrative to explicate these tensions. Personal narrative serves as a testimony to the prolific possibilities that personal experience has in developing a liberatory praxis, that is, "action and reflection upon the world [and our interactions with it] in order to change it" (hooks, 1994, p. 14). As social studies educators, we play a critical role in engendering in our students the sense that their personal experiences are meaningful, valuable, and critical to understanding the world, while simultaneously asking our students to interrogate their own taken-for-granted un/conscious conceptualizations of the world. To effectively do this, I believe that we have to undergo a similar process. Hence, I am sharing in this chapter teacher interactions and reflections of their engagement with South Africa. These reflections are part of data collected as a result of a larger teacher educator exchange between South African and Ohio teachers that began in 2001 and is ongoing. For this chapter, I focus specifically on my interactions with two teachers before and during the exchange visits, and their interaction with South African educators in the United States and South Africa. I also analyze the teachers' reflections after the trip.

The teacher reflections presented in this chapter represent critical implications for the ways in which we can rethink curriculum that are included in school textbooks and dominant curricula resources and the ways in which focused international partnerships can provide opportunities for U.S. educators to challenge the history and legacy of imperialism in their teaching. In thinking about the often stereotypical ways in which regions outside of the United States are imaged and presented, the critical engagement and reflection of U.S. educators experiences in South Africa and with South African society/peoples is crucial to dismantling these dominant stereotypical constructions.

Methodologically this chapter can be described as a decolonizing project (Smith, 1999; Subreenduth, 2006) that troubles traditional and imperial categories of global Others. Such a troubling is intended to open up alternative spaces to discuss the practice and performance of such colonial/imperial ideologies via "multiple layers of struggle[s] across multiple sites" (Smith, 2005, p. 88). According to Smith, the decolonizing project is about "unmasking and [the] deconstruction of imperialism, and its aspects of colonialism, in its old and new formations; for the reclamation of knowledge, language, and culture; and for the social transformation of the colonial relations between the native and the settler" (p. 88).

In order to rupture the underpinnings of oppression, one needs to counter and disrupt the operations of Othering and objectification within classrooms. More urgently there is the need for decolonizing interventions to offer traveling counternarratives and discourses about marginalized regions, peoples, and societies. I see the educator exchanges that I direct working toward the nature of deconstruction that Smith (2005) calls for. My personal narrative and the experiences of the educators participating in the educator exchanges highlight the significant impact of travel on our curricular decisions and teacher identity. In this chapter I present three narratives (mine, Mark, and Jenna) to offer the different ways in which meaningful educational travel and interactions can provide transformative personal and pedagogical possibilities. My autobiography is not directly connected to the educators' perspectives on travel to South Africa, but it addresses and overlaps with the history of race in South Africa and the United States. The teacher reflections particularly help us understand the nature of competing perspectives on global issues and the politics of knowledge production, including the challenges faced by educators who teach about global societies such as South Africa.

DIVERSE TRAVEL NARRATIVES
IN AND OUT OF SOUTH AFRICA

From Shantytown to Downtown: An Autobiography[2]

I begin with the struggle to find a way to express the implications of my paralysis of articulating Third World narratives of identity and difference that is implicated in the politics and discourse of race, power, and knowledge production. My paralysis has to do with the risk of misinterpretation, consumption of exoticism, and making public what is not supposed to be public, as well as the possibility of further violent symbolic acts. My hope for such transnational narratives is an alternative lens through which we (as dominant/marginalized) can examine the discursive nature of race, power, and knowledge and its possibilities for creating and engendering productive and healing spaces. As Third World transnational subjects, categories of race, identity, difference, and Othering become convoluted, complex, and contested both in the West and global South (see Daza, 2008). Such complexities are particularly enhanced as these locations become more psychological spaces than simply geographic or temporal categories (John, 1989). This psychological conceptualization is further complicated within social, economic, and cultural discourses that particularize these psychological spaces (John, 1989). This very complexity compels me to use the metaphor "From Shantytown to Downtown" in my title above. I use this as a metaphor to demonstrate the spaces of where *my* body, *my* politics, *my* knowledge intermingles within the transnational politics of location, power, and race (i.e., my movement from the global South—Shantytown (South Africa)—to the West—Downtown, USA). However, this metaphor also encapsulates and has implications for the thousands of immigrant children and youth who find themselves in U.S. classrooms—as foreign Others, often voiceless and who share many of my own tensions of being foreigner/Otherized.

I can clearly remember and identify the emergence of my politicized and racialized identity in apartheid South Africa. The year was 1978 and I was a 14-year-old eighth grader. The senior students were screaming at us, banging on the classroom doors and windows, urging us to get out of our classrooms and join the student protests. That marked the moment of stepping out of my sheltered and naive childhood and into the conundrum of racialized politics. We were Indian students protesting in solidarity with African students all across the country.[3] The student protests began with the historic 1976 Soweto student uprising[4] and culminated in South Africa's first democratic election in 1994. But I am moving too quickly across two crucial decades in South Africa's contemporary history. I am writing not to situate South Africa's history, but rather to contextualize my identity politics within the politics of race in South Africa as well as the reflections of the U.S. educators. Like all other brown-skinned Indians in South Africa, I had to, for example, attend an all Indian school, live in an all-Indian residential area, and visit all-Indian beaches and other public places. My segregated, racialized existence was normal—a naturalized routine of my life in apartheid South Africa, until my eighth-grade experiences.

The policy of apartheid (literally meaning apartness) was a shrewd political device to preserve regimented racial identities while securing and bolstering white supremacy and privilege (Saunders & Southey, 2001). From "cradle to grave," apartheid officially commanded the quality and the nature of life for every white, African, colored, and Indian South African[5] (Beck, 2000, p. 125). The paramount plan of the apartheid regime was complete white control and domination. Hence, a string of apartheid legislations beginning in 1948 was passed to ensure the total subjection of blacks[6] (Govender, Mnynaka, & Pillay, 1997). Race in its realist version, determined by the physical and genetic code (see Hall, 2002), served to categorize and classify difference in apartheid South Africa. Such differentiated categorizations were connected to economic, political privileges or discriminations and power and knowledge was intricately embedded and contorted with race (see Subreenduth 2003, 2006).

My eighth-grade political awareness and activism provided a space within which I could articulate my lived politics. Every year of my studies—from eighth grade until my exit from university—was interrupted with my participation in student boycotts, marches, and community awareness campaigns.

I am not sure at what point exactly my Indianness within South Africa start-ed becoming more blurry—even with the apartheid system of neat racial categorizations, it no longer remained so cleanly and clearly demarcated for me. As a third-generation South African Indian, how did color rather than culture shape my identity and ways of knowing?

Through my solidarity with the black protest movements, the apartheid system of racialization was interrupted and my (racialized/cultural) subject positions shifted. Still embracing multiple identities and subject positions, a more definitive sense of self began emerging as a black student activist. As Omi and Winant (1986) state, social (and political) movements create col-lective identities through the process of "*rearticulation*" that produces new subjectivity (p. 93, original emphasis). Eventually I became a teacher, with a commitment to social justice and national liberation. South Africa's rac-ist ideology, practice, and governance shaped and fueled my ideological, pedagogical, and lived stance against oppression. My experiences in South Africa continue to inform and affect my work toward a practice of social justice and decolonization both in the global South and the West.

Leaving apartheid South Africa in the early 1990s, I entered the "First World" as a graduate student who desired to learn about global and multi-cultural pedagogy in the hope of preparing to deal with such issues in post-apartheid South Africa. This move proved to be rewarding, challenging, and ambiguous. During apartheid, anti-oppressive intellectual work and writings were banned and so its availability in the United States was inspir-ing, comforting, and reinvigorating. However, this "affair" with "freedom" was short lived, as racialized experiences (of self and others) became more and more a common occurrence (see Rhee, 2006; Rhee & Sagaria, 2004). What was often different about these racialized experiences, as compared to mine in South Africa, was its lack of blatancy. These racialized interac-tions were often masked in statements of wonder, approval, or dismissal of my "exotic" self—from not being aware of Indian presence in South Africa (and thus surprised that I was not from India), to my ability to speak English fluently though with a "foreign" accent. My combined racialized identities—African/Indian/English-speaking—served to bolster exoticism, rather than produce a complex reading of Africa, particularly South Africa, as a place with a diverse population of people who are fully human, complex, and complicated as any other. I continuously found myself being called upon to speak on behalf of South Africa and even the African continent, serving as "expert" or not (if the U.S. person had him- or herself visited Africa, then he or she became "expert"), and to make palatable and exotic our culture, food, and social practices. While frustrating, such experiences and interac-tions were easier to deal with and negotiate than my own complicity in the ongoing construction of exotica. I could explain the complexity of South African society and its politics, even if in my view it did not mean anything to the audience. But these attempts to intervene in the audiences' limited and exotic knowledge constructions of South Africa left me only somewhat satisfied. Tensions of sharing Third World knowledge and experiences left me conflicted as I sensed that its acceptance was because of its exoticism. That is, a voyeuristic glimpse into Otherness that may have been sustained by my own sharing about what I valued as authentic events, experiences, and practices. My complicity was a heavy burden that I carried around with me. I often felt defensive and found it frustrating to continuously address stereotypes and to defend "Africa" against the multitude of generalizations and inaccuracies.

The longer I remained as a graduate student and later faculty—Third Worlding (Spivak, 1996) the Western intellectual field—I felt the impact of my Western education on my Third World community and self. As Smith (2006) explains, "The [Western] university experience transforms the gaze of the [Third World] student who return[s] home to study the 'other' that is themselves" (p. 551). Also, the mirror reflection of one's community changes—refracting instead our own complicities and investments in our Western education. In addition, the suspicions of the West's political, economic, and global dynamics in the global South often is transferred to Western-educated Third World subjects within their Third World communities. Hence, the interactions that transpire when these Western-educated transnational Third World graduate students and academics negotiate their shuttling between their "native home" and their adopted Western homes are intricate and complex. This transnational complexity urges a reconsideration of the dominant racial categories and the ways racialized encounters are performed within Western settings.

As described above, my subject positions are multiple and their contexts diverse. They can be described, crudely of course, as Third World transnational immigrant women of color studying, teaching, and working within predominantly white middle-class Midwestern universities in the United States and researching, identifying, and working with Third World communities and subjects. I frame my narrative within Narayan's (1997) inclusion of

Third World subjects as individuals from Third-World countries temporarily living and working in Western contexts, to individuals who are immigrants to the West from Third-World countries, to individuals who were born and have lived in Western contexts but have social identities that link them to immigrant communities of color, and to all individuals who are members of communities of color in Western contexts and do not have any sense of an "immigrant" identity. What all these individuals have in common ... is the fact that their communities, achievements, and culture have not been regarded as part of mainstream western culture. (p. 121)

I have built upon Narayan's thesis as a way to incorporate a less static transnational identity that constantly shuttles through ideological, material, imagined, and re/membered nations. I am the racial "Other" as my autobiography suggests in the imaginary of the (U.S.) nation (Anderson, 2006; Bhabha, 1994; Dolby, 2004). Like most "Others" our lives remain marginalized, our experiences undervalued, and our knowledge disregarded or contested within the mainstream. This marginalization often silences our haunting voices as what we have to say exposes the everyday practices of the dominant society and simultaneously creates our own vulnerability that often leads to undesirable consequences.

What role do I, as a Third World transnational immigrant woman of color, play in complicating Third/First World discourse on race? How does my constant shuttling (material, ideological, and imagined) between First and Third Worlds disrupt racial categories, immigrant issues, and complicate societal configurations within the location of community, academia, and research? Thus, articulating a transnational narrative that identifies and theorizes hybrid racialized particularities (as in a mixing of west/global south) further complicates the multiple imagined spaces and locations of living, learning, and teaching.

TRAVELING TO THE OTHER: DISRUPTING PERCEPTIONS OF IDENTITY, RACE, AND POLITICS

I have described above how my transnational experiences have (re)shaped, confronted, and challenged others and myself to think about issues of race, color, ethnicity, Africa, and Third World knowledge within U.S. settings. In the remaining chapter, I share how two U.S. pre-service and practicing educators reflect on their transnational experiences with South African educators both in the United States and in South Africa. In sharing their experiences, I intersperse my own reflections on my engagement with the U.S. educators prior, during, and after their travels to South Africa. The two teacher narratives presented here are from Mark, a white male pre-service educator who was completing his master's program in language arts. He also served as a graduate assistant for the South Africa project. The second educator was Jenna, a white female middle-level educator in social studies and science. She participated in the South Africa project and educator exchange both as a pre-service and practicing educator. She continues to be actively engaged in the project.

While these two teacher narratives are implicated within larger travel narratives, I present them as alternative travel narratives in that these travels produce significant impact on teacher identity and pedagogy. My key intention here is not to romanticize the transformative possibilities of face-to-face encounters with the Other. Despite many instances of prolific stereotypes upheld by these travels, for this chapter, I want to dwell on the possibilities of such encounters at decolonizing the Eurocentric notions of the Other—in this case South Africans—by the U.S. educators. So, in what ways can their travel to South Africa and engagement with South Africans, particularly prolonged engagement with South African educators, assist in recognizing how authentic marginalized perspectives can enable us to rethink and decolonize mainstream curriculum knowledge about global societies?

Unnerving Interpellation of (White Male) Self

While Mark was not the typical white male graduate student and pre-service teacher, his sense of interpellation (see Bhabha, 1994) of self in understanding the impact of close encounters with postcolonial environments is key to understanding the impact of focused interaction and dialogue with the postcolonial Other. Mark can best be described as a deeply reflective white male who was acutely aware of his white male privilege before working with me on the project as well as traveling to South Africa. I share Mark's story because his reflection captures what he calls his "reverse culture shock." For me, his narrative captures the heightened pain and suffering this travel brings to the fore as it coerces him into an interrogation of self/identity. Even though Mark has always been aware of his white male privilege, he has not, as his reflection indicates, come face to face with the colonized Other in the global context. And, more importantly, it seems to him that the encounter in particular (forced) him into the category of colonizer. He writes:

> Coming back to this country [U.S.] after the trip has been...surreal??? bizarre??? unnerving??? Somehow, the "me" of now has been subsequently interpellated in a different way, a way that feels familiar yet foreign at the same time. Partially, I think this new interpellation of self has to do with a kind of intimate engagement with and within a postcolonial environment. Previously, I had been on the fringes of postcolonial environments in Ireland, Morrocco, and Egypt (by "fringes," I don't mean that I wasn't "there"; at the same time, as a tourist, one is never completely "there" because one assumes and maintains a kind of "outside" or distance within the subjectivity of the tourist mentality).

In addition to Mark's personal travels, he also took courses in postcolonial studies and literature. His above reflection alludes to what has been known to him in an untangible way (through his personal travel and academic work) and how these previous deliberations become much more tangible when he travels to South Africa and is forced into role of colonizer.

Mark goes on to explain how his travels to/in South Africa triggered a split self-reflection—almost a schizophrenic sense of self that had previously precluded any significant analysis about his white male self:

> Maybe I have partially internalized the sense of the split self that characterizes and/or is reported by some theorists when speaking on the colonial subject; I often find myself attempting to bridge the gap between sympathy and empathy by adopting what I perceive intuitively as mindsets, modes of being, points of view, neuroses, psychoses, or (in this case) internal schisms, whether conscious or unconscious, that haunt, hound, or (to go further) interpellate those (now) postcolonial subjects. It may be a ruse of the mind, an attempt at ridding myself of some guilt associated with my unintended membership in the class of folk that have typically dominated in the colonial paradigm.

Mark's above encounters with South Africa as a postcolonial nation as well as with its postcolonial citizens can be read in many ways. What is clear is the tensions his newly interpellated self creates in (psycho)analyzing the colonized (in this case South Africa/South Africans) and the colonizer (in this case Mark himself). His reflections on the physical and psychological interactions help us rethink how privilege can/not be escaped but, rather, complicated. And by complicating privilege and "colonizer," he helps us in decolonizing the colonizer/colonized binary in same way that complicating "colonized" is helpful in disrupting homogenous formulations of both.

Mark's reflections on the impact of his trip on his classroom practice indicate his struggle with his own biases toward other white males:

> My experiences in South Africa have confirmed certain beliefs I already held about the prejudices and pre-conceived notions a teacher brings into the classroom about certain "kinds" of students; these notions seem rooted in ideas a teacher may hold about certain ethnic/racial groups or those in a particular socioeconomic group....I realized myself that even though I identify myself as a white male, I have serious prejudices against other white males, and this may interfere with how I interact with such students in my classroom; this may sound sort of counterintuitive but it's true.

I have deliberately presented large chunks of Mark's reflections because it captures the emotions of his interpellation and introspection. Mark's reflections offer a more complex reading of the category of white male. Mark's desire for some completeness, for making sense seems to be part of his struggle to rethinking his identity as more complex than "white male." He often apologizes for what he calls his "ramblings" but I think these ramblings symbolize the ways in which such interactions can't exude clarity, definiteness, or coherence that we are socially and academically engineered to make or expect. Yet, this very nonsense or the lack of coherence (see, e.g., Kumashiro, 2004, 2008; Lather, 2007; Mignolo, 2000; Spivak, 1993, 1999, 2000a, 2000b, 2001, 2004) and the complexities that he struggles with is exactly what makes the encounter a productive one for him—personally and as an educator. The productive learning for him is in the various points of his coming apart and coming together: not in coagulation. I am not sure if Mark intended to convey through his reflections his disillusionment with the simple idea of white male privilege—but he does and in so doing he helps us find tangible ways to understand or catch a glimpse of the complexities of white male privilege. Toward the end of Mark's reflections, he states that he has learned about "humanity—their similarities, the universal themes and struggles. Here, I believe, lies the greatest answer to creating and developing a world of peace and tolerance." This has always been my intent for the educator exchanges—to connect to the humanizing piece of the international collaborations. This is a way for U.S. educators to see and talk to real people—like themselves—and use these experiences to disrupt the perception of the Other as being savage subjects. Mark's narrative also demonstrates that when both privileged/oppressed are too simplified and narrowly defined then subjects are dehumanized, but complicating both is humanizing in that it allows us to consider that human responses and experiences are far more complex than what may appear on the surface.

REREADING HISTORICAL EVENTS THROUGH GLOBAL OTHERS

Jones and Jenkins (2004) write about their attempt at getting indigenous, colonizer, and immigrant other students in their class to reread historical events as a way to inculcate cross-cultural pedagogy. I utilize the authors' framework to examine how a U.S. teacher's (Jenna) travel and engagement with South African educators assisted her in the development of a more authentic multiperspective cross-cultural pedagogy. I present here Jenna's professional development and worldview from a naive pre-service student to a confident, collaborative, and interrogative practicing teacher, who clearly has been impacted by her travel and collaborations with South Africans. This narrative affirms the intention of the educator exchanges in that her personal and professional development is not simply with regards to knowing, extending her understanding, or developing sympathy about South Africa and thus presenting her students with a more authentic perspective about South African history. More importantly, this narrative evidences her deep reflective engagement with her own learning. I first met Jenna, a white midwestern female student, in my pre-service undergraduate methods class. I was one of her first interactions with the Other. I was struck by her naivety yet desire to offer her students more authentic and critical perspectives in teaching social studies. In class, she did not shy away from discussions on multicultural, global, and diversity topics. In fact, she seemed to relish the opportunity of discussing these in a formal setting. Her strong sense of self—to some of her peers it seemed arrogance—kept her away from being sucked into many of the other students' annoyances with such discussions. We kept in touch during her graduate studies and she applied for and was chosen to participate in an exchange to South Africa. Other than traveling to Mexico for spring break, this was her first international trip and the fact that it was to the continent of Africa raised concerns for her family. I recall the almost daily e-mails and requests for information—Jenna even created a FAQ and information sheet that I started using with other participants. Information solicited was mainly to soothe her family that she will be safe from civil war–type activities in Africa, diseases like malaria, and whether there would be American-type food available. She researched different aspects of South Africa and she worked on a presentation with another peer and faculty member. This is the usual fervor from which most of the educator participants begin—huge concerns about safety, availability of food that they can eat, living conditions, access to daily amenities, and so on. Despite Jenna's family concerns about these, her enthusiasm and excitement about traveling seemed to supersede her own concerns. The above interaction occurred more than 5 years ago. Since then Jenna reworked one of her graduate research papers to more critically examine and critique the conceptualization of Freire's (1970) *Pedagogy of Hope* and she graduated, and then began teaching and continued to find ways to engage herself and students in the study of South Africa. She organized visits of South African educators to her school and got other colleagues, her principal, and community involved in a number of initiatives with South African educators. We worked collaboratively for almost 2 years to establish a school partnership with her school and one in South Africa. It was actualized last year, and Jenna was instrumental in organizing their first school exchange, which coincided with an international conference where teachers from both schools presented on their partnership.

As a result of her engagement with South African educators, travel to South Africa as a pre-service educator, she continues her engagement with South Africa through her curriculum development. Over the last few years, she developed a unit on South Africa (for her sixth-grade social studies classes), particularly the impact of apartheid. Evidenced by her students' work, she clearly engaged them in critical inquiry about the role of apartheid in South Africa. She used her own experiences in South Africa, her artifacts and her and her students' research to challenge their thinking. One of the collaborations Jenna has being instrumental in spearheading is with a South African elementary school. Once the getting-to-know-you type of communication was completed, Jenna and the South African educators began discussions about developing a collaborative curriculum project on apartheid using the book *Journey to Jo'burg* by Beverly Naidoo. The South African teachers had not used the book before, so they purchased and read the books before the further development of the unit. During one of our organizational teleconferences and in the midst of discussions about curricular timelines, one of the South African teachers interrupted the current conversation to ask: "Can you tell me, how did you come to choose *Journey to Jo'Burg?*" Jenna explained that she wanted to push her students to think about apartheid through a text that could appeal to them as well as provide authentic information—as a tool to have them investigate/research South Africa. Jenna explained that she found a website that had an already developed unit on this topic and the book used was *Journey to Jo'Burg*.[7] The South African teacher listened and then said, "The book is very mild . . . that is not what apartheid was really about . . . so we look forward to discussing with you and your students about what really happened during apartheid."

The South African teacher's response was met with a little tension, but Jenna remarked that this would be an opportunity for more authentic perspectives. It also pushed Jenna and the other U.S. teachers to rethink and rearticulate the meaning of (their) radical pedagogy. The South African teacher insists, as hooks (1996) does, that marginalized people acknowledge and confront their marginality by creating oppositional explanations for texts that explore different ways of being and provide alternatives to prevailing unjust social practices. My intent in sharing this interaction is to demonstrate how educator transnational travel and prolonged meaningful interactions can be tapped as a way to complicate, disrupt, and challenge their/our construction of Africa and Others.

Pushing Y/Our Comfort Zones

In offering U.S. educators' opportunities to reexamine themselves within the convoluted terrain of their travels, I also hope that this engagement will yield more critical educators who would become cognizant of the complexity of culture, race, politics, and history in South Africa. However, it is clear as in Mark's case and for many of the other participants that this experience pushes them out of their comfort zones. While this is true for many, Mark believes it is insufficient, and that I should afford more opportunities for more

> pointed, purposeful, and ongoing discussions among group members (possibly moderated and directed by a South African participant). . . . I think that sometimes it would have been beneficial and constructive to kind of "push

the issue" (if you will) to engage ourselves in critical and problematic analyses of experiences. When the "issue" isn't forced upon you, in a sense, then the possibility exists to ignore what made you uncomfortable or upset in a particular situation or scenario, and I think one can construct profound meaning from actually interrogating that sense of discomfort or "troubledness" or what have you.

Mark's narrative conveyed the ways in which he troubled his sense of self—it is a painful process but only one that can be undertaken through conscious reflection and interrogation. There are useful studies in the educational literature that address issues of identity, beliefs, and experiences (Britzman, 1994; Olsen, 1997). Research on teacher perspectives and teacher decision making traces how teachers' beliefs and values shape their practices (Clark & Peterson, 1986; Cornett et al., 1992). Scholarship on teachers' personal accounts or beliefs help us understand the complicated ways teachers' beliefs are enacted in the classroom (Carter & Doyle, 1987; Clandidin, 1992). Research also indicates how teachers' and students' knowledge and experiences influence teaching and learning in a particular setting (Subedi, 2008).

Mark's call for more explicit troubling of the U.S. teachers' experiences harkens Giroux's (1998) critical pedagogy stance that "learning is [not] a neutral and transparent process removed from the juncture of power, history, and social context" (p. ix). Giroux's insistence that schools and thus societies be viewed as sites of struggle and possibility (for resistance) is key to understanding South Africa's political struggles. If we are to transform the ways in which we teach about other geographies, peoples, culture, and histories, we need to develop what Giroux calls "transformative intellectuals" and that we need to formulate "counterhegemonic pedagogies" (p. xxxiii) that will empower our students. This means educators will not only provide students the knowledge and social skills they will need to effectively function in the larger society as critical agents, but more importantly, educators will educate students for transformative action. For teachers to both become transformative intellectuals and to help their students become the same, they have to move away from the view that teaching–learning knowledge is simply routinized, technocratic, and neutral. Teacher work should be seen as a form of "intellectual labor" (Giroux, 1988, p. 125)—the kind that Mark is pushing me to include—the kind of troubledness that he talks about, suggesting that teaching involves an integration of thinking and practice as a means for teachers to become more critical reflective practitioners who engender the same from their students.

Various scholars in the field of social studies have argued for the need to examine how local and global discourses are interconnected and how global perspectives can create spaces for intellectual development and pedagogical decision making (Hanvey, 1975; Kniep, 1986; Woyach & Remy,

1982). Scholars such as Merryfield (2002) point out that the lack of global perspective in curriculum leads learners to develop entrenched stereotypes and prejudice about societies and people considered the Other. For this reason, educators have argued for the need to further infuse controversial global issues when teaching about topics on culture and history (Gaudelli, 2003). Without the knowledge of critical global history and current political climate, it would indeed be difficult for students to recognize how issues of power, knowledge, and politics are embedded within how the United States is connected to global societies. Just as Mark and Jenna evidence in their narratives, educators cannot ignore how discussions on colonialism and the contemporary unequal global exchanges have shaped how we have come to understand and interpret the meaning of the world (see, e.g., McCarthy, 1998; Merryfield, 2001; Willinsky, 1998; Wilson, 1998).

REIMAGINING CURRICULUM KNOWLEDGE

In offering the three contextualized travel case studies, if you will, it is my hope that social studies educators use this experience to inform the ways in which they teach about other cultures, histories, and politics. I envision the educators' travels to South Africa as provocative pedagogical, political, and personal experiences that forced them to take a different approach to understanding issues of democratization, citizenship, race, and politics in non-Western societies, and more critically about the ways in which they were implicated within historical discourses on race and colonialism. Such an approach to offering transnational educational experiences situates particular historical and contemporary educational conditions as effects of Western colonialism/imperialism and as development of various curricula in national and transnational contexts. This also offers a space to examine the ways in which individuals and groups of people within the same geographic and Othered location construct, challenge, negotiate, and interpret the political, cultural, and historical aspects of their country.

While the dominant imagination of curriculum knowledge and power is always present in interactions, the possibilities presented in this chapter offer insights into the process by which U.S. educators can reimagine, reconceptualize, and disrupt their ways of knowing and subsequently of teaching about non-Western societies in social studies classrooms. Such purposeful pedagogical experiences challenge U.S. educators to create curriculum knowledge that is more critically presented to their students. These interactions also remind us that teachers do not serve a sanitized role in the learning process (as lead presenters of knowledge or as facilitators in the learning process or learners for that matter) but their preexisting attitudes and past experiences will also color the learning process—making it far from being simplistic and homogenous. Thus, schooling and learning opportunities must be sensitive to differences and must account for the social/historical context of learning and knowledge production.

As evidenced in ongoing interaction of Jenna and the South African educators, collaborative dialogue across differences is possible. This chapter calls for continued, sorely needed dialogue and purposeful, focused interaction among international educators to enable a more nuanced understanding of the complex interrelationships between local, national, and international knowledge systems. Such an approach will provide educators a much-needed forum that challenges them to pay attention to ideological, imperial, and personal curricular decisions. For educators like me, this examination of how purposeful educator traveling encounters that challenge dominant curricula knowledge in U.S. classrooms provides insights into how educators consume this knowledge during their travels and the productive possibilities for how they reproduce this for their students.

ACKNOWLEDGMENTS

I would like to thank Stephanie Daza and Jeong-eun Rhee for their feedback on this chapter.

NOTES

1. I thank Omiunota Ukpokodu for her feedback on the original version of this revised section.
2. This section of the paper is a revised version that appeared in: Subreenduth (2008).
3. I use the apartheid racial categorization white, African, colored, and Indian in this chapter not as an essentialized concept or category but as a means to illustrate apartheid ideology/practices based on race.
4. The Soweto student insurrection of 1976 was a tragic national moment in South Africa. More than 1,000 black students were killed in demonstrations (Kunnie, 2000). Students were protesting against the Bantu education system and the government's policy of mandating Afrikaans as a second medium of instruction in black schools (this in addition to black students already having English as a medium of instruction).
5. The apartheid racial categorization of white, African, colored, and Indian are used here not as an essentialized concept or category, but as a means to illustrate apartheid ideology/practices based on race.
6. The term black has its roots in the Black Consciousness Movement (BCM) of the 1960s in South Africa. It was an inclusive term to refer to all of those who were marginalized and oppressed under the apartheid regime. It was used to collectively refer to Africans, coloreds, and Indians during the struggle. But

the apartheid government appropriated this term in the late 1970s to refer to Africans only. However, the term black remained an inclusive term for the oppressed and those aligned with the liberation (Nkomo, 1990).

7. Synopsis of story: Mma lives and works in Johannesburg, far from the village 13-year-old Naledi and her younger brother, Tiro, call home. When their baby sister suddenly becomes very sick, Naledi and Tiro know, deep down, that only one person can save her. Bravely, they set off alone on a journey to find Mma and bring her back. It isn't until they reach the city that they come to understand the dangers of their country, and the painful struggle for freedom and dignity that is taking place all around them (retrieved June 19, 2009, from (www.harpercollins.com/books/9780064402378/Journey_to_Joburg/index.aspx–66k -).

REFERENCES

Anderson, B. (2006). *Imagined communities: Reflections on the origin and spread of nationalism*. New York: Verso.

Apple, M. (1996). *Cultural politics and education*. New York: Teachers College Press

Asher, N., & Crocco, M.S. (2001). Engendering multicultural identities and representation in education. *Theory and Research in Social Education, 29*(1), 129–151.

Banks, J. A. (Ed.). (1996). *Multicultural education, contemporary perspectives*. New York: Teachers College Press.

Banks, J. (2004). *Diversity and citizenship education: Global perspectives*. San Francisco: Jossey-Bass.

Beck, R. (2000). *The history of South Africa*. London: Greenwood Press.

Bhabha, H. (1994). *The location of culture*. London: Routledge.

Britzman, D. P. (1994). Is there a problem with knowing thyself?: Towards a poststructuralist view of teacher identity. In T. Shanahan (Ed.), *Teachers thinking, teachers knowing* (pp. 53–75). Urbana, IL: NCRE.

Carter, K., & Doyle, W. (1987). Teachers' knowledge structures and comprehension processes. In J. Calderhead (Ed.), *Exploring teachers' thinking* (pp. 147–160). London: Cassell.

Clandinin, D. J. (1985). Personal practical knowledge: A study of teachers' classroom images. *Curriculum Inquiry, 15*, 361–385.

Clark, C. M., & Peterson, P. L. (1986). *Teachers thought processes: Research in teaching and learning*. New York: Macmillan.

Cornett, J. W., Chase, S. K., Miller, P., Schrock, D., Bennett, B. J., Goins, A., et al. (1992). Insights from the analysis of our own theorizing: The viewpoints of seven teachers. In E. W. Ross, J. W. Cornett, & G. McCutcheon (Eds.), *Teacher personal theorizing: Connecting curriculum practice, theory, and research* (pp. 137–157). Albany: State University of New York Press.

Daza, S. (2008). Decolonizing researcher authenticity. *Race Ethnicity and Education, 11*(1), 7–86.

Dolby, N. (2004). Encountering an American self: Study abroad and national identity. *Comparative Education Review, 48*(2), 150–173.

Faulconer, T., & Freeman, A.C. (2005). Teachers, classroom controversy and the media. *Social Education. 69*(6), 323–327.

Freire, P. (1970). *Pedagogy of the oppressed.* New York: Continuum.

Gaudelli, W. (2003). *World class: Teaching and learning in global times.* Mahwah, NJ: Erlbaum.

Giroux, H. A. (1988). *Teachers as intellectuals: Toward a critical pedagogy of learning.* Granby, MA: Bergin & Garvey.

Giroux, H. A. (1992). *Border crossings: Cultural workers and the politics of education.* New York: Routledge.

Govender, S., Mnynaka, M., & Pillay, G. (1997). *New generation history standard 10.* Musgrave: New Generation.

Hall, S. (2002). *Race: The floating signifier.* Northampton, MA: Media Education Foundation.

Hanvey, R.G. (1975). *An attainable global perspective.* New York: Center for War/Peace Studies.

hooks, b. (1994). *Teaching to transgress: Education as the practice of freedom.* New York: Routledge.

hooks, b. (1996). Choosing the margin as a space of radical openness. In A. Garry & M. Pearsall (Eds.), *Women, knowledge, and reality: Explorations in feminist philosophy* (pp. 48–56). New York: Routledge.

John, M. (1989). Postcolonial feminists in the western intellectual field: Anthropologists and native informants. *Inscriptions, 5,* 49–73.

Jones, A., & Jenkins, K. (2004). Pedagogical events: Re-reading shared moments in educational history. *Journal of Intercultural Studies, 25*(2), 143–158.

Kniep, W. M. (1986). Defining global education by its content. *Social Education, 50*(1), 437–466.

Kumashiro, K. K. (2004). *Against common sense: Teaching and learning toward social justice.* New York: Routledge Falmer.

Kumashiro, K. K. (2008). *The seduction of common sense: How the right has framed the debate on America's schools.* New York: Teachers College Press.

Kunnie, J. (2000). *Is apartheid really dead?: Pan-Africanist working-class cultural critical perspectives.* Boulder, CO: Westview Press.

Ladson-Billings, G. (1993). Through the looking glass: Politics and the social studies curriculum. *Theory and Research in Social Education, 21,* 84–92.

Lather, P. (2007). *Getting lost: Feminist efforts toward a double(d) science.* New York: State University of New York Press.

Mahalingam, R., & McCarthy, C. (Eds.). (2000). *Multicultural curriculum: New directions for social theory, practice, and policy.* London: Routledge.

McCarthy, C. (1998). *The uses of culture: Education and the limits of ethnic affiliation.* New York: Routledge.

McLaren, P. (1997). *Revolutionary multiculturalism: Pedagogies of dissent for the new millennium.* Boulder, CO: Westview Press.

Merryfield, M. M. (2000). Why aren't teachers being prepared to teach for diversity, equity, and global interconnectedness? A study of lived experiences in the making of multicultural and global educators. *Teaching and Teacher Education, 16,* 429–443.

Merryfield, M. M. (2001). Moving the center of global education: From imperial worldviews that divide the world to double consciousness, contrapuntal pedagogy, hybridity, and cross-cultural competence. In W. B. Stanley (Ed.), *Critical issues in social studies research for the 21st century* (p. 179–208). Greenwich, CT: Information Age.

Merryfield, M. M. (2002). Rethinking our framework for understanding the world. *Theory and Research in Social Education, 30*(1), 148–152.

Merryfield, M. M., & Wilson, A. (2005). *Social studies and the world: Teaching global perspectives.* Silver Spring, MD: National Council for Social Studies.

Mignolo, W. (2000). *Local histories/global designs: Coloniality, subaltern knowledges, and border thinking.* Princeton, NJ: Princeton University Press.

Narayan, U. (1997). *Dislocating cultures: Identities, traditions, and third world feminism.* New York: Routledge.

Nkomo, M. (1990). *Pedagogy of domination: Toward a democratic education in South Africa.* Trenton, NJ: Africa World Press.

Olsen, L. (1997). *Made in America: Immigrant students in our public schools.* New York: New Press.

Omi, M., & Winant, H. (1986). *Racial formation in the United States.* New York: Routledge.

Parker, W. C. (2003). *Teaching democracy: Unity and diversity in public life.* New York: Teachers College Press.

Patterson, N. C., & Chandler, P. T. (2008). Free speech in the balance: What do we know about the rights of public school teachers. *Social Studies Research and Practice, 3*(2), 90–102.

Rhee, J. (2006). Re/membering (to) shifting alignments: Korean women's transnational narratives in US higher education. *International Journal of Qualitative Studies in Education, 19*(5), 595–615.

Rhee, J., & Sagaria, M. (2004). International students: Constructions of imperialism in the *Chronicle of Higher Education. The Review of Higher Education, 28*(1), 77–96.

Rizvi, F. (2004). Debating globalization and education after September 11. *Comparative Education, 40*(2), 157–171.

Ross, E.W. (Ed.). (2001). *The social studies curriculum: Purposes, problems and possibilities.* Albany: State University of New York Press

Saunders, C., & Southey, N. (2001). *A dictionary of South African history.* Cape Town, South Africa: David Phillip Publisher.

Smith, L. T. (1999). *Decolonizing methodologies: Research and indigenous people.* London: Zed Books.

Smith, L. T. (2005). On tricky ground: Researching the native in the age of uncertainty. In N. Denzin & Y. Lincoln (Eds.), *Handbook of qualitative research* (pp. 85–107). Thousand Oaks, CA: Sage.

Smith, L. T. (2006). Introduction. *International Journal of Qualitative Studies in Education, 19*(5), 549–552.

Spivak, G. C. (1993). *Outside in the teaching machine.* New York: Routledge.

Spivak, G. C. (1996). Subaltern studies: Deconstructing historiography. In G. C. Spivak, D. Landry, & G. M. MacLean (Eds.), *The Spivak reader: Selected works of Gayatri Chakravorty Spivak* (pp. 3–33). New York: Routledge.

Spivak, G. C. (1999). *A critique of postcolonial reason: Toward a history of the vanishing present.* Cambridge, MA: Harvard University Press.

Spivak, G. C. (2000a). From Haverstock Hill Flat to US classroom, what's left of theory. In J. Butler, J. Guillory, & K. Thomas (Eds.), *What's left of theory?: New work on the politics of literary theory* (pp. 1–39). New York: Routledge.

Spivak, G. C. (2000b). The new subaltern: A silent interview. In V. Chaturvedi (Ed.), *Mapping subaltern studies and the postcolonial* (pp. 324–340). London: Verso.

Spivak, G. C. (2001). Questioned on translation: Adrift. *Public Culture, 13*(1), 13–22.

Spivak, G. C. (2004). Globalicities: Terror and its consequences. *CR: The New Centennial Review, 4*(1), 73–94.

Subedi, B. (2008). Contesting racialization: Asian immigrant teachers' critiques and claims of teacher authenticity. *Race Ethnicity and Education, 11*(1), 57–70.

Subreenduth, S. (2003). Using a needle to kill an elephant: The politics of race and education in post-apartheid South Africa. *Inquiry: Critical Thinking Across the Disciplines, 22*(2), 65–73.

Subreenduth, S. (2006). "Why, why are we not even allowed...?": A de/colonizing narrative of complicity and resistance in post/apartheid South Africa. *International Journal of Qualitative Studies in Education, 19*(5), 617–638.

Subreenduth, S. (2008). Deconstructing the politics of a differently colored transnational identity. *Race Ethnicity and Education, 11*(1), 41–55.

Willinsky, J. (1998). *Learning to divide the world: Education at empire's end.* Minneapolis: University of Minnesota Press.

Wilson, A. (1998). Oburoni outside the whale: Reflections on an experience in Ghana. *Theory and Research in Social Education, 26*(3), 410–429.

Woyach, R. B., & Remy, R.C., (1982). A community-based approach to global education. *Theory into Practice, 21*, 177–183.

CPSIA information can be obtained
at www.ICGtesting.com
Printed in the USA
JSHW030217020620
5917JS00002BA/10

9 781607 523864